We Who Dared to Say No to War

American Antiwar Writing from 1812 to Now

MURRAY POLNER

THOMAS E. WOODS, JR.

BASIC
BOOKS

A Member of the Perseus Books Group
New York

Copyright © 2008 by Murray Polner and Thomas E. Woods, Jr.

Published by Basic Books
A Member of the Perseus Books Group

All rights reserved. Printed in the United States of America. No part of this
book may be reproduced in any manner whatsoever without written permission
except in the case of brief quotations embodied in critical articles and reviews.

Books published by Basic Books are available at special discounts for bulk
purchases in the United States by corporations, institutions, and other
organizations. For more information, please contact the Special Markets
Department at the Perseus Books Group, 2300 Chestnut Street, Suite 200,
Philadelphia, PA 19103, or call (800) 810-4145, ext. 5000, or e-mail
special.markets@perseusbooks.com.

Designed by Brent Wilcox

A CIP catalog record for this book is available from the Library of Congress.
ISBN-13: 978-1-56858-385-3

10 9 8 7 6 5 4 3 2 1

Murray Polner dedicates this book to his grandchildren—
Jesse, Rachel, Aliza, Cody, Molly, and Catherine—
and hopes they will always be inspired by those memorable
words "Justice, justice shalt thou pursue." (Deuteronomy 16:20)

Thomas Woods dedicates this book to his daughters,
Regina, Veronica, and Amy.
May they inherit a world in which reason and truth
finally triumph against propaganda and hatred.

"What difference does it make to the dead, the orphans and the homeless, whether the mad destruction is wrought under the name of totalitarianism or the holy name of liberty and democracy?"

—Mohandas Gandhi,
Non-Violence in Peace and War

Contents

10 Americans Confront War   295

Introduction

We Who Dared to Say No to War brings together some of the most memorable, if largely neglected, writings and speeches by those Americans who have opposed our government's addiction to war, from the War of 1812 to the present. Coedited by a man of the left (Murray Polner) and a man of the right (Thomas Woods), this cross-ideological book reveals how fascinatingly broad and diverse is the American antiwar tradition. We intend it as a surprising and welcome change from the misleading liberal-peace/conservative-war dichotomy that the media and even our educational establishment and popular culture have done so much to foster.

We have assembled some of the most compelling, vigorously argued, and just plain interesting speeches, articles, poetry, and book excerpts. We feature Daniel Webster, one of our history's great orators, denouncing military conscription in 1814 as unconstitutional and immoral two years after President James Madison and congressional war hawks eager to grab Canada declared war against Great Britain. Our treatment of the Mexican-American War includes a forgotten speech by Abraham Lincoln opposing the war, together with remarks by others who feared the war would only help expand slavery into the newly conquered formerly Mexican lands. For the Civil War we include a letter by a southern Christian theologian to Confederate president Jefferson Davis urging that Christians be exempted from the draft, and an abolitionist assailing the resort to yet another war, which in the end cost hundreds of thousands of lives, not to mention those wounded in body and mind.

After Appomattox, the victorious Union then turned its attention to slaughtering Indians.

Some of the most perceptive and significant, if now long-forgotten, antiwar writings in our history appeared in the wake of the Spanish-American War of 1898 and especially as the savage Philippine-American War raged (and in which an estimated two hundred thousand Filipinos as well as some four thousand U.S. soldiers perished). Labor leaders, businessmen, clergymen, and freethinkers alike condemned these adventures. The American Anti-Imperialist League, a national organization that opposed the war and annexations, believed an expansive America was unfaithful to her finest traditions of peace, nonintervention, and anticolonialism. Among the most prominent of these dissenters were Jane Addams, Ambrose Bierce, William Jennings Bryan, Andrew Carnegie, Eugene V. Debs, John Dewey, Emma Goldman, William James, Helen Keller, Carl Schurz, William Graham Sumner, Mark Twain, and two former presidents, Grover Cleveland and Benjamin Harrison. Shortly before Sumner—a carping critic, scholar, and Social Darwinist—died in 1910 after the rise of an American empire in the Caribbean and the Pacific, he sensed what lay ahead: "I have lived through the best years of this country's history," he wrote. "The next generations are going to see war and social calamities."

How right he was, from World War I to repeated interventions in the Caribbean and Latin America to the Korean War to the antidemocratic intrigues in Iran, Guatemala, and beyond. And while World War II may have been a necessary war, we remind readers that (1) that war was but a continuation of the unnecessary World War I, and (2) there were always critics of the war—"noninterventionists" to its partisans and "isolationists" to its opponents—before and after the attack on Pearl Harbor. Some of the most articulate opponents of the foreign-policy consensus, then and now, among Washington's elite are those who recognize that American military power needs to be narrowly restricted to *defense*—specifically, an end to the stationing of U.S. troops throughout the world, a sharp reduction in military budgets, a restoration of constitutional parity between the three branches of government, and a refusal to inject the nation into conflicts without end, all over the world.

The Korean War (with nearly thirty-eight thousand Americans killed and many more wounded, some grievously, and the deaths of several million Koreans) has received little or no attention—perhaps because it was only another abattoir in which no side could rightly claim victory.* It was not so with the defeat in Vietnam; after the United States invaded Vietnam, some fifty-eight thousand GIs died in as pointless a war as has ever been fought by this country. "Had American leaders not thought that all international events were connected to the Cold War," writes historian Robert D. Schulzinger, "there would have been no American war in Vietnam."** As in the early stages of every war fought by this country, a majority of trusting and believing majorities rallied round the flag and their leaders. Even so, some of the writings we include in this book mention the fabricated Tonkin Gulf "assault" by North Vietnamese torpedo boats (much like the lie spread about Spaniards sinking the USS *Maine* in Havana's harbor in 1898), including Senator Wayne Morse's denunciation of the rush to war without the benefit of a congressional declaration of war. It was a war that millions protested and during which college students at Kent State and Jackson State universities were slain and J. Edgar Hoover's FBI repeatedly violated civil liberties. Nevertheless, the war dragged on until 1975, when U.S. helicopters were forced to rescue retreating escapees huddled atop the American embassy in Saigon.

Senator George McGovern's memorable speech on the Senate floor during the Vietnam War in support of the McGovern-Hatfield amendment to end the war was perhaps the most trenchant denunciation of that failed war and its supporters. McGovern, a World War II Army Air Force combat pilot and recipient of a Silver Star and Distinguished Flying

---

*See, for example, "Unearthing War's Horrors Years Later in South Korea," *New York Times* (December 3, 2007), A9. All sides killed civilians, but this dispatch reports the finding of South Korea's Truth and Reconciliation Commission.

**Robert D. Schulzinger, *A Time for War: The United States and Vietnam, 1941–1975* (New York: Oxford University Press, 1997), 329.

© Paul Tick. Courtesy of Paul Tick Collection.

Cross, turned to his colleagues in the Senate and told them, "Every senator in this chamber is partly responsible for sending fifty thousand young Americans to an early grave. This chamber reeks of blood."

Finally, and inevitably, we turn to Iraq, where impassioned supporters invoke a future consumed by "World War IV." As usual, our present and future wars are aided and abetted by the intimate relationship between weapons manufacturers (which in the good old days were called "merchants of death")* and contractors and far too many policy makers and legislators. We offer here the testimonies of serious opponents of

---

*H. C. Engelbrecht and F. C. Hanighen, *Merchants of Death* (New York: Dodd, Mead, 1934).

our government's foreign policy as a rebuke to the limited and narrow debate that takes place among Washington's elites, think tanks, and (with few exceptions) our servile and incurious mass media.

The conventional wisdom about the Iraq War is that it was begun under false pretenses, that a supine media drilled those falsehoods into Americans' heads, and that this was all very unusual. Well, as they say, two out of three ain't bad.

What the reader of this book will discover is that what we have endured over the past five years in the Iraq campaign is not unusual at all. The history of American wars is littered with propaganda, falsehoods, a compliant media, the manipulation of patriotic sentiment—everything we've seen recently, we've seen before. Time and again.

That's not encouraging at all, of course. But we can at least be consoled that we are not alone, that for two centuries thoughtful Americans have struggled against the very things that confront us today. We belong to a noble lineage of thought and action—and it is that great tradition, in all its ideologically diverse glory, that we celebrate here.

—Murray Polner and Thomas Woods, Jr.,
Great Neck, New York, and Auburn, Alabama

1

The War of 1812

Where is it written in the Constitution, in what article or section is it contained, that you may take children from their parents, and parents from their children, and compel them to fight the battles of any war, in which the folly or the wickedness of Government may engage it?

—SENATOR DANIEL WEBSTER, December 1814, opposing a bill introduced by war hawks to enact a military draft with an eye to conquering Canada

Among the official rationales for the War of 1812 against Britain were her offenses on the high seas. Britain and France were both guilty of harassing neutral shipping during the Napoleonic Wars, and the British were additionally guilty of impressing sailors on American ships into service in the British navy. The men who were thus seized were said to be deserters, but in some cases they had never been in the British navy at all, or at the very least had become American citizens in the meantime (and thus were presumably no longer subject to British authority). Yet something else must have been at work, since New England, the part of the country most reliant on maritime concerns, was also the most opposed to war with Britain. The situation vis-à-vis international trade was undesirable, to be sure, but it would improve once the war concluded, and in the meantime ship captains could and did take out insurance against war-related troubles at sea. Another factor contributing to the drive for war was a desire to annex Canada—which, as a British possession, would be fair game in a war against Britain. As the war went on, in fact, much of New England became convinced that "Mr. Madison's War" was really a war of conquest, and they refused to take part. The state of Connecticut declared that the president had no authority to call upon the militia of that state "to assist in carrying on an offensive war," and that it would comply with the federal order only if New England should be threatened "by an actual invasion of any portion of our territory."

Among the documents we reproduce here is the lengthy address against war that Representative Samuel Taggart drafted for delivery before Congress. Especially chilling, because so eerily familiar to Americans who lived through the Bush years and the Iraq war, is Congressman Taggart's discussion of the invasion of Canada, and all the promises of an easy victory that its advocates put forth. It would, its supporters said, be just a matter of marching in and watching the Canadians, yearning for liberation at the hands of Americans, flock to our banner. We have, it has been said, nothing to do but to march an army into the country and display the standard of the United States, and the Canadians will immediately flock to it and place themselves under our protection. From another angle, supporters of invading Canada also proposed that if the Canadians should turn out to be "a debased race of poltroons" uninterested in American liberation, the "mere sight of an army of the United States would immediately put an end to all thoughts of resistance."

There was to be no cakewalk in Canada, as it turned out.

Among the war's domestic consequences was the Panic of 1819. With the New England banks unwilling to lend money for the war effort, financially unsound banks had popped up around the country, lending out notes with little if any backing in specie. When those banks inevitably collapsed, the result was an economic downturn that turned many people against fractional-reserve banking and even against banking itself.

The Treaty of Ghent, which officially ended the war in December 1814, included not a single word about any of the grievances for which the U.S. government had allegedly fought. But just as war opponents predicted, with the return of peace the British stopped harassing Americans anyway.

The Draft Is Unconstitutional

DANIEL WEBSTER

Massachusetts congressman Daniel Webster (who later served as a U.S. senator and secretary of state) delivered this speech before the House of Representatives on December 9, 1814.

When the present generation of men shall be swept away, and that this government ever existed shall be a matter of history only, I desire that it may be known that you have not proceeded in your course unadmonished and unforewarned. Let it then be known, that there were those who would have stopped you, in the career of your measures, and held you back, as by the skirts of your garments, from the precipice over which you are now plunging and drawing after you the government of your country. . . .

It is time for Congress to examine and decide for itself. It has taken things on trust long enough. It has followed executive recommendation, 'til there remains no hope of finding safety in that path. What is there, sir, that makes it the duty of this people now to grant new confidence to the Administration, and to surrender their most important rights to its discretion? On what merits of its own does it rest this extraordinary claim? When it calls thus loudly for the treasure and lives of the people, what pledge does it offer that it will not waste all in the same preposterous pursuits which have hitherto engaged it? In the failure of all past promises, do we see any assurance of future performance? Are we to measure out our confidence in proportion to our disgrace and now at last to grant away everything, because all that we have heretofore granted has been wasted or misapplied? What is there in our condition that bespeaks a wise or an able government? What is the evidence that the protection of the country is the object principally regarded? In every quarter that protection has been more or less abandoned to the States. That every town on the coast is not now in possession of the enemy, or in ashes, is owing to the vigilance and exertions of the States themselves, and to no protection granted to them by those on whom the whole duty of their protection rested. . . .

Let us examine the nature and extent of the power which is assumed by the various military measures before us. In the present want of men and money, the Secretary of War has proposed to Congress a military conscription. For the conquest of Canada, the people will not enlist; and if they would, the treasury is exhausted, and they could not be paid. Conscription is chosen as the most promising instrument, both of overcoming reluctance to the service, and of subduing the difficulties of the exchequer. The Administration asserts the right to fill the ranks of the regular army by compulsion. It contends that it may now take one out of every twenty-five men, and any part, or the whole of the rest, whenever its occasions require. Persons thus taken by force, and put into an army, may be compelled to serve during the war, or for life. They may be put on any service, at home or abroad, for defense or for invasion, accordingly to the will and pleasure of the government. The power does not grow out of any invasion of the country, or even out of a state of war. It belongs to government at all times, in peace as well as in war, and it is to be exercised under all circumstances, according to its mere discretion. This, sir, is the amount of the principle contended for by the Secretary of War.

Is this, sir, consistent with the character of a free government? Is this civil liberty? Is this the real character of our Constitution? No, sir, indeed it is not. The Constitution is libeled. The people of this country have not established for themselves such a fabric of despotism. They have not purchased at a vast expense of their own treasure and their own blood a Magna Carta to be slaves. Where is it written in the Constitution, in what article or section is it contained, that you may take children from their parents, and parents from their children, and compel them to fight the battles of any war in which the folly or the wickedness of government may engage it? Under what concealment has this power lain hidden which now for the first time comes forth, with a tremendous and baleful aspect, to trample down and destroy the dearest rights of personal liberty? Who will show me any Constitutional injunction which makes it the duty of the American people to surrender everything valuable in life, and even life itself, not when the safety of their country and its liberties may demand the sacrifice, but whenever the purposes of an ambitious and mischievous government may require it? Sir, I almost disdain to go to quotations and references to prove that such an abominable doctrine has no foundation in the Constitution of the country. It is enough to know that that instrument was intended as the basis of a free government, and that the power contended for is incompatible with any notion of personal liberty. An attempt to maintain this doctrine upon the provisions of the Constitution is an exercise of perverse ingenuity to extract slavery from the substance of a free government. It is an attempt to show, by proof and argument, that we ourselves are subjects of despotism, and that we have a right to chains and bondage, firmly secured to us and our children by the provisions of our government. . . .

Congress having, by the Constitution, a power to raise armies, the Secretary [of War] contends that no restraint is to be imposed on the exercise of this power, except such as is expressly stated in the written letter of the instrument. In other words, that Congress may execute its powers, by any means it chooses, unless such means are particularly prohibited. But the general nature and object of the Constitution impose as rigid a restriction on the means of exercising power as could be done by the most explicit injunctions. It is the first principle applicable to such a case, that no construction shall be admitted which impairs the general nature and character of the instrument. A free constitution of government is to be construed upon free principles, and every branch of its provisions is to receive such an interpretation as is full of its general spirit. No means are to be taken by implication which would strike us absurdly if expressed. And what would have been more absurd than for this Constitution to have said that to secure the great blessings of liberty it gave to government uncontrolled power of military conscription? Yet such is the absurdity which it is made to exhibit, under the commentary of the Secretary of War.

But it is said that it might happen that an army could not be raised by voluntary enlistment, in which case the power to raise armies would be granted in vain, unless they might be raised by compulsion. If this reasoning could prove anything, it would equally show, that whenever the legitimate power of the Constitution should be so badly administered as to cease to answer the great ends intended by them, such new powers may be assumed or usurped, as any existing Administration may deem expedient. This is the result of his own reasoning, to which the Secretary does not profess to go. But it is a true result. For if it is to be assumed, that all powers were granted, which might by possibility become necessary, and that government itself is the judge of this possible necessity, then the powers of government are precisely what it choose they should be. Apply the same reasoning to any other power granted to Congress, and test its accuracy by the result. Congress has power to borrow money. How is it to exercise this power? Is it confined to voluntary loans? There is no express limitation to that effect, and, in the language of the secretary, it might happen, indeed it has happened, that persons could not be found willing to lend. Money might be borrowed then in any other mode. In other words, Congress might resort to a forced loan. It might take the money of any man by force, and give him in exchange exchequer notes or certificates of stock. Would this be quite constitutional, sir? It is entirely within the reasoning of the Secretary, and it is a result of his argument, outraging the rights of individuals in a far less degree than the practical consequences which he himself draws from it.

A compulsory loan is not to be compared, in point of enormity, with a compulsory military service.

If the Secretary of War has proved the right of Congress to enact a law enforcing a draft of men out of the militia into the regular army, he will at any time be able to prove, quite as clearly, that Congress has power to create a Dictator. The arguments which have helped him in one case, will equally aid him in the other, the same reason of a supposed or possible state necessity, which is urged now, may be repeated then, with equal pertinency and effect.

Sir, in granting Congress the power to raise armies, the people have granted all the means which are ordinary and usual, and which are consistent with the liberties and security of the people themselves, and they have granted no others. To talk about the unlimited power of the government over the means to execute its authority, is to hold a language which is true only in regard to despotism. The tyranny of arbitrary government consists as much in its means as in its ends; and it would be a ridiculous and absurd constitution which should be less cautious to guard against abuses in the one case than in the other. All the means and instruments which a free government exercises, as well as the ends and objects which it pursues, are to partake of its own essential character, and to be conformed to its genuine spirit. A free government with arbitrary means to administer it is a contradiction; a free government without adequate provisions for personal security is an absurdity; a free government with an uncontrolled power of military conscription, is a solecism, at once the most ridiculous and abominable that ever entered into the head of man. . . .

Who shall describe to you the horror which your orders of conscription shall create in the once happy villages of this country? Who shall describe the distress and anguish which they will spread over those hills and valleys, where men have heretofore been accustomed to labor, and to rest in security and happiness? Anticipate the scene, sir, when the class shall assemble to stand its draft, and to throw the dice for blood. What a group of wives and mothers and sisters, of helpless age and helpless infancy, shall gather round the theatre of this horrible lottery, as if the stroke of death were to fall from heaven before their eyes on a father, a brother, a son, or a husband. And in a majority of cases, sir, it will be the stroke of death. Under present prospects of the continuance of the war, not one half of them on whom your conscription shall fall will ever return to tell the tale of their sufferings. They will perish of disease or pestilence or they will leave their bones to whiten in fields beyond the frontier. Does the lot fall on the father of a family? His children, already orphans, shall see his face no more. When they behold him for the last time, they shall see him lashed and fettered, and dragged away from his own threshold, like a felon and an outlaw. Does it fall on a son, the hope and the staff of aged parents? That hope shall fail them. On that staff they shall lean no longer. They shall not enjoy the happiness of dying before their children. They shall totter to their grave, bereft of their offspring and unwept by any who inherit their blood. Does it fall on a husband? The eyes which watch his parting steps may swim in tears forever. She is a wife no longer. There is no relation so tender or so sacred that by these accursed measures you do not propose to violate it. There is no happiness so perfect that you do not propose to destroy it. Into the paradise of domestic life you enter, not indeed by temptations and sorceries, but by open force and violence. . . .

Nor is it, sir, for the defense of his own house and home, that he who is the subject of military draft is to perform the task allotted to him. You will put him upon a service equally foreign to his interests and abhorrent to his feelings. With his aid you are to push your purposes of conquest. The battles which he is to fight are the battles of invasion—battles which he detests perhaps, and abhors, less from the danger and the death that gathers over them, and the blood with which they drench the plain, than from the principles in which they have their origin. Fresh from the peaceful pursuits of life, and yet a soldier but in name, he is to be opposed to veteran troops, hardened under every scene, inured to every privation, and disciplined in every service. If, sir, in this strife he fall—if, while ready to obey every rightful command of government, he is forced from his home against right, not to contend for the defense of his country, but to prosecute a miserable and detestable project of invasion, and in that strife he fall 'tis murder. It may stalk above the cognizance of human law, but in the sight of Heaven it is murder; and though millions of years may roll away, while his ashes and yours lie mingled together in the earth, the day will yet come when his spirit and the spirits of his children must be met at the bar of omnipotent justice. May God, in his compassion, shield me from any participation in the enormity of this guilt. . . .

The operation of measures thus unconstitutional and illegal ought to be prevented by a resort to other measures which are both constitutional and legal. It will be the solemn duty of the State governments to protect their own authority over their own militia, and to interpose between their citizens and arbitrary power. These are among the objects for which the State governments exist; and their highest obligations bind them to the preservation of their own rights and the liberties of their people. I express these sentiments here, sir, because I shall express them to my constituents. Both they and myself live under a constitution which teaches us that "the doctrine of nonresistance against arbitrary power and oppression is absurd, slavish, and destructive of the good and happiness of mankind" (New Hampshire Bill of Rights). With the same earnestness with which I now exhort you to forebear from these measures, I shall exhort them to exercise their unquestionable right of providing for the security of their own liberties. . . .

What Republicanism Is This?

JOHN RANDOLPH DENOUNCES THE WAR OF 1812

December 10, 1811
U.S. House of Representatives

Congressman John Randolph of Roanoke, chairman of the Ways and Means Committee during Thomas Jefferson's presidency, was a states' rights, strict-constructionist Virginian who feared that the Republican (sometimes called

Democratic-Republican) Party of his day was abandoning its limited-government stance. Offensive war, he said, was not compatible with that posture.

But is war the true remedy? Who will profit by it? Speculators—a few lucky merchants who draw prizes in the lottery—commissaries and contractors. Who must suffer by it? The people. It is their blood, their taxes, that must flow to support it. . . .

The Government of the United States was not calculated to wage offensive foreign war—it was instituted for the common defence and general welfare; and whosoever should embark it in a war of offence, would put it to a test which it was by no means calculated to endure. . . .

Ask these self-styled patriots where they were during the American [revolutionary] war (for they are for the most part old enough to have borne arms), and you strike them dumb—their lips are closed in eternal silence. . . .

He called upon [n.b.: Congressional speeches used to be recorded in the third person] those professing to be Republicans to make good the promises held out by their Republican predecessors when they came into power—promises which for years afterwards they had honestly, faithfully fulfilled. We had vaunted of paying off the national debt, of retrenching useless establishments; and yet had now become as infatuated with standing armies, loans, taxes, navies, and war, as ever were the Essex Junto. What Republicanism is this?

With Good Advice Make War

CONGRESSMAN SAMUEL TAGGART

Representative Samuel Taggart, a Massachusetts Federalist and a Presbyterian pastor, served in the U.S. Congress from 1803 until 1817. Protesting the closed-door debate over war, Taggart refused to deliver this speech on the House floor. It was instead published in the Alexandria Gazette *on June 24, 1812.*

. . . Believing, as I most conscientiously do, that a war, at this time, would jeopardize the best, the most vital interests, of the country which gave me birth, and in which is contained all that I hold near and dear in life, I have, so far as depended upon my vote, uniformly opposed every measure which I believed had a direct tendency to lead to war. . . .

Among many very wise observations of the wisest of men, who, although an absolute and very powerful monarch, it is observable, never engaged in any war, this is one. *With good advice make war.* This is a maxim which is peculiarly applicable to offensive wars. With respect to such wars as are purely defensive, nations are, many times, not left to their own choice. Another nation, either more ambitious or more powerful, invades an inoffensive neighbor, with a view to conquest. The nation invaded has no choice left but either resistance or submission. No doubt such unprovoked aggressions legalize war. Whether offensive war is in any case, and under any circumstances, justifiable, is a question which ought to be maturely considered. Without attempting to either a decision, or a discussion of it, at this time, I shall take it for granted, that it will be on all hands conceded that offensive war ought not to be waged, unless where the causes are great, and the call peculiarly urgent. No one pretends that the war in which we propose to engage is purely defensive. No hostile armament that I know of is upon our border, menacing invasion, or endeavoring to effect a lodgement on our soil. No hostile fleet is hovering on our coast and menacing our cities with either plunder or destruction. None of our cities are besieged, nor is our internal tranquillity threatened by a foreign invader. As it respects any disturbance from the foreign enemy with whom we contemplate to be at war, we may both lie down in peace, and sleep in safety in the most exposed situation in the country without anyone to disturb our repose. We contemplate the invasion of a foreign territory, to which no one pretends we have any right, unless one to be acquired by conquest. It is to be a war of conquest upon land, undertaken with a view to obtain reparation for injuries we have sustained on the water. In the first place, although our honor is said to be concerned in it, and that it is a war which cannot, consistent with honor, be avoided, I can see nothing very honorable in it. . . .

It seems that, while we tamely submit to the injuries of other nations, we are disposed to select that nation alone for our enemy with whom we have the greatest interest in being at peace, and who is able to do us the most harm in the event of a war. I have no disposition to appear the advocate of either the Orders in Council, the blockading system, or the impressments of the one Power, or of the Berlin and Milan decrees, the treacherous seizure of our property in port, where the owner supposed it secure under the protection of the laws, or the immuring of our seamen in dungeons, and compelling them, as the only alternative, to serve on board her privateers, practiced by the other. . . .

In the remarks which I am about to make, I know not but I shall be denounced as a British partisan, not only in the slang of unprincipled newspapers, but by some members of this House. Being conscious of having no interest to serve [but] that of my country, I shall not be deterred by that consideration from making the observations I had contemplated. War is, on all hands, allowed to be a great evil, as well as uncertain in its issue, a state of things in which might frequently takes the place of right, and in every view of it, is attended with such calamities that it never ought to be resorted to, unless in cases of the most urgent necessity. The true policy of nations, therefore, who are desirous of maintaining peace, ought to be to narrow down the subjects in dispute as much as possible; and, instead of enlarging upon and aggravating every subject of difference, instead of a constant brooding over the injuries they have received, to explore ways and means, and cultivate a disposition in every practicable way to effect an accommodation, and it may not be amiss sometimes to take a rapid glance at causes of difference which have originated with themselves. Whenever either a nation or an individual takes the high ground of complete self-justification in every particular, and will receive nothing short of the most explicit submission from the opposite party, the prospect of an amicable accommodation is very small. When there is a disposition in either, or in both parties, to distort, or to represent everything in the worst possible light, it has ever been found a very easy thing to produce a quarrel either between nations or individuals, even in cases where, by a mutual and candid explanation, the difference might have been easily adjusted. . . .

I wish it to be kept in view that I have no intention, neither do I entertain a wish to vindicate the Orders in Council. Every neutral, and especially every American, must view the principles contained in these orders as injurious to his rights. . . .

It is said to be necessary to go to war, for the purpose of securing our commercial rights, of opening a way for obtaining the best market for our produce, and in order to avenge the insults which have been offered to our flag. But what is there in the present situation of the United States, which we could reasonably expect would be ameliorated by war? In a situation of the world which is perhaps without a parallel in the annals of history, it would be strange indeed, if the United States did not suffer some inconveniences, especially in their mercantile connexions and speculations. In a war which has been unequalled for the changes which it has effected in ancient existing establishments, and for innovations in the ancient laws and usages of nations, it would be equally wonderful, if, in every particular, the rights of neutrals were scrupulously respected. But, upon the whole, we have reaped greater advantages, and suffered fewer inconveniences from the existing state of things, than it was natural to expect. During a considerable part of the time, in which so large and fair a portion of Europe has been desolated by the calamities of war, our commerce has flourished to a degree surpassing the most sanguine calculations. Our merchants have been enriched beyond any former example. Our agriculture has been greatly extended, the wilderness has blossomed like a rose, and cities and villages have sprung up, almost as [if] by the force of magic. It is true that this tide of prosperity has received a check. The aggressions and encroachments of foreign nations have set bounds to our mercantile speculations; heavy losses have been sustained by the merchant, and the cotton planter of the South and West can no longer reap those enormous profits, those immense golden harvests, from that species of agriculture which he did a few years ago. But, if the shackles which we have placed upon commerce by our own restrictive system were completely done away, and the enterprise of the merchant was left free to explore new channels, it is probable that it would at this moment be more extensive and more gainful than in times of profound peace in Europe. . . .

Embarrassed as is the present situation of the United States, would you exchange that situation, or wish this nation to exchange situations with that of any of those countries who have been so long and so arduously engaged in the pursuit of war and glory? Have the peaceful citizens of this Confederated Republic any reason to envy the subjects of the great Emperor, arrayed in all the plenitude of his power and the splendor of his victories? Look at the present situation of Great Britain, France, Spain, Holland, Germany, Sweden, Denmark, Switzerland, Russia, Prussia, etc., who have been so long either tasting the sweets, or groaning under the calamities of war; and would you be willing that this country would exchange situations with either of them? No, you would not. Every principle of humanity, as well as every dictate of common sense would revolt at the idea. Why then, in the name of Heaven, shall we plunge ourselves into a war, which cannot fail to involve us in the vortex of all their ills, without the prospect, or even the possibility of securing to us one solitary good? . . .

If the recruits of the regular army are in numbers so scanty, and if at the beginning of a war which needs the full glow of national enthusiasm to give it éclat, recourse must be had to a compulsive process not very different in principle from the conscription of France, to drag our citizens reluctantly into the service, it is a practical comment upon the correctness of an opinion which has been frequently advanced within these walls, as well as elsewhere, that the present war was necessary to comport with the sentiments, and meet the wishes of the people at large. No, sir; this conduct speaks louder than any words can do: that the people neither see nor feel the necessity of this war. A thousand resolutions, and noisy pledges of lives and fortunes, which cost nothing, can never rebut the impression. I am afraid that it will be found that we have mistaken the sentiments of licentious journalists, many of them foreigners without a single American feeling or attachment, and of officers, contractors, purveyors, and office hunters, who expect to make a gain of war, at the public expense, for the voice of the people. The substantial yeomanry of the country do not, they cannot, wish for this war. . . . We appear to be selecting a time to begin a war, when our Treasury is empty, and we are destitute of resources to replenish it. Some appear disposed to scout all calculations of expense, and to rely upon patriotism and a high sense of honor to carry on the war. But however good a topic patriotism may be, to furnish materials for an harangue in a bar-room, for a newspaper or electioneering essay, or to embellish a war speech on the floor of Congress, we must have money— money in large sums—to carry on the war. . . .

At all events, Canada must be ours [say those who support war]; and this is to be the sovereign balm, the universal panacea, which is to heal all the wounds we have received either in our honor, interest, or reputation. This is to be the boon which is to indemnify us, for all past losses on the ocean, secure the liberty of the seas hereafter, protect our seamen from impressments, and remunerate us for all the blood and treasure which is to be expended in the present war. Our rights on the ocean have been assailed, and, however inconsistent it may seem to go as far as possible from the ocean to seek redress, yet this would appear to be the policy. We are to seek it, it seems, by fighting the Indians on the Wabash or at Tippecanoe, or the Canadians at Fort Malden, at Little York, at Kingston, at Montreal, and at Quebec. . . .

The conquest of Canada has been represented to be so easy as to be little more than a party of pleasure. We have, it has been said, nothing to do but to march an army into the country and display the standard of the United States, and the Canadians will immediately flock to it and place themselves under our protection. They have been represented as ripe for revolt, panting for emancipation from a tyrannical Government, and longing to enjoy the sweets of liberty under the fostering hand of the United States. On taking a different view of their situations, it has been suggested that, if they should not be disposed to hail us on our arrival as brothers, come to emancipate and not to subdue them, that they are a debased race of poltroons, incapable of making anything like a stand in their own defense, that the mere sight of an army of the United States would immediately put an end to all thoughts of resistance, that we had little else to do only to march, and that in the course of a few weeks one of our valiant commanders, when writing a dispatch to the President of the United States, might adopt the phraseology of Caesar: *Veni, Vidi, Vici.* This subject deserves a moment's consideration. To presume on the disaffection or treasonable practices of the inhabitants for facilitating the conquest, will probably be to reckon without our host. The Canadians have no cause of disaffection with the British Government. They have ever been treated with indulgence. They enjoy all that security and happiness, in their connexion with Great Britain, that they could reasonably expect in any situation. Lands can be acquired by the industrious settlers at an easy rate, I believe for little more than the office fees for issuing patents, which may amount to three or four cents per acre. They have few or no taxes to pay. . . . They have a good market for their surplus produce, unhampered with embargoes or commercial restrictions of any kind, and are equally secure in both person and property, both in their civil and religious rights, with the citizens of the United States. What have they, therefore, to gain by a connexion with the United States? . . .

Should the present war prove disastrous and unsuccessful; should we neither take Canada, nor obtain one single object for which we make war; yet, if we only make war, and fight, and show our spirit, whatever may be the consequences, we may have a consolation similar to that of the gallant Francis, which he communicated in a note to the Queen Regent, after he was defeated and taken prisoner by his enemy and rival, Charles V, in the fatal battle of Pavia: "Madam, we have lost all but our honor." But, will such a saving of our honor dry up the tears of the parent, the mother, or the sister—the widow or the orphan? Will it console the survivor for the loss of a husband, a parent, a son, a brother, or an intimate friend? Will it rebuild our ruined cities and restore life to our slaughtered citizens? Will it either administer comfort or give compensation to the many thousands who will be reduced from affluence to the utmost distress by the operations of war? Will it procure to us the unmolested enjoyment of any of those rights we are going to war to assert? Will it render us more respected among foreign nations, or them less disposed to make encroachments on our rights in [the] future? No, sir; it will have none of these effects. But I will venture to state some of the effects which it will have. It will expose the authors of this war to the execration of their fellow citizens, and it will afford us sufficient leisure to mourn over our follies when it is too late. Let that kind of honor perish from among nations. Let that principle in a particular manner be expunged, both from the moral and political code of this nation, which would involve the ruin of millions for no other cause than a mere point of honor.

I shall trouble the House with but one single appeal more, and that is merely to make a solemn appeal to the principles and feelings of a large proportion of the members of this House. Indeed, I would wish to single out no man as being of a character different from that of those which I address. I mean by this an appeal to Christians—men whose hopes and expectations extend beyond the fleeting, transitory things of time—men who believe the doctrines of Christianity, and who have imbibed a portion of the spirit of its meek and lowly founder. Can it be agreeable to the principles of that religion which you profess, and the hopes you entertain, to vote in favor of this war? Can we look to that God in whose presence we stand, and before whom we must shortly appear, to grant his blessing upon the act, when we give a vote which may, in its consequences, send thousands and ten thousands of immortal human beings, suddenly, uncalled, and probably unprepared into the presence of their God? It is to be recollected, too, that we are about to draw the sword against a Christian nation. Perhaps in no other part of the world of equal extent is there so much real Christianity as in Great Britain and the United States. The voice of that heaven-born religion is peace and good will to men. Its author and founder came from heaven to preach and publish peace. He hath pronounced a blessing on the peace-makers, and is himself the Prince of Peace. How inconsistent then is it with the characters of Christian nations and Christian rulers to deluge their country with blood, stimulated by the calls of either ambition or avarice, and in contempt of the dictates of humanity as well as the principles of Christianity. How solemn, how affecting is the thought that children of the same family, heirs of the same promises, persons engaged in the same design, and influenced by the same desires, hopes, and fears, should, in the chances of the war, slaughter each other in the field. I have not the talent at description which is adequate to place the calamities of war in a light which is sufficiently strong; but I thank God that I have none of that certain something which some, perhaps, would call firmness of mind, in my constitution—none of that stoical apathy which can survey these calamities, even in imagination, with indifference, nor can I appreciate the character of the man, call him hero, warrior, or philosopher, or what you please, who can fiddle over a city in flames, or survey the calamities of war with calm indifference. I would, therefore, beseech gentlemen to forget for a single moment the warmth of political discussion, and listen to the claims of humanity, and turn their views to the blood-stained field of slaughter, to the scattered and mangled limbs of thousands of slain, and to the piercing groans of the wounded and dying. These are some of the bloody sacrifices paid to the Moloch of honor and ambition. Turn away from this part of the picture, and take a survey of cities in flames, of thousands and ten thousands, not only of men, but of helpless women and children, who, if not involved in the flaming ruins, are turned out naked, houseless, and penniless into the world, without a garment to cover them or a morsel of bread to support them. Take, in the next place, a glance at the mansions of private life, lately the abodes of plenty, innocence, and domestic peace, and view the sad reverse. View the tears of the parent bowed down under a load of years, deprived of a son, perhaps the last earthly stay and support of the evening of life, and of the widow and the orphan, bewailing the stay and support of helpless infancy, and of the more tender and affectionate, although weaker and more dependent sex, gone by the ruthless sword, and of the brother, the sister, or intimate acquaintance, bewailing the loss of a brother or a friend. But the picture is too horrible to dwell on. Let us draw a veil over the remainder. These, some of them at least, and many times, all of them combined, are the attendant calamities of war, a war which, in the present case, if it is once begun, we can neither calculate the extent nor the duration. These may be all the fruits of a single vote. A solitary *aye* may decide the question. I beseech gentlemen to pause, and seriously to consider this before they give their votes in favor of the proposition now on the table. Whatever may be the decision, I have this one consolation, that I shall, when I have given my vote, have exonerated myself of all responsibility for the consequences. Believing as I do, that this war is both unnecessary and impolitic in the outset, that there is no adequate object which we can reasonably expect to obtain by war, and that, in every view, it is contrary to the best, the most vital interests of my country, I shall, when I have recorded my vote against it, have done my duty.

"Thou Hast Done a Deed Whereat Valor Will Weep"

ALEXANDER HANSON

Congress declared war against Britain on June 18, 1812; on June 20, the Federal Republican, *a Baltimore newspaper, published the following editorial by Alexander Hanson. Two days later, an angry mob destroyed the paper's offices. When the* Federal Republican *relocated to another office, that one was destroyed by a mob as well. Hanson served as a U.S. congressman from Maryland from 1812 until his untimely death in 1816.*

"Thou hast done a deed whereat valor will weep." Without funds, without taxes, without an army, navy, or adequate fortifications—with one hundred and fifty millions of our property in the hands of the declared enemy, without any of his in our power, and with a vast commerce afloat, our rulers have promulged [*sic*] a war against the clear and decided sentiments of a vast majority of the nation. As the consequences will soon be felt, there is no need of pointing them out to the few who have not sagacity enough to apprehend them. Instead of employing our pen in this dreadful detail, we think it more apposite to delineate the course we are determined to pursue as long as the war shall last. We mean to represent in as strong colors as we are capable, that it is unnecessary, inexpedient, and entered into from a partial, personal, and as we believe, motives bearing upon their front marks of undisguised foreign influence, which cannot be mistaken. We mean to use every constitutional argument and every legal means to render as odious and suspicious to the American people, as they deserve to be, the patrons and contrivers of this highly impolitic and destructive war, in the fullest persuasion that we shall be supported and ultimately applauded by nine-tenths of our countrymen, and that our silence would be treason to them. We detest and abhor the endeavors of faction to create civil contest through the pretext of a foreign war it has rashly and premeditatedly commenced, and we shall be ready cheerfully to hazard everything most dear, to frustrate anything leading to the prostration of civil rights, and the establishment of a system of terror and proscription announced in the Government paper at Washington as the inevitable consequence of the measure now proclaimed. We shall cling to the rights of freemen, both in act and opinion, till we sink with the liberties of our country, or sink alone. We shall hereafter, as heretofore, unravel every intrigue and imposture which has beguiled or may be put forth to circumvent our fellow-citizens into the toils of the great earthly enemy of the human race. We are avowedly hostile to the presidency of James Madison, and we never will breathe under the dominion, direct or derivative, of Bonaparte, let it be acknowledged when it may. Let those who cannot openly adopt this confession, abandon us; and those who can, we shall cherish as friends and patriots, worthy of the name.

2

The Mexican War

I went about preparing myself to give the vote understandingly when it should come. I carefully examined the President's messages, to ascertain what he himself had said and proved upon the point. The result of this examination was to make the impression, that taking for true, all the President states as fact, he falls far short of proving his justification; and that the President would have gone farther with his proof, if it had not been for the small matter, that the truth would not permit him.

—ABRAHAM LINCOLN,
speech against the Mexican War,
January 12, 1848

The United States annexed Texas, which had once belonged to Mexico, in 1845, nine years after that province had declared its independence. Since Mexico had never officially recognized Texan independence, it viewed the annexation as a provocative act. Adding to the diplomatic tension was an unresolved border dispute: Mexico claimed the Nueces River as the southern border of Texas, while the Texans (and with them the U.S. government) pointed to the Rio Grande.

In addition, President James Polk was interested in purchasing additional territory from Mexico in what would later become the American southwest. Efforts to negotiate proved fruitless, owing largely to the instability of the Mexican government. Stymied on all fronts, the Polk administration looked to a military solution. It hoped the Mexican government might initiate hostilities, in order that the U.S. government's decision to go to war would seem like an act of self-defense.

The incident the Polk administration was looking for occurred on April 24, 1846, when Mexican troops attacked their American counterparts in Texas. Once Polk learned what had happened, he declared to Congress, "Mexico has shed American blood upon American soil." Two days later, war was officially declared on Mexico.

Abraham Lincoln, a congressman from Illinois, became suspicious of the official rationale given for the war. His "spot resolution," introduced into Congress, demanded that Polk clarify for the country the exact spot on which American forces had been attacked. Lincoln and others suspected that American soldiers had been placed not along the Nueces River but in the disputed area between the two proposed borders of Texas. Posted there, Americans were far more likely to provoke an attack, since Mexico had never acknowledged the loss of the disputed territory and could not abide the presence of foreign troops there.

It turned out that the shots had indeed been fired in the disputed area, and that Polk had placed American troops in a territory in which the likelihood of a violent confrontation was relatively high. In 1848, the year the war ended, Congress voted 85 to 81 to censure President Polk, declaring that the war had been "unnecessarily and unconstitutionally begun by the President of the United States."

Historian John Armstrong Crow (1906–2001) said of the Mexican War, "In justice be it said that the people of the United States supported this war less than they have ever supported any campaign in their history. [Historian Samuel Eliot Morison bestows that designation on the War of 1812.] Some North American newspapers decried the conflict in terms which in other days would have bordered on treason. The famous New England writer, Henry David Thoreau, became so public in his complaints that they sent him to jail. Nevertheless, the people by and large did believe in their Manifest Destiny, did want Texas and California," were imperialistic-minded both in fact and in principle." The controversies that later ensued over the disposition of slavery in the territories won from Mexico played no small role in bringing on the American Civil War. Such are the unintended consequences of war.

Annexation and War with Mexico Are Identical

HENRY CLAY

Henry Clay, longtime congressman and senator from Kentucky and an influential figure in national politics, opposed the acquisition of Texas on the grounds that it would provoke war with Mexico. This letter was addressed to the National Intelligencer *of Raleigh, North Carolina, on April 17, 1844.*

Annexation and war with Mexico are identical. Now, for one, I certainly am not willing to involve this country in a foreign war for the object of acquiring Texas. I know there are those who regard such a war with indifference and as a trifling affair, on account of the weakness of Mexico, and her inability to inflict serious injury upon this country. But I do not look upon it thus lightly. I regard all wars as great calamities, to be avoided, if possible, and honorable peace as the wisest and truest policy of this country. What the United States most need are union, peace, and patience. Nor do I think that the weakness of a power should form a motive, in any case, for inducing us to engage in or to depreciate the evils of war. Honor and good faith and justice are equally due from this country towards the weak as towards the strong. . . .

I do not think that Texas ought to be received into the Union, as an integral part of it, in decided opposition to the wishes of a considerable and respectable portion of the confederacy. I think it far more wise and important to compose and harmonize the present union, as it now exists, than to introduce a new element of discord and distraction into it. . . .

It is useless to disguise that there are those who espouse and those who oppose the annexation of Texas upon the ground of the influence which it would exert, in the balance of political power, between two great sections of the Union. I conceive that no motive for the acquisition of foreign territory would be more unfortunate than that of obtaining it for the purpose of strengthening one part against another part of the common confederacy. Such a principle, put into practical operation, would menace the existence, if it did not certainly sow the seeds of a dissolution of the Union.

Annexation would be to proclaim to the world an insatiable and unquenchable thirst for foreign conquest or acquisition of territory. For if today Texas be acquired to strengthen one part of the confederacy, tomorrow Canada may be required to add strength to another. Finally, the part of the confederacy which is now weakest, would find itself still weaker from the impossibility of securing new territory for those peculiar institutions (slavery) which it is charged with being desirous to extend. . . .

I consider the annexation of Texas, at this time, without the assent of Mexico, as a measure compromising the national character, involving us certainly in war with Mexico, probably with other foreign powers, dangerous to the integrity of the Union, inexpedient in the present financial condition of the country, and not called for by any general expression of public opinion.

The True Grandeur of Nations

CHARLES SUMNER

Charles Sumner, a lawyer, orator, and politician, was for many years a U.S. senator from Massachusetts and a leading figure among the Radical

Republicans during the Reconstruction period. Sumner delivered these antiwar remarks on July 4, 1845, in Boston. His opposition to war notwithstanding, Sumner did support the U.S. Civil War.

By an act of unjust legislation, extending our power over Texas, peace with Mexico is endangered—while, by petulant assertion of a disputed claim to a remote territory [Oregon] beyond the Rocky Mountains, ancient fires of hostile strife are kindled anew on the hearth of our mother country [England].

Mexico and England both avow the determination to vindicate what is called the *National Honor;* and our Government calmly contemplates the dread Arbitrament of War, provided it cannot obtain what is called an honorable peace.

Far from our nation and our age be the sin and shame of contests hateful in the sight of God and all good men, having their origin in no righteous sentiment, no true love of country, no generous thirst for fame, "that last infirmity of noble mind," but springing manifestly from an ignorant and ignoble passion for new territory, strengthened, in our·case, in a republic whose star is Liberty, by unnatural desire to add new links in chains destined yet to fall from the limbs of the unhappy slave!

In such contests God has no attribute which can join with us.

Who believes that the national honor would be promoted by a war with Mexico or a war with England? What just man would sacrifice a single human life to bring under our rule both Texas and Oregon?. . .

A war with Mexico [to conquer and annex Texas, California, Arizona, etc.] would be mean and cowardly; with England [for Oregon] it would be bold at least, though parricidal. The heart sickens at the murderous attack upon an enemy [Mexico] distracted by civil feud, weak at home, impotent abroad; but it recoils in horror from the deadly shock between children of a common ancestry, speaking the same language, soothed in infancy by the same words of love and tenderness, and hardened into vigorous manhood under the bracing influence of institutions instinct with the same vital breath of freedom.

Can there be in our age any peace that is not honorable, any war that is not dishonorable? The true honor of a nation is conspicuous only in deeds of justice and beneficence, securing and advancing human happiness.

In the clear eye of that Christian judgment which must yet prevail, vain are the victories of War, infamous its spoils. He is the benefactor, and worthy of honor, who carries comfort to wretchedness, dries the tear of sorrow, relieves the unfortunate, feeds the hungry, clothes the naked, does justice, enlightens the ignorant, unfastens the fetters of the slave, and finally, by virtuous genius, in art, literature, science, enlivens and exalts the hours of life, or, by generous example, inspires a love for God and man. This is the Christian hero; this is the man of honor in a Christian land.

He is no benefactor, nor worthy of honor, whatever his worldly renown, whose life is absorbed in feats of brute force, who renounces the great law of Christian brotherhood, whose vocation is blood. Well may the modern poet exclaim, "The world knows nothing of its greatest men!"—for thus far it has chiefly honored the violent brood of Battle, armed men springing up from the dragon's teeth sown by Hate, and cared little for the truly good men, children of Love, guiltless of their country's blood, whose steps on earth are noiseless as an angel's wing.

It will not be disguised that this standard differs from that of the world even in our day. The voice of man is yet given to martial praise, and the honors of victory are chanted even by the lips of woman. The mother, rocking the infant on her knee, stamps the images of War upon his tender mind, at that age more impressible than wax; she nurses his slumber with its music, pleases his waking hours with its stories, and selects for his playthings the plume and the sword.

From the child is formed the man; and who can weigh the influence of a mother's spirit on the opinions of his life? The mind which trains the child is like a hand at the end of a long lever; a gentle effort suffices to heave the enormous weight of succeeding years. As the boy advances to youth, he is fed like Achilles, not on honey and milk only, but on bears' marrow and lions' hearts. He draws the nutriment of his soul from a literature whose beautiful fields are moistened by human blood. Fain would I offer my tribute to the Father of Poetry, standing with harp of immortal melody on the misty mountain-top of distant Antiquity—to those stories of courage and sacrifice which emblazon the annals of Greece and Rome—to the fulminations of Demosthenes and the splendors of Tully—to the sweet verse of Virgil and the poetic prose of Livy; fain would I offer my tribute to the new literature, which shot up in modern times as a vigorous forest from the burnt site of ancient woods—to the passionate song of the Troubadour in France and the Minnesinger in Germany—to the thrilling ballad of Spain and the delicate music of the Italian lyre: but from all these has breathed the breath of War, that has swept the heart-strings of men in all the thronging generations.

And when the youth becomes a man, his country invites his service in war, and holds before his bewildered imagination the prizes of worldly honor. For him the pen of the historian and the verse of the poet. His soul is taught to swell at the thought that he, too, is a soldier— that his name shall be entered on the list of those who have borne arms for their country; and perhaps he dreams that he, too, may sleep, like the Great Captain of Spain, with a hundred trophies over his grave.

The law of the land throws its sanction over this frenzy. The contagion spreads beyond those subject to positive obligation. Peaceful citizens volunteer to appear as soldiers, and affect, in dress, arms, and deportment, what is called the "pride, pomp, and circumstance of glorious war." The ear-piercing fife has to-day filled our streets, and we have come to this church, on this National Sabbath [Fourth of July], by the thump of drum and with the parade of bristling bayonets. . . .

Mean and Infamous

THEODORE PARKER

February 4, 1847

Theodore Parker (1810–1860) was an abolitionist, social reformer, and Unitarian minister. He was one of the Secret Six who supported abolitionist John Brown in 1859. Parker delivered this speech at an antiwar meeting at Boston's Faneuil Hall on February 4, 1847.

We are in a war; the signs of war are seen here in Boston. Men needed to hew wood and honestly serve society are marching about your streets; they are learning to kill men, men who never harmed us nor them; learning to kill their brothers. It is a mean and infamous war we are fighting. It is a great boy fighting a little one, and that little one feeble and sick. What makes it worse is, the little boy is in the right, and the big boy is in the wrong, and tells solemn lies to make his side seem right. He wants, besides, to make the small boy pay the expenses of the quarrel. . . .

The war had a mean and infamous beginning. It began illegally, unconstitutionally. The Whigs say, "The President made the war." Mr. Webster says so! It went on meanly and infamously. Your Congress lied about it. Do not lay the blame on the Democrats; the Whigs lied just as badly. Your Congress has seldom been so single-mouthed before. Why, only sixteen voted against the war, or the lie. I say this war is mean and infamous, all the more because waged by a people calling itself democratic and Christian. . . .

I say, I blame not so much the volunteers as the famous men who deceived the nation! . . .

It is time for the people of Massachusetts to instruct their servants in Congress to oppose this war; to refuse all supplies for it; to ask for the recall of the army into our own land. It is time for us to tell them that not an inch of slave territory shall ever be added to the realm. Let us remonstrate; let us petition; let us command. If any class of men have hitherto been remiss, let them come forward now and give us their names—the merchants, the manufacturers, the Whigs and the Democrats. If men love their country better than their party or their purse, now let them show it. . . .

Your President tells us it is treason to talk so! Treason, is it? Treason to discuss a war which the government made, and which the people are made to pay for? If it be treason to speak against the war, what was it to make the war, to ask for 50,000 men and $74,000,000 for the war? Why, if the people cannot discuss the war they have got to fight and to pay for, who under heaven can? Whose business is it, if it is not yours and mine? If my country is in the wrong, and I know it, and hold my peace, then I am guilty of treason, moral treason. Why, a wrong—it is only the threshold of ruin. I would not have my country take the next step. Treason is it, to show that this war is wrong and wicked? Why, what if George III, any time from '75 to '83, had gone down to Parliament and told them it was treason to discuss the war then waging against these colonies! What do you think the Commons would have said? What would the Lords say? Why, that king, foolish as he was, would have been lucky, if he had not learned there was a joint in his neck, and, stiff as he bore him, that the people knew how to find it. . . .

I call on the men of Boston, on the men of the old Bay State, to act worthy of their fathers, worthy of their country, worthy of themselves! Men and brothers, I call on you all to protest against this most infamous war, in the name of the state, in the name of the country, in the name of man—yes, in the name of God; leave not your children saddled with a war debt, to cripple the nation's commerce for years to come. Leave not your land cursed with slavery, extended and extending, palsying the nation's arm and corrupting the nation's heart. Leave not your memory infamous among the nations, because you feared men, feared the government; because you loved money got by crime, land plundered in war, loved land unjustly bounded; because you debased your country by defending the wrong she dared to do. . . .

The Half-Insane Mumbling of a Fever Dream

ABRAHAM LINCOLN

Abraham Lincoln, an Illinois Whig then serving in his one term as a U.S. congressman, delivered this speech in the House of Representatives on January 12, 1848.

Let him [President James Polk] remember he sits where Washington sat, and so remembering, let him answer as Washington would answer. As a nation should not, and the Almighty will not, be evaded, so let him attempt no evasion—no equivocation. And if, so answering, he can show that the soil was ours where the first blood of the war was shed—that it was not within an inhabited country, or, if within such, that the inhabitants had submitted themselves to the civil authority of Texas or of the United States, and that the same is true of the site of Fort Brown—then I am with him for his justification. In that case I shall be most happy to reverse the vote I gave the other day. I have a selfish motive for desiring that the President may do this—I expect to give some votes, in connection with the war, which, without his so doing, will be of doubtful propriety in my own judgment, but which will be free from the doubt if he does so. But if he can not or will not do this—if on any pretense or no pretense he shall refuse or omit it—then I shall be fully convinced of what I more than suspect already—that he is deeply conscious of being in the wrong; that he feels the blood of this war, like the blood of Abel, is crying to Heaven against him; that originally having some strong motive—what, I will not stop now to give my opinion concerning—to involve the two countries in a war, and trusting to escape scrutiny by fixing the public gaze upon the exceeding brightness of military glory—that attractive rainbow that rises in showers of blood—that serpent's eye that charms to destroy—he plunged into it, and has swept on and on till, disappointed in his calculation of the ease with which Mexico might be subdued, he now finds himself he knows not where.

How like the half-insane mumbling of a fever dream, is the whole war part of his late message! At one time telling us that Mexico has nothing whatever that we can get but territory; at another, showing us how we can support the war by levying contributions on Mexico. At one time urging the national honor, the security of the future, the prevention of foreign interference, and even the good of Mexico herself, as among the objects of the war; at another telling us that "to reject indemnity, by refusing to accept a cession of territory, would be to abandon all our just demands, and to wage the war bearing all its expenses, without a purpose or definite object." So then this national honor, security of the future, and everything but territorial indemnity may be considered the no-purpose and indefinite objects of the war! But, having it now settled that territorial indemnity is the only object, we are urged to seize, by legislation here, all that he was content to take a few months ago, and the whole province of Lower California to boot, and to still carry on the war—to take all we are fighting for, and still fight on. Again, the President is resolved under all circumstances to have full territorial indemnity for the expenses of the war; but he forgets to tell us how we are to get the excess after those expenses shall have surpassed the value of the whole of the Mexican territory. So again, he insists that the separate national existence of Mexico shall be maintained; but he does not tell us how this can be done, after we shall have taken all her territory.

Lest the questions I have suggested be considered speculative merely, let me be indulged a moment in trying to show they are not. The war has gone on some twenty months; for the expenses of which, together with an inconsiderable old score, the President now claims about one half of the Mexican territory, and that, by far the better half, so far as concerns our ability to make anything out of it. It is comparatively uninhabited; so that we could establish land offices in it, and raise some money in that way. But the other half is already inhabited, as I understand it, tolerably densely for the nature of the country; and all its lands, or all that are valuable, already appropriated as private property.

How then are we to make anything out of these lands with this encumbrance on them? Or how remove the encumbrance? I suppose no one will say we should kill the people, or drive them out, or make slaves of them, or confiscate their property. How, then, can we make much out of this part of the territory? If the prosecution of the war has in expenses already equaled the better half of the country, how long its future prosecution will be in equaling the less valuable half is not a speculative, but a practical, question, pressing closely upon us. And yet it is a question which the President seems to never have thought of.

As to the mode of terminating the war and securing peace, the President is equally wandering and indefinite. First, it is to be done by a more vigorous prosecution of the war in the vital parts of the enemy's country; and after apparently talking himself tired on this point, the President drops down into a half-despairing tone, and tells us that "with a people distracted and divided by contending factions, and a government subject to constant changes by successive revolutions, the continued success of our arms may fail to secure a satisfactory peace." Then he suggests the propriety of wheedling the Mexican people to desert the counsels of their own leaders, and trusting in our protestations, to set up a government from which we can secure a satisfactory peace; telling us that "this may become the only mode of obtaining such a peace." But soon he falls into doubt of this too; and then drops back onto the already half-abandoned ground of "more vigorous prosecution." All this shows that the President is in nowise satisfied with his own positions. First he takes up one, and in attempting to argue us into it he argues himself out of it, then seizes another and goes through the same process, and then, confused at being able to think of nothing new, he snatches up the old one again, which he has some time before cast off. His mind, tasked beyond its power, is running hither and thither, like some tortured creature on a burning surface, finding no position on which it can settle down and be at ease.

Again, it is a singular omission in this message that it nowhere intimates when the President expects the war to terminate. At its beginning,

General Scott was by this same President driven into disfavor, if not disgrace, for intimating that peace could not be conquered in less than three or four months. But now, at the end of about twenty months, during which time our arms have given us the most splendid successes, every department and every part, land and water, officers and privates, regulars and volunteers, doing all that men could do, and hundreds of things which it had ever before been thought men could not do—after all this, this same President gives us a long message, without showing us that as to the end he himself has even an imaginary conception. As I have before said, he knows not where he is. He is a bewildered, confounded, and miserably perplexed man. God grant he may be able to show there is not something about his conscience more painful than all his mental perplexity.

This Is a War for Slavery

WILLIAM GOODELL

William Goodell was active in the abolitionist movement, and opened a nonsectarian church in 1843 where he delivered antislavery sermons. Most influential among his writings was the book Slavery and Anti-Slavery: A History of the Great Struggle in Both Hemispheres; with a View of the Slavery Question in the United States, *an 1852 book from which the excerpt below is drawn.*

The first paragraph of the following excerpt contains a reference to "Mr. Jay." Goodell is speaking of William Jay, author of A Review of the Causes and Consequences of the Mexican War *(1849). In that book, Jay made an observation that will sound eerily familiar to modern Americans: "We have been taught to ring our bells, and illuminate our windows and let off fireworks as manifestation of our joy, when we have heard of great ruin and devastation, and misery, and death, inflicted by our troops upon a people who never injured us, who never fired a shot on our soil, and who were utterly incapable of acting on the offensive against us."*

The only ostensible cause of complaint against Mexico, was the claims of certain American citizens for depredations committed on their property by Mexicans, or by subordinate officials of the Mexican government. Mr. Jay has thoroughly sifted these claims, and shown that they constituted no just ground or necessity of war.

The first claim, in July, 1836, under President [Andrew] Jackson [1829–1837], consisted of fifteen distinct specifications of alleged facts, requiring time for their proper investigation. Of the existence of many of them, the Mexican *Government* may well be supposed to have been wholly ignorant, as they claimed to have been, until the complaint was presented. Yet the American Minister, Mr. Ellis, was directed to obtain a satisfactory answer within *three weeks,* or announce that, unless satisfaction was made without unnecessary delay, his further residence would be useless. If this threat proved unavailing, he was to give notice that, unless he received a satisfactory answer in *two weeks,* he should demand his passports and return home. Mr. Ellis was a Mississippi slaveholder, eager to extend the area of slavery by a dismemberment of Mexico.

Another remarkable feature of this demand was, that Mr. Ellis was informed by our government that it was not in possession of "*the proof* of all the circumstances of the wrong done in the above cases!" The reparation was to be demanded *first,* under a threat of war, and the justice of the claim ascertained *afterwards!* Mr. Ellis was to be sole judge whether there was "unnecessary delay," and whether the answers were "satisfactory." The alleged aggressions were mostly of recent date.

Similar claims on France and England had been matter of negotiation for ten or twenty years, without a threat of war, but Mexico was required to finish up the whole business in *five weeks!* . . .

Mr. Ellis thought proper to add five more complaints, without waiting for any directions from his Government. These, added to the thirteen remaining original ones, made the number eighteen. In respect to each of these, the Mexican government returned suitable explanations and assurances *within the time specified.* Some of them were shown to be unfounded. Others of them required proof. Others required further time for investigation. Others of them having been investigated, and being found just, the claimants should be compensated. Others of them were under litigation, and the results would soon be ascertained.

In one case, an American vessel had been seized by the custom-house officers and condemned for want of the proper papers, but an appeal having been taken to a higher court, before whom the missing papers were produced, the vessel had been discharged. The detention was not the fault of the Mexican officers, but of the master of the vessel, in losing his papers. In every case the answer appeared to be fair and reasonable.

Mr. Ellis, nevertheless, as had been determined beforehand, *demanded his passports* and returned home, refusing to give the Mexican Government a reason for so extraordinary a course. And on his return home the country was made to ring with the falsehood that Mexico had refused to pay our just demands! . . .

The President evidently intended WAR. Indeed his message affirmed, distinctly, that these injuries justified an "IMMEDIATE WAR." But, in a semi-official letter to Governor Cannon of Tennessee, only six months before, which had somehow got into print, he had distinctly said "It does not seem that offenses of this character" (i.e., such as would justify war) "have been committed by Mexico."

But, thanks (under God) to the little band of northern agitators against slavery, the people of the North were not yet prepared for such a measure, and the war proposition of President Jackson received little favor by their representatives in Congress. There needed to be new machinations and a more favorable opportunity, before the desired result could be reached.

The treaty between the two countries forbade any act of reprisal, by either party, on account of grievances or damages until they had been "verified by competent proof," and until the demand for satisfaction "refused, or unreasonably delayed." We have seen that, the eighteen complaints against Mexico had *not* been thus verified, nor had the demand for satisfaction been "refused or unreasonably delayed." Yet the President, as we have seen, desired authority to make "reprisals" unless prompt reparation should be made, on a renewal of the demand from on board one of our armed vessels on the coast of Mexico.

And in making this request, he laid before Congress a list of grievances amounting to FORTY-SIX, making twenty-eight new cases that had never been presented to the Mexican Government at all! Some of these additional claims—strange to tell—dated back as far as 1816 and 1817, when Mexico was a province of Spain! And some of them were claims for insurrectionary services against the Spanish Government!

Mr. Ellis was then re-appointed Minister to Mexico, but he remained at home, and a courier was dispatched with the budget of grievances, with an allowance of ONE WEEK to examine and determine upon them all. By incredible zeal and industry, the list of grievances was now swelled to FIFTY-SEVEN. This was in July, 1837, under the administration of Mr. [Martin] Van Buren. Many of these demands, as Mr. Jay well observes, and has clearly shown, "were in the highest degree insolent and ridiculous."

The messenger to Mexico tarried his "*one week*" and returned. But before the list of these fifty-seven grievances reached Mexico, the Mexican Government, intent upon an equitable settlement of all the difficulties it *had heard* anything about, viz.: the *eighteen* specifications made by Mr. Ellis, had passed an act offering to submit to the award of a friendly power, the claims of the United States. In the same peaceful spirit, another Mexican Minister was sent to Washington, and the arbitration proposed, in December, 1837.

The warlike designs of the Federal Administration were thus again baffled. The offer was too fair to be rejected, in the face of the nation and the world, yet for four months no notice was taken of it, but the *new* claims were three times distinctly urged by our Secretary, Mr. Forsyth. Not until the offer had become public, and Congress plied with northern petitions to accept it, and remonstrances against the annexation of Texas, was the overture heeded, and negotiations commenced.

At length an arrangement was made, by which the claims were to be presented to Commissioners to sit at Washington, two to be appointed by each party; the board to sit not more than eighteen months, the decision, of cases by it to be final, and the cases on which they could not agree, to be determined by an umpire to be named by the King of Prussia.

Here, then, were allowed *eighteen months* to go through with an investigation, which Mexico had been required to complete in *three weeks!*

After many delays, the Commission assembled two years after their appointment, giving ample time for all the claimants to collect their evidences.

After sitting *nine* months, they passed upon all the claims that had sufficient vouchers; but, in order to give further time for collecting evidence, the Commission was kept open the remaining nine months, when it was dissolved. The King of Prussia named as umpire his Minister at Washington, Baron Roenne. Now notice the result.

. . . Our government had been demanding of Mexico nearly *twelve millions of dollars,* had demanded a prompt settlement on pain of "reprisals" and war. And here, after the most laborious investigation, and giving ample time, twice over, for proving the claims, they are dwindled down to a little over *two millions,* not much more than ONE-SIXTH PART of the claim. It is true that only about SEVEN AND A HALF millions were acted upon; but this was the fault of the claimants, if they had any valid evidences to bring forward. Again, of the claims brought forward in season and investigated, viz.: about seven and a half millions, only about one-fourth was adjudged to be due.

The award of over two millions remained unpaid, in consequence of the pecuniary embarrassments of the Mexican treasury. Adding to this the amount of claims that had not been adjudicated, the Federal Government was furnished with another opportunity of urging its claims upon Mexico. Another arbitration treaty was negotiated; the commissioners, for this time, were to sit in Mexico, and Mexican citizens having claims against the United States were also to have an opportunity of presenting their claims for adjudication. . . .

So much for our claims against Mexico. Except for delay of payment growing out of its poverty, it does not appear that there was any backwardness on the part of the Mexican Government to do all that could reasonably be asked at its hands. And this is the sum total of all our causes of war against Mexico. . . . And this debt was collected, by the war process, at an expense of above one hundred millions of dollars!

It was territory, not money, that the Federal Government wanted of Mexico, and territory for the extension of slavery. Every step in the entire process affords evidence of this. . . .

The refusal of Mexico to acknowledge the independence of Texas was an obstacle, in the minds of the Northern people, to the annexation of the latter, and hence the Senate, as we have seen, had refused the ratification of Messrs. Tyler and Calhoun's treaty for that object.

The next step was to intimidate Mexico into a recognition of Texan independence. Accordingly, in October, 1844, our Minister to Mexico, Mr. Shannon, in conformity with his instructions, presented an insolent remonstrance on that subject. In reference to a projected attempt of Mexico to reduce her refractory province, Mr. Shannon represented the importance of Texas to this country, and intimated that his Government could not see it invaded, without taking part in the controversy. The Mexican Minister replied that his government was not capable of yielding to a menace which the President of the United States, *"exceeding the powers given to him by the fundamental law of his nation,* has directed against it." He added:

> While one power is seeking more ground to stain by the SLAVERY of an unfortunate branch of the human family, the other is endeavoring, by preserving what belongs to it, to diminish the surface which the former wants for this detestable traffic. Let the world now say which of the two has justice and reason on its side.

Mr. Shannon demanded a retraction of this language. The Mexican Government nobly refused to retract, but repeated it. And President Tyler laid the correspondence before Congress, complaining of the language of the Mexican Government as an affront, that "might well justify the United States in a resort to any measure to vindicate the national honor." He contented himself, however, with urging "prompt and immediate action, on the subject of annexation."

The successful annexation of Texas in 1845, encouraged the slaveholding party in Congress to broach, openly, the project of entering into negotiations for the cession of Cuba. Their papers began also to dwell on the importance of adding California to the United States, and President [James] Polk [1845–1849] was evidently determined to obtain that province, either by negotiation or war. A new bluster was made about our claims upon Mexico, and Mr. Slidell was dispatched on a mission to that Government to make an offer for New Mexico and California. He was to offer *the claims* and *five millions* for New Mexico, and the claims and twenty-five millions for both New Mexico and California.

To facilitate this land speculation, *"the claims"* were conveniently swelled to upwards of eight millions, although Mexico had paid the interest of the award, and above three hundred thousand dollars of the principal, by forced loans, and notwithstanding her financial embarrassments, so anxious was she to retain her relations of peace with this country.

How much *ought* to have been claimed the reader will judge when he sees, not only (as already exhibited) the amount of above five and a half millions rejected by the Commissioners and Umpire, but when he sees, likewise, how the whole matter was settled when Mexico was afterwards dismembered by our forces, when we had her in our power, and when we had obtained all the slave territory we wanted! We could afford to be honest then, in respect to these claims. In the final settlement, at the close of the war, the award of the Commissioners was put down at TWO MILLIONS of dollars, and the remainder of the claim, above six millions, was put down at only THREE AND A QUARTER millions, the Federal Government stipulating to pay the claimants all "valid claims" *not exceeding* the latter sum, yet releasing the Mexican Government from further responsibility! Thus our Government itself repudiated above three millions. But this is not all.

As five-sevenths of the claims investigated were found spurious, and as the claims presented later were evidently of a still worse character, it is calculated by Judge Jay, who has presented and studied these statistics, that "one million will be more than sufficient to meet every equitable demand," that is (as we understand it) in addition to the award of two millions; thus reducing the FOURTEEN millions claimed, to THREE millions, and repudiating ELEVEN millions of it as spurious!

Such were "the claims" of which EIGHT MILLIONS were to be used as purchase money to obtain California and New Mexico, through the mission of Mr. Slidell. In his person, the American Government presented itself before Mexico in the character of an importunate creditor demanding more than double his just due, with a bowie knife in one hand and a purse, with his bill, in the other. Now, says he, sell me half of your land at my own price, and take this purse and my bill receipted, for your pay. If not, receive this knife into your bosom. The offer of Mr. Slidell was rejected, as was foreseen, and he returned home. The correspondence, with the attendant circumstances, betray the extreme anxiety of the Federal Administration to provoke Mexico into a war, and raise a clamor against her in this country.

Another occasion or pretext of quarrel with Mexico was sought in a pretended question respecting the western boundary of Texas. Mr. Jay has clearly shown that the acts of this Government had recognized, in several ways, a boundary far to the eastward of that which, on his accession to the Presidency, about the time of the annexation of Texas, was resolutely maintained, and with a military force, by President [James] Polk. Under pretense of defending Texas, which needed no defense, General [Zachary] Taylor was stationed beyond the real borders of Texas, with discretion even to cross the Rio Grande, the new boundary now claimed by the President, in case hostilities were commenced by Mexico. The slightest skirmish on the newly claimed territory, would sufficiently answer the purpose of throwing on Mexico the odium of commencing the war. All this was sheer Executive usurpation, without the authority or knowledge of Congress. In the meantime, five states were required to be in readiness to furnish aid to Gen. Taylor, though the documents show that our Cabinet were not under the least apprehension of any invasion from Mexico.

On the very *next day* after the reception at Washington of advices from Mr. Slidell, Jan. 12, 1846, from which it was inferred, that there was no hope of a cession of California, peremptory orders were given to Gen. Taylor to advance to the Rio Grande, and the "points *opposite* Metamoras and Mier, and the vicinity of Laredo, were suggested for his consideration." The evident object was to provoke a collision. After a variety of ineffectual manœuvres to provoke the Mexicans to strike the first blow, it was in fact given by our own army, and Gen. Taylor announced to his government that HOSTILITIES HAD COMMENCED; on the receipt of which President Polk announced to Congress and to the world the untruth that "*Mexico had passed the boundary of the United States, had invaded our territory, and shed American blood on American soil.*" Congress, thereupon, (rejecting a motion to read the documents) and sustaining a call for the "previous question," which precluded discussion, adopted a vote asserting the existence of war by *act of Mexico!* This was on May 11, 1846, the same day the House received the President's war message!

Gen. Taylor immediately took possession of Metamoras; and the war was vigorously pushed westward to its intended destination, the conquest of New Mexico and California. In anticipation of these military movements, by land, a naval force had been stationed in the Pacific, near the coast of California, with secret orders to Com. Sloat, June 24, 1845, to possess the port of San Francisco, and blockade or occupy other ports, *as soon as he should hear of an inland war with Mexico.* These orders were now carried into effect, possession taken of Monterey, and a proclamation immediately issued announcing that "*California now belongs to the United States.*" This was on the 7th of July, 1846. Two days after, San Francisco was also in our possession.

All this in less than two months after the declaration of war by Congress, plainly showing that the conquest of California had been

determined upon and provided for, a year beforehand, and while neither the people of the United States nor Congress were permitted to
know the designs of the President. The declaration of war by Congress
did not reach the squadron in the Pacific till the 28th of August, fifty-
two days after the Commodore, by proclamation, had annexed California to the United States. . . .

Mr. Jay introduces into his volume some confessions of Mr. Thomp-
son, our Minister in Mexico, clearly showing the designs of the Federal
Government, in 1843, under the administration of Mr. Tyler, to get
possession of California, and to provoke Mexico into a war for that purpose. He cites also Mr. Calhoun, as having said in the Senate of the
U.S., Feb. 24, 1847, (in reference to the precipitate action of Congress
in declaring, May 11, 1846, that "war existed by act of Mexico")—"*We
had not a particle of evidence that the Republic of Mexico had made war
against the United States.*"

Mr. C. J. Ingersoll, as chairman of the Committee on Foreign Relations, in Feb., 1847, made a report avowing the sentiment that the war
was necessary, in order to get possession of territories that "*every American administration has been striving to get by purchase.*"

And in the same report, as well as in a previous speech (Jan. 19) in
the House, Mr. Ingersol has the robber-like effrontery to throw the
blame of the war and its continuance upon Mexico, because she refused
to sell us her provinces, which, says he, "*she has now constrained us to take
by force, though even yet we are disposed to pay for them, not by blood merely,
but by money too!*"

Mr. Stanton of Tennessee, Mr. Beddinger of Virginia, Mr. Sevier of
Arkansas, and Mr. Giles of Maryland, openly avowed, on the floor of
Congress, that the war was a war of conquest. Mr. Polk had, however, in
his message, a little time previous, adventured the extraordinary assertion, that "the war has not been waged with a view to conquest." In echo
to this declaration, a resolution was introduced in the House (Jan.,
1847), disclaiming a view to conquest, *but the House refused to adopt the
resolution.*

The Southern press abounded in gratulations at the prospect of conquest, and of the extension of slavery. Henry Clay, in a speech in Kentucky, declared that the bill of Congress, of May 11, 1846, "attributing the commencement of the war to the act of Mexico," was "a bill with a PALPABLE FALSEHOOD stamped on its face." A new House of Representatives, "fresh from the people," elected *after* the declaration of May 11, 1846, "Resolved," in the December following, "that *the war was unnecessarily and unconstitutionally begun by the President of the United States.*" That portions of Mexico, including California, were unconstitutionally conquered, and *treated and governed* as conquered territory by the President, before the treaty of peace, was strongly affirmed and clearly shown in the U.S. Senate, in March, 1848, by both Mr. Webster and Mr. Calhoun.

Of the *manner* in which the war was prosecuted, we have not room to say much. The reader of Mr. Jay's *Review* will find some sickening details of lawlessness, of rapacity, of plunder, and of outrage, disgraceful to the American name. Barbarities were committed which should make humanity weep and blush. General [Zachary] Taylor himself, in a communication to the War Department, said: "I deeply regret to report that many of the twelve months' volunteers, in their route hence of the lower Rio Grande, have committed extensive outrages and depredations upon the peaceable inhabitants. THERE IS SCARCELY ANY FORM OF CRIME THAT HAS NOT BEEN REPORTED TO ME AS COMMITTED BY THEM." General Kearney communicated a similar statement. The Californians, he says, "*have been shamefully abused by our own people.*"

When such testimonies come from such witnesses, we may conjecture the rest. . . .

The Congress that had declared the beginning of the war unconstitutional, and the members who had denounced the measure as criminal and wicked, were nevertheless so corrupt and hardened as to vote money for its continuance! A few only had the consistency and honesty to record their votes in the negative.

Though Mr. Polk had declared our title to the whole of Oregon to be "clear and unquestionable," yet he had surrendered much of it to

Great Britain, to maintain relations of peace. For Oregon was too far North for the convenient use of the slaveholders, and it might be made into free States. But without the slightest claim to New Mexico and California, he prosecuted a war of conquest to obtain them, because the slaveholders desired them, and they were expected to add to the number of slave States, to help govern the Union. These objects were openly avowed by the Southern press.

All wars of conquest have their limits. It is not certain that the administration sought to conquer and retain all Mexico. The central and southern provinces might be difficult to be managed—might be found too populous and too refractory to admit, at present, the quiet restoration of slavery. The war was expensive. The administration (and partly on account of the war, and its attendant usurpations) was becoming unpopular. Desirous of securing permanently what was in his power, and what was originally contemplated by the war, Mr. Polk turned his thoughts on peace. For this purpose, August 8, 1846, he recommended to Congress an appropriation of two millions of dollars, to be placed at his disposal for that purpose. This request plainly indicated his desire to make an offer of money for a cession of territory, and gave the lie to his former pretense, that war was not waged for conquest. A bill was introduced into the House for this object and was passed, but with the celebrated proviso offered by Mr. Wilmot, that the territory thus acquired should be free from the polluting touch of slavery. The bill went to the Senate the last day of the session, but was not acted upon, and Congress adjourned. . . .

In August, 1847, negotiations were opened with Mexico through our agent, Mr. Trist. The Mexican Commissioners were instructed, by their government to insist that "the United States shall engage not to permit slavery in that part of the territory which they shall acquire by treaty." Mr. Trist promptly refused to negotiate a treaty under such restrictions, declaring them as obnoxious as "an order to establish the INQUISITION," that "the *bare mention* of such a treaty was an impossibility," and that no American President "would dare to present any such treaty to the Senate."

"I assured them," says Mr. Trist, (in his official dispatch to our Secretary of State,) "that if it were in their power to offer me the whole territory described in our project, increased ten-fold in value, and, in addition to that, covered *a foot thick all over with pure gold,* upon THE SINGLE CONDITION THAT SLAVERY SHOULD BE EXCLUDED THEREFROM, I could not entertain the offer for a moment, nor even think of communicating it to Washington.". . .

In the final close of the Mexican war, these territories were obtained at a cost of FIFTEEN MILLIONS of dollars paid to Mexico, in addition to the relinquishment of our long contested "claims." Besides this, the direct expenditures of the war are estimated at over ONE HUNDRED MILLIONS. Adding extra pay, pensions, bounties of land, etc., Mr. Jay puts down the money cost of our new territory at ONE HUNDRED AND THIRTY MILLIONS OF DOLLARS. And all this to extend the area of slavery beyond Texas.

Address on War

ALEXANDER CAMPBELL

Born in Ireland, Alexander Campbell made his home in Virginia for many years and was involved in a nineteenth-century movement to heal the divisions between the various Christian denominations. He delivered this address in Wheeling, Virginia, (West Virginia not yet having been created) in 1848, at a time when the subject of war was very much on Americans' minds.

Some years ago . . . an elaborate investigation [was undertaken] of the real causes for which the wars of Christendom had been undertaken from the time of Constantine the Great down to the present century. From the results furnished by the Peace Society of Massachusetts it appeared that, after subtracting a number of petty wars long since carried on and those waged by Christian nations with tribes of savages, the wars of real magnitude amounted in all to 286.

The origin of these wars, on a severe analysis, appeared to have been as follows: 22 for plunder and tribute; 44 for the extension of territory; 24 for revenge or retaliation; 6 for disputed boundaries; 8 respecting points of honor or prerogative; 6 for the protection or extension of commerce; 55 civil wars; 41 about contested titles to crowns; 30 under pretense of assisting allies; 23 for mere jealousy of rival greatness; 28 religious wars, including the Crusades. Not one for defense alone, and certainly not one that an enlightened Christian man could have given one cent for, in a voluntary way, much less have volunteered his services or enlisted into its ranks.

If the end alone justifies the means, what shall we think of the wisdom or the justice of war, or of the authors and prominent actors of these scenes? A conscientious mind will ask, Did these 286 wars redress the wrongs, real or feigned, complained of? Did they in all cases, in a majority of the cases, or in a single case, necessarily determine the right side of the controversy? Did they punish the guilty, or the more guilty, in the ratio of their respective demerits? No one can, indeed, no one will, contend that the decision or termination of these wars naturally, necessarily, or even probably, decided the controversy so justly, so rationally, so satisfactorily as it could have been settled in any one case of the 286 by a third or neutral party.

War is not now, nor was it ever, a process of justice. It never was a test of truth—a criterion of right. It is either a mere game of chance or a violent outrage of the strong upon the weak. Need we any other proof that a Christian people can in no way whatever countenance a war as a proper means of redressing wrongs, of deciding justice, or of settling controversies among nations? On the common conception of the most superficial thinkers on this subject, not one of the 286 wars which have been carried on among the "Christian nations" during 1,500 years was such as that an enlightened Christian man could have taken any part in it, because, as admitted, not one of them was for defense alone; in other words, they were all aggressive wars.

But to the common mind, as it seems to me, the most convincing argument against a Christian becoming a soldier may be drawn from the fact that he fights against an innocent person—I say an innocent person, so far as the cause of the war is contemplated. The men that fight are not the men that make the war. Politicians, merchants, knaves, and princes cause or make the war, declare the war, and hire men to kill for them those that may be hired on the other side to thwart their schemes of personal and family aggrandizement.

The soldiers on either side have no enmity against the soldiers on the other side, because with them they have no quarrel. Had they met in any other field, in their citizen dress, other than in battle array, they would, most probably have not only inquired after the welfare of each other, but would have tendered to each other their assistance if called for. But a red coat or a blue coat, a tri-colored or a two-colored cockade, is their only introduction to each other, and the signal that they must kill or be killed! . . .

By the "horrors of war" I do not mean the lightning and the thunder of the battlefield, the blackness and darkness of those dismal clouds of smoke, which like death's own pall, shroud the encounter; it is not the continual roar of its cannon, nor the agonizing shrieks and groans of fallen battalions, of wounded and dying legions; nor is it, at the close of the day, the battlefield itself, covered with the gore and scattered limbs of butchered myriads, with here and there a pile, a mountain heap of slain heroes in the fatal pass, mingled with the wreck of broken arms, lances, helmets, swords, and shattered firearms, amidst the pavement of fallen balls that have completed the work of destruction, numerous as hailstones after the fury of the storm; nor, amidst these, the sight of the wounded lying upon one another, weltering in their blood, imploring assistance, importuning an end of their woes by the hand of a surviving soldier, invoking death as the only respite from excruciating torments.

But this is not all; for the tidings are at length carried to their respective homes. Then come the bitter wail of widows and orphans, the screams and the anguish of mothers and sisters deprived forever of the consolations and hopes that clustered round the anticipated return of those so dear to them, that have perished in the conflict.

But even these are not the most fearful desolations of war. Where now are the 200,000 lost by England in our Revolutionary War; the 70,000 who fell at Waterloo and Quatre-Bros; the 80,000 at Borodino; the 300,000 at Arbela; or where the 15,000,000 Goths destroyed by Justinian in 20 years; the 32,000,000 by Genghis Khan in 41 years; the 60,000,000 slain by the Turks; the 80,000,000 by the Tartars, hurried away to judgment in a paroxysm of wrath, amid the fury of the passions? What can we think of their eternal destiny? Besides all these, how many have died in captivity?. . .

But these, multiplied by myriads, are but specimens of the countless millions slain, the solitary exiles, the lonely captives. They tell the least portion of the miseries of war. Yet even these say to the Christian, "How can you become a soldier? How countenance and aid this horrible work of death?"

For my own part, and I am not alone in this opinion, I think that the moral desolations of war surpass even its horrors. And amongst these I do not assign the highest place to the vulgar profanity, brutality, and debauchery of the mere soldier, the professional and licensed butcher of mankind, who, for his $8 a month or his 10 sous per day, hires himself to lay waste a country, to pillage, burn, and destroy the peaceful hamlet, the cheerful village, or the magnificent city, and to harass, wound, and destroy his fellow man, for no other consideration than his paltry wages, his daily rations, and the infernal pleasure of doing it, anticipating hereafter "the stupid stares and loud huzzas" of monsters as inhuman and heartless as himself. And were it not for the infatuation of public opinion and popular applause, I would place him, as no less to be condemned, beside the vain and pompous volunteer, who for his country, "right or wrong," hastens to the theater of war for the mere plaudits of admiring multitudes, ready to cover himself with glory, because he has aided an aspirant to a throne or paved the way to his own election to reign over a humbled and degraded people.

I make great allowance for false education, for bad taste, for the contagion of vicious example; still, I cannot view those deluded by such sophistry, however good their motives, as deserving anything from contemporaries or posterity except compassion and forgiveness. Yet, behold its influence on mothers, sisters, and relatives; note its contagion, its corruption of public taste. See the softer sex allured, fascinated by the halo of false glory thrown around these worshipped heroes! See them gazing with admiration on the "tinselled trapping," the "embroidered ensigns," of him whose profession it is to make widows and orphans by wholesale! Sometimes their hands are withdrawn from works of charity to decorate the warriors' banners and to cater to these false notions of human glory! Behold, too, the young mother arraying her proud boy "with cap and feather, toyed with a drum and sword, training him for the admired profession of a man killer."

This is not all. It is not only at home, in the nursery, and infant school that this false spirit is inspired. Our schools, our academies, our colleges echo and reecho with the fame of an Alexander, a Caesar, a Napoleon, a Wellington. Forensic eloquence is full of the fame of great heroes, of military chieftains, of patriotic deliverers whose memory must be kept forever verdant in the affections of a grateful posterity, redeemed by their patriotism or rescued from oppression by their valor.

The pulpit, too, must lend its aid in cherishing the delusion. There is not infrequently heard a eulogium on some fallen hero, some church service for the mighty dead, thus desecrating the religion of the Prince of Peace by causing it to minister as the handmaid of war. . . .

But how are all national disputes to be settled? Philosophy, history, the Bible, teach that all disputes, misunderstandings, alienations are to be settled, heard, tried, adjudicated by impartial, that is, by disinterested, umpires. No man is admitted to be a proper judge in his own case. Wars never make amicable settlements, and seldom, if ever, just decisions of points at issue. We are obliged to offer preliminaries of peace at last. Nations must meet by their representatives, stipulate and restipulate, hear and answer, compare and decide.

In modern times we terminate hostilities by a treaty of peace. We do not make peace with power and lead. It is done by reason, reflection, and negotiation. Why not employ these at first? But it is alleged that war has long been, and must always be, the *ultima ratio regum*—the last argument of those in power. For ages a father inquisitor was the strong argument for orthodoxy; but light has gone abroad and he has lost his power. Illuminate the human mind on this subject also, create a more rational and humane public opinion, and wars will cease.

But, it is alleged, all will not yield to reason or justice. There must be compulsion. Is war then the only compulsory measure? Is there no legal compulsion? Must all personal misunderstandings be settled by the sword?

Why not have a *by-law-established umpire?* Could not a united national court be made as feasible and as practicable as a United States court? Why not, as often proposed, and as eloquently, ably, and humanely argued, by the advocates of peace, have a congress of nations and a high court of nations for adjudicating and terminating all international misunderstandings and complaints, redressing and remedying all wrongs and grievances?

There is not, it appears to me, a physical or a rational difficulty in the way. But I do not now argue the case. I merely suggest this expedient, and will always vote correspondingly, for reasons as good and as relevant as I conceive them to be humane and beneficial.

To sum up the whole we argue:

(1) The right to take away the life of the murderer does not of itself warrant war, inasmuch as in that case none but the guilty suffer,

whereas in war the innocent suffer not only with, but often with-out, the guilty. The guilty generally make war and the innocent suffer from its consequences.

(2) The right given to the Jews to wage war is not vouchsafed to any other nation, for they were under a theocracy, and were God's sheriff to punish nations; consequently no Christian can argue from the wars of the Jews in justification or in extenuation of the wars of Christendom. The Jews had a Divine precept and author-ity; no existing nation can produce such a warrant.

(3) The prophecies clearly indicate that the Messiah himself would be "the Prince of Peace," and that under his reign "wars should cease" and "nations study it no more."

(4) The gospel, as first announced by the angels, is a message which results in producing "peace on earth and good will among men."

(5) The precepts of Christianity positively inhibit war—by showing that "wars and fightings come from men's lusts" and evil passions, and by commanding Christians to "follow peace with all men."

(6) The beatitudes of Christ are not pronounced on patriots, heroes, and conquerors but on peacemakers, on whom is conferred the highest rank and title in the universe: "Blessed are the peacemak-ers, for they shall be called the sons of God."

(7) The folly of war is manifest in the following particulars: First. It can never be the criterion of justice of a proof of right. Second. It can never be a satisfactory end of the controversy. Third. Peace is always the result of negotiation, and treaties are its guaranty and pledge.

(8) The wickedness of war is demonstrated in the following particulars:
    First. Those who are engaged in killing their brethren, for the most part, have no personal cause of provocation whatever.
    Second. They seldom, or never, comprehend the right or the wrong of the war. They, therefore, act without the approbation of conscience.

Third. In all wars the innocent are punished with the guilty.

Fourth. They constrain the soldier to do for the state that which, were he to do it for himself, would, by the law of the state, involve forfeiture of his life.

Fifth. They are the pioneers of all other evils to society, both moral and physical. In the language of Lord Brougham, "Peace, peace, peace! I abominate war as un-Christian. I hold it the greatest of human curses. I deem it to include all others—violence, blood, rapine, fraud, everything that can deform the character, alter the nature, and debase the name of man." Or with Joseph Bonaparte, "War is but organized barbarism—an inheritance of the savage state." With Franklin I, therefore, conclude, "There never was a good war, or a bad peace."

No wonder, then, that for two or three centuries after Christ all Christians refused to bear arms. So depose Justin Martyr, Tatian, Clement of Alexandria, Tertullian, Origen, and so forth.

In addition to all these considerations, I further say, were I not a Christian, as a political economist even, I would plead this cause. Apart from the mere claims of humanity, I would urge it on the ground of sound national policy.

Give me the money that's been spent in wars and I will clear up every acre of land in the world that ought to be cleared, drain every marsh, subdue every desert, fertilize every mountain and hill, and convert the whole earth into a continuous series of fruitful fields, verdant meadows, beautiful villas, hamlets, towns, cities, standing along smooth and comfortable highways and canals, or in the midst of luxuriant and fruitful orchards, vineyards, and gardens, full of fruits and flowers, redolent with all that pleases the eye and regales the senses of man. I would found, furnish, and endow as many schools, academies, and colleges as would educate the whole human race, would build meeting houses, public halls, lyceums, and furnish them with libraries adequate to the wants of a thousand millions of human beings.

Beat your swords into plowshares, your spears into pruning hooks, convert your warships into missionary packets, your arsenals and munitions of war into Bibles, school books, and all the appliances of literature, science, and art, and then ask, "What would be wanting on the part of man to 'make the wilderness and solitary peace glad,' to cause 'the desert to rejoice and blossom as the rose,' to make our hills 'like Carmel and Sharon,' and our valleys as 'the garden of God'?" All this being done, I would doubtless have a surplus for some new enterprise. . . .

Let everyone, then, who fears God and loves man put his hand to the work; and the time will not be far distant when—

No longer hosts encountering hosts
Shall crowds of slain deplore:
They'll hang the trumpet in the hall,
And study war no more.

3

The Civil War

Slavery was doomed politically even if Lincoln had permitted the small Gulf Coast Confederacy to depart in peace.

—JEFFREY ROGERS HUMMEL,
in *Emancipating Slaves, Enslaving Free Men:
A History of the American Civil War*

Although the general public is liable to believe that Abraham Lincoln waged war on the seceding southern states in order to end the horror of slavery, professional historians know full well that the abolition of slavery was not a war aim until well into the conflict. In fact, Lincoln supported a constitutional amendment that would have prevented the federal government from ever abolishing slavery, if that was what it would take to persuade the southern states to remain in the Union, and perhaps for the already seceded ones to return. In his first inaugural he said, "I understand a proposed amendment to the Constitution—which amendment, however, I have not seen—has passed Congress, to the effect that the Federal Government shall never interfere with the domestic institutions of the States, including that of persons held to service. To avoid misconstruction of what I have said, I depart from my purpose not to speak of particular amendments so far as to say that, holding such a provision to now be implied constitutional law, I have no objection to its being made express and irrevocable." First and foremost, Lincoln's aim was to "save the Union."

Jeffrey Hummel's book *Emancipating Slaves, Enslaving Free Men*, which received the endorsements of a great many distinguished American historians, makes a strong case that slavery was doomed to a natural death in any event. Every other country in the Western hemisphere that abolished slavery in the nineteenth century managed to do so without war. "The fact that emancipation overwhelmed such entrenched plantation economies as Cuba and Brazil," Hummel writes, "suggests that slavery was politically moribund anyway."

> Slavery was doomed politically even if Lincoln had permitted the small Gulf Coast Confederacy to depart in peace. The Republican-controlled Congress would have been able to work toward emancipation within the border states, where slavery was already declining. In due course the Radicals could have repealed the Fugitive Slave Law of 1850. With chattels fleeing across the border and raising slavery's enforcement costs, the peculiar institution's destruction within an independent cotton South was inevitable.

Years earlier, Congressman Joseph Rogers Underwood of Kentucky had warned of precisely this: "How could we retain our slaves, when they, in one hour, one day, or a week at the furthest, could pass the boundary? Sooner or later, this process would extend itself farther and farther south, rendering slave labor so precarious and uncertain that it could not be depended upon. . . . Slavery in the States would fall with the Union."

This point recalls the earlier suggestion of William Lloyd Garrison, perhaps the most famous abolitionist in American history: a division of the Union would have hastened the end of slavery. It was not merely a desire for moral purity that inspired so many abolitionists to favor dissolving the Union with the South. Doing so would also have made the enforcement costs of slavery prohibitive. No longer part of a common nation with the South, the northern states would have been under no obligation to permit, much less actively cooperate in, the recapture of runaway slaves. Maintaining the slave system under such conditions, particularly in the border states, would not have been easy.

It so happens that this is precisely how slavery was destroyed in Brazil. The institution essentially collapsed there after being abolished in the Brazilian state of Ceará in 1884. A hastily passed fugitive slave law was largely ignored, the value of slaves fell dramatically, and within four years the Brazilian government had acknowledged the reality of the situation by enacting immediate and uncompensated emancipation.

Lysander Spooner was a radical abolitionist who supported John Brown, and also favored the right of secession. And in 1870, looking back on recent history, he dismissed the federal government's flattering claims about its wondrous deeds as so much propaganda: "All these cries of having 'abolished slavery,' of having 'saved the country,' of having 'preserved the union,' of establishing 'a government of consent,' and of 'maintaining the national honor,' are all gross, shameless, transparent cheats—so transparent that they ought to deceive no one—when uttered as justifications for the war, or for the government that has succeeded the war, or for now compelling the people to pay the cost of the war, or for compelling anybody to support a government that he does not want."

But even those who contend that diplomacy and politics had failed and thus the war ultimately had to be fought must still guard against any glorification of war, and recall its grisly human costs: in this case, some 1.5 million people dead, wounded, or missing. What kind of insatiable Moloch is this "Union," a mere political abstraction, to which so many had to be sacrificed? Furthermore, Lincoln's record on civil liberties—hundreds of newspapers closed and many thousands of citizens arrested without trial, among other offenses—has been a godsend to today's war party: when caught in any kind of mischief, they confidently explain that even Lincoln did thus-and-so, and that is that.

Indeed, the Lincoln legacy can be and has been cited on behalf of all manner of political atrocities, from assaults on civil liberties to the waging of war against civilian populations. The religious veneer of Lincoln's political rhetoric seared into the American consciousness the idea of the U.S. government as an instrument of God's will, to be employed without mercy against any force so impious as to resist it. This conception of the federal government works even for politicians who might feel uncomfortable with openly religious language: the idea of a righteous central authority steamrolling all opposition—ipso facto wicked and perverse, of course—as part of the inevitable forward march of history fits quite nicely into just about any nationalist agenda, left or right. This is why the standard narrative is so stubborn, so resistant to evidence, and so difficult to overturn: the entire American political class has a vital stake in its preservation.

One's view on the war notwithstanding, there is an undeniable moral seriousness in the arguments that follow, and they deserve thoughtful consideration.

The War Method of Peace

EZRA HEYWOOD

Ezra Heywood (1829–1893) was an individualist anarchist and abolitionist. Although most of the abolitionist movement, including those who had favored a peaceful end to slavery, supported the Civil War on the grounds that it would bring about a swift end to human bondage, Heywood belonged to a minority that believed two wrongs did not make a right; he alludes below to St. Paul's admonition not to do evil that good may come. He published this essay on June 14, 1863.

A resort to war to put down slavery is a resort to lying to put down falsehood, a resort to stealing to put down theft. Indeed, slavery is an advance on war, since its victims, first prisoners of war, were formerly killed at once, afterwards held to service as an act of humanity.

Then war is wrong—wrong yesterday, wrong today, wrong forever; not an evil merely, but a sin and a crime. To Christians, the character of Jesus should be decisive on this point. Was he right in going to Calvary, or should he have marched against Pilate as a Major-General? It was the Cross that made him the moral lawgiver of his race, and has affixed his name to the highest civilization of history. I saw Orthodox epaulettes, wealth and fashion, in a soft attire and shining equipage, rolling in gorgeous splendor to church, in the name of the Prince of Peace, who went barefoot! Yet this going to luxurious pews in "Christian" epaulettes is the homage which vice pays to virtue; since, because it was noble for men to be saints in Jerusalem, it is fashionable for sinners to be hypocrites in Boston. Men will worship Love, though they work blood—will preach Jesus, though, as a "necessary evil," they practise Joshua. Lying is one of the "fine arts" of war; they call it "strategy"; that is, falsehood in military boots. Yorktown in the Revolution was won by a lie, and Washington told it. John Brown went to Harper's Ferry under a false name, —but because he was an Abolition saint, we did not say much about it! Murder is the gravest crime man commits; yet war is murder multiplied by the majority. By what ethics, then, is the man a criminal, and the mass heroes? Can we "serve God individually, and the devil collectively"? If the whole is greater than a part, to kill a man is a greater sin than to enslave him; for life bases and includes all other human rights. Self-defence is right; but how much of yourself will you save? Self is composed of soul and body; to save your life by sin, you lose your soul; to lose your life for truth, you save your soul. I go for the soul. You would not do wrong, would not lie, would not steal, to save your life; will you commit the gravest sin to live? To argue that animal instinct prevail; that when the lion and the lamb lie down together, "the lamb must be inside the lion," and hence men are under the dominion of brutish instincts, and cannot resist them, is practical atheism; makes free agency a fiction. The claim that war comes in society as earthquakes come in nature is equally ir-relevant. If earthquakes are free moral agents, if earthquakes vote and join the church, that argument is in point—otherwise, it is imperti-nent and absurd. . . .

My friends, among radicals you must allow me to be a little con-servative. The principles of the Anti-Slavery Society, which I have read to you, plainly forbid the use of the sword as an agent of eman-cipation;—rapine and havoc set loose. States desolated, cities sacked, whole populations driven forth to squalor and starvation, beneath skies lurid with the glare of their burning homes, a million Americans still urged to mutual and unrelenting slaughter—no principles I have endorsed necessitate such barbarous measures! For I aspire to be a man as well as an Abolitionist, and slaveholders are my brothers not less than slaves. I know the grand purpose that inspires freemen in this tremendous conflict,—that this red evening cloud may announce a fair dawn to America; that, through the wall of sorrow and desola-tion, we may hear the music of breaking choirs, the joy of a race re-stored from slaves to men! But I would not do evil that good may come; I scout the horrid doctrine, that the end justifies the means; therefore, I do not believe in this war. The Abolitionists initiated the true policy, the only policy which liberty has had in this struggle,— the policy of principle. Justice as the duty of the master, and the right of the slave, which would have quietly removed the whole cause of disturbance; for immense as is this darkening cloud of war, all its bolts would have dropped harmless into the earth at the heaven-tipped virtue of emancipation. That refused, then separation as a moral duty, repudiating oppressors as the criminals they are, and erecting the North into a nationality on the basis of "No union with slaveholders"; putting the opposite systems each on its own merits, and letting the laws of nature which are all anti-slavery, and God who was always an Abolitionist, take care of the consequences. Thus to wash our hands of the guilt of slavery, and strangle forever the very thought of com-promise with it.

A Christian Appeal to the Confederacy

DAVID LIPSCOMB

David Lipscomb (1831–1917), a Church of Christ minister, was the author of On Civil Government: Its Origin, Mission and Destiny and the Christian's Relation to It *(1889), which made a biblical case for a voluntary society along libertarian lines. Here he appeals to various authorities in the Confederacy to exempt Christians from military service.*

To His Excellency the President of the Confederate States of America:

WHEREAS, A large number of the members of the churches of Jesus Christ throughout this and the adjoining counties of the State of Tennessee, feel a deep sense of the responsibility they are under to recognize the Bible in its teachings, as the only infallible guide of their life, and the supreme authoritative rule of action, and as being of superior authority to and more binding upon the subjects of the Kingdom of Jesus Christ, than the rules and regulations of any human government or power, they would respectfully represent.

(1) That they are fully satisfied that God, through the Scriptures of Sacred Truth, demands of his servants that they should submit quietly, heartily and cheerfully to the government under which they may live, in all cases, except when compliance with the civil law would involve a violation of the law of God. They are deeply impressed with the truth that when there is a conflict between the requirements of worldly government and the law of God, the duty of the Christian, is, upon the peril of his well-being, to obey God first, let the consequences be to him what they may.

(2) They are firm in the conviction of the truth, that no man who regards the authority of God, the spirit and letter of the Sacred Scriptures in their proper division and application, the life and teachings of the Son of God, or his Holy Apostles, as given for

the guidance of his followers, can in any manner engage in, aid, foment, or countenance the strifes, animosities and bloody conflicts in which civil governments are frequently engaged, and in which they often involve their subjects.

The measure and limit of their duty to, and connexion with the governments under which they live, as laid down in the Sacred Scriptures, is not an active participation in its affairs to destroy or upbuild, but simply a quiet and cheerful submission to its enactments, in the payment of tribute and any demands on our property or time, modified only, by the first and highest obligation to obey God.

With these considerations of what our duty to God requires at our hands, the enforcement of the "Conscript Act" for the purpose of raising and maintaining an army, for the carrying on of this unhappy war, in which our country is involved, cannot fail to work indescribable distress to those members of our churches holding these convictions. Some of them will be driven as exiles from their homes, for no political preferences, but because they dare not disobey the commandments of God. Others may be thrown into seeming opposition to your government, suffering imprisonment and punishment as may be inflicted on them. Others still by the pressure of circumstances, may be driven to a deeply sadder fate, the violation of all their conscientious convictions of duty to their Maker and Master, whom they have under the most solemn vows, pledged themselves to serve.

In view of these things, we are induced to make a statement of these facts to you, with the hope that some relief may be afforded to those of our members thus distressed.

We are the more encouraged, too, in this hope, from the fact that we perceive that the Congress of the Confederate States of America, with a commendable regard for the conscientious convictions of its subjects, made provision upon certain conditions for the exemption of the members of certain denominations of professed Christians, from the performance of requirements repulsive to their religious faith. With the view, too, that this law might not act invidiously with reference to individuals or bodies of individuals, not specially named in said act, the power was vested in the Honorable President, of making such further exemptions as, in his judgement, justice, equity or necessity might demand. We respectfully petition of you that those members of our churches, who are now, and have been striving to maintain a position of Christian separation from the world, its strifes and conflicts, may be relieved, on terms equitable and just, from requirements repulsive to their religious faith, and that they may be, at least, placed upon a footing similar to that in which denominations holding a like faith are placed.

To the Ruling Authorities of the State of Tennessee:

WHEREAS, A large number of the members of the Churches of Jesus Christ feel a deep sense of the responsibility they are under to recognize the Bible in its teachings, as the only infallible guide and au thoritative rule of action, and as being of superior authority to, and more binding upon the subjects of the kingdom of Jesus Christ than any human rules or regulations, they would most respectfully represent.

(1) That they recognize the necessity for the existence of civil government, so long as a considerable portion of the human family fails to submit to the government of God.

(2) That while God demands of his servants that they should submit cheerfully and heartily, to the government under which they may live, in all cases, except when compliance with the requirements of civil government, involves the violation of God's law, they are deeply impressed with the truth that when there is a conflict between the requirements of civil government and the law of God, the duty of the Christian is, upon peril of his eternal well-being, to obey God first, let the consequences be to him what they may.

(3) They are satisfied that the measure of their duty to civil government, as defined in the Bible, is to submit, not by personal participation in affairs of government, to uphold or destroy, pull down or upbuild, but simply, as a duty they owe to God, to

submit, and in that submission, modified only as above to discharge the offices of good citizens in all the relations of life.

(4) They are firmly impressed with the truth that no man who regards the authority of God, or of his Holy Apostles, as set forth in example and precept, for the instruction and guidance of his followers in the future ages of the world, can engage in, or in any way aid, foment or countenance the strifes, animosities and bloody conflicts in which civil governments are frequently engaged, and in which they involve their subjects.

(5) The spirit of the Church of Christ and the spirit of civil government are different. The one is a spirit of force, as all history attests, that no civil government ever did arise except by force, violence and the destruction of life. So they must maintain that existence by force. We suppose the future, with but slight variations, will repeat the history of the past. But Christianity permits not its subjects to use force or do violence, even in defence of its own existence; its guiding spirit is one of love, "peace on earth and good will toward man."

(6) This difference in the spirit of the two institutions, the government of God and the government of man, together with the diversity of the means essential to the prosperity and success of each respectively, necessarily, at times, involves a conflict in their respective requirements. We, therefore, in behalf of the churches of which we are members, respectfully petition of you that the requirements which, as we believe, conflict with our duties to God, may be remitted to those members of our churches who have been, and are now, striving to maintain a position of Christian separation from the world, its conflicts and strifes, as set forth in the preceding articles.

(7) We firmly believe that the oaths of allegiance, and the oaths to support and defend the governments of the world, now imposed as necessary to the transaction of the common affairs of life, are contrary to the spirit and teachings of the Savior and his inspired

Apostles, and involve, if strictly complied with, a violation of some of the plainest precepts of the Christian religion. We therefore, feel that in taking these oaths and obligations, and in performing those requirements that have an appearance of countenancing bloodshed and violence, we are violating the obligations of fealty we have taken to our Heavenly Master. We imperil the well-being of the church, dishonor God, and involve ourselves in eternal ruin. We, therefore, respectfully ask a release from the performance of these requirements, and others of a similar character, assuring you again, that we recognize it as a solemn duty we owe to God, to submit to the government under which we may live, in all its requirements, save when that government requires of us something contrary to the letter and spirit of the Christian religion, as revealed in the Bible.

To His Excellency Andrew Johnson, Governor of the State of Tennessee:

We, the undersigned, having been appointed a committee by an assembly of members of churches of Jesus Christ, met at Leiper's Fork, Williamson county, Tenn., to present to your Excellency their grievances, and in their and our behalf to petition of you a release from certain requirements made at their hands, would most respectfully represent that the mass of the members of the churches of Jesus Christ, in the counties of Davidson, Williamson, Maury and Hickman, and many scattered through other counties of Middle Tennessee, believe that all military service, or connexion with military service, is utterly incompatible with the spirit and requirements of the Christian religion. Believing this, they cannot comply with the requisition recently made of them in common with other residents of the State, for enrolling themselves for military service without a violation of their solemn conscientious convictions of duty to their Lord and Master, and a violation of their vows of fealty to him. We, therefore, in behalf of these churches and members of churches, respectfully petition of you, in the exercise of your authority, a release from those requirements, that are repugnant to their religious faith, upon terms that you may consider just and right. We desire to assure you in this request and movement, upon the faith and integrity of Christians, we are acting from no factious or political motive, but from the single desire of preserving our faith and profession of Christianity pure. Praying earnestly that your counsels and the counsels of the rulers of our country may be so conducted as to restore to our country a speedy and lasting peace, we are most obediently and respectfully yours.

<hr>

War or Constitution

CLEMENT L. VALLANDIGHAM

Clement L. Vallandigham was a congressman from Ohio who belonged to the "peace Democrats" who favored a nonviolent resolution of the issues that separated North and South. He was highly critical of Abraham Lincoln and the various deviations from the Constitution that marked the prosecution of the war. The speech below was declared to be an act of treason, and Vallandigham, seized from his home by sixty-seven federal soldiers in the middle of the night, was convicted by a military tribunal and deported from the Union.

All kinds of propaganda were disseminated at the time about Vallandigham's alleged wickedness, in order to devise some kind of justification for the deportation of a congressman; twentieth-century historian Frank Klement debunked the case against Vallandigham in Lincoln's Critics: The Copperheads of the North *and* The Limits of Dissent: Clement Vallandigham and the Civil War.

Mr. Chairman, in the Constitution of the United States, which the other day we swore to support, and by the authority of which we are here assembled now, it is written, "All legislative powers herein granted shall be vested in a Congress of the United States." It is further written, also, that the Congress to which all legislative powers granted, are thus committed: "Shall make no law abridging the freedom of speech or of the press." And, it is yet further written, in protection of Senators and Representatives, in that freedom of debate here, without which there can be no liberty that: "For any speech or debate in either House they shall not be questioned in any other place."

Holding up the shield of the *Constitution,* and standing here in the place, and with the manhood of a Representative of the people, I propose to myself, to-day, the ancient freedom of speech used within these walls, though with somewhat more, I trust, of decency and discretion than have sometimes been exhibited here. Sir, I do not propose to discuss the direct question of this civil war in which we are engaged. Its present prosecution is a foregone conclusion; and a wise man never wastes his strength on a fruitless enterprise. My position shall, at present, for the most part, be indicated by my votes, and by the resolutions and motions which I may submit. But there are many questions incident to the war and to its prosecution, about which I have somewhat to say now.

Mr. Chairman, the President, in the message before us, demands the extraordinary loan of $400,000,000—an amount nearly ten times greater than the entire public debt, State and Federal, at the close of the Revolution, in 1783, and four times as much as the total expenditures during the three years' war with Great Britain, in 1812.

Sir, that same Constitution which I again hold up, and to which I give my whole heart, and my utmost loyalty, commits to Congress alone the power to borrow money, and to fix the purposes to which it shall be applied, and expressly limits army appropriations to the term of two years. Each Senator and Representative, therefore, must judge for himself, upon his conscience and his oath, and before God and the country, of the justice and wisdom and policy of the President's demand; and whenever this House shall have become but a mere office wherein to register the decrees of the Executive, it will be high time to abolish it.

But I have a right, I believe, sir, to say that, however gentlemen upon this side of the Chamber may differ finally as to the war, we are yet firmly and inexorably united in one thing, at least, and that is in the determination that our own rights and dignities and privileges, as the Representatives of the people, shall be maintained in their spirit, and to the very letter. And, be this as it may, I do know that there are some here present who are resolved to assert, and to exercise these rights with becoming decency and moderation, certainly, but, at the same time, fully, freely, and at every hazard.

Sir, it is an ancient and wise practice of the English Commons, to precede all votes of supplies by an inquiry into abuses and grievances, and especially into any infractions of the Constitution and the laws by the Executive. Let us follow this safe practice. We are now in Committee of the Whole *on the State of the Union;* and in the exercise of my right and my duty as a Representative, and availing myself of the latitude of debate allowed here, I propose to consider *the present State of the Union,* and supply, also, some few of the many omissions of the President in the message before us. Sir, he has undertaken to give us information of the state of the Union, as the *Constitution* requires him to do; and it was his duty, as an honest Executive, to make that information full, impartial, and complete, instead of spreading before us a labored and lawyerly vindication of his own course of policy—a policy which has precipitated us into a terrible and bloody revolution. He admits the fact; he admits that, to-day, we are in the midst of a general civil war, not now a mere petty insurrection, to be suppressed in twenty days by a proclamation and a *posse comitatus* of three months' militia. . . .

Thus, sir, the case stood, at twelve o'clock on the 4th of March last, when, from the eastern portico of this capitol, and in the presence of twenty thousand of his countrymen, but enveloped in a cloud of soldiery, which no other American President ever saw, Abraham Lincoln took the oath of office to support the Constitution, and delivered his inaugural—a message, I regret to say, not written in the direct and straightforward language which becomes an American President and an

American statesman, and which was expected from the plain, blunt, honest man of the Northwest—but with the forked tongue and crooked counsel of the New York politician leaving thirty millions of people in doubt whether it meant peace or war. But, whatever may have been the secret purpose and meaning of the inaugural, practically, for six weeks, the policy of peace prevailed; and they were weeks of happiness to the patriot, and prosperity to the country. Business revived; trade returned; commerce flourished. Never was there a fairer prospect before any people. Secession in the past, languished, and was spiritless, and harmless; secession in the future, was arrested, and perished. By overwhelming majorities, Virginia, Kentucky, North Carolina, Tennessee, and Missouri—all declared for the old Union, and every heart beat high with hope that, in due course of time, and through faith and patience and peace, and by ultimate and adequate compromise, every State could be restored to it. It is true, indeed, sir, that the Republican party, with great unanimity, and great earnestness and determination, had resolved against all conciliation and compromise. But, on the other hand, the whole Democratic party, and the whole Constitutional-Union party, were equally resolved that there should be no civil war, upon any pretext: and both sides prepared for an appeal to that great and final arbiter of all disputes in a free country—the people. . . .

One of the last and worst acts of a Congress which, born in bitterness and nurtured in convulsion, literally did those things which it ought not to have done, and left undone those things which it ought to have done, was the passage of an obscure, ill-considered, ill-digested, and unstatesmanlike high protective tariff act, commonly known as "The Morrill Tariff." Just about the same time, too, the Confederate Congress, at Montgomery, adopted our old tariff of 1857, which we had rejected to make way for the Morrill act, fixing their rate of duties at five, fifteen, and twenty percent lower than ours. The result was as inevitable as the laws of trade are inexorable. Trade and commerce—and especially the trade and commerce of the West—began to look to the South. Turned out of their natural course, years ago, by the canals and railroads of Pennsylvania and

New York, and diverted eastward at a heavy cost to the West, they threatened now to resume their ancient and accustomed channels—the watercourses—the Ohio and the Mississippi. And political association and union, it was well known, must soon follow the direction of trade and interest. The city of New York, the great commercial emporium of the Union, and the North-west, the chief granary of the Union, began to clamor now, loudly, for a repeal of the pernicious and ruinous tariff. Threatened thus with the loss of both political power and wealth, or the repeal of the tariff, and, at last, of both, New England—and Pennsylvania, too, the land of Penn, cradled in peace—demanded, now, coercion and civil war, with all its horrors, as the price of preserving either from destruction. Ay, sir, Pennsylvania, the great key-stone of the arch of the Union, was willing to levy the whole weight of her iron upon that sacred arch, and crush it beneath the load. The subjugation of the South—ay, sir, the *subjugation* of the South!—I am not talking to children or fools; for there is not a man in this House fit to be a Representative here, who does not know that the South can not be forced to yield obedience to your laws and authority again, until you have conquered and subjugated her—the subjugation of the South, and the closing up of her ports—first, by force, in war, and afterward, by tariff laws, in peace—was deliberately resolved upon by the East. And, sir, when once this policy was begun, these self-same motives of waning commerce, and threatened loss of trade, impelled the great city of New York, and her merchants and her politicians and her press—with here and there an honorable exception—to place herself in the very front rank among the worshipers of Moloch. Much, indeed, of that outburst and uprising in the North, which followed the proclamation of the 15th of April, as well, perhaps, as the proclamation itself, was called forth, not so much by the fall of Sumter—an event long anticipated—as by the notion that the "insurrection," as it was called, might be crushed out in a few weeks, if not by the display, certainly, at least, by the presence of an overwhelming force. . . .

But, whatever may have been the causes or the motives of the act, it is certain that there was a change in the policy which the Administration meant to adopt, or which, at least, they led the country to believe they intended to pursue. I will not venture, now, to assert, what may yet, some day, be made to appear, that the subsequent acts of the Administration, and its enormous and persistent infractions of the Constitution, its high-minded usurpations of power, formed any part of a deliberate conspiracy to overthrow the present form of Federal-republican government, and to establish a strong centralized Government in its stead. No, sir; whatever their purposes now, I rather think that, in the beginning, they rushed, heedlessly and headlong into the gulf, believing that, as the seat of war was then far distant and difficult of access, the display of vigor in re-enforcing Sumter and Pickens, and in calling out seventy-five thousand militia, upon the firing of the first gun, and above all, in that exceedingly happy and original conceit of commanding the insurgent States to "disperse in twenty days," would not, on the one hand, precipitate a crisis, while, upon the other, it would satisfy its own violent partisans, and thus revive and restore the failing fortunes of the Republican party. . . .

But, whatever may have been the purpose, I assert here, to-day, as a Representative, that every principal act of the Administration since has been a glaring usurpation of power, and a palpable and dangerous violation of that very Constitution which this civil war is professedly waged to support. . . .

But, sir, Congress was not assembled at once, as Congress should have been, and the great question of civil war submitted to their deliberations. The Representatives of the States and of the people were not allowed the slightest voice in this, the most momentous question ever presented to any government. The entire responsibility of the whole work was boldly assumed by the Executive, and all the powers required for the purposes in hand were boldly usurped from either the States or the people, or from the legislative department; while the voice of the judiciary, that last refuge and hope of liberty, was turned away from with contempt.

Sir, the right of blockade—and I begin with it—is a belligerent right, incident to a state of war, and it can not be exercised until war has been declared or recognized; and Congress alone can declare or recognize war. But Congress had not declared or recognized war. On the contrary, they had, but a little while before, expressly refused to declare it, or to arm the President with the power to make it. And thus the President, in declaring a blockade of certain ports in the States of the South, and in applying to it the rules governing blockades as between independent powers, violated the Constitution.

But if, on the other hand, he meant to deal with these States as still in the Union, and subject to Federal authority, then he usurped a power which belongs to Congress alone—the power to abolish and close up ports of entry; a power, too, which Congress had, also, but a few weeks before, refused to exercise. And yet, without the repeal or abolition of ports of entry, any attempt, by either Congress or the President, to blockade these ports, is a violation of the spirit, if not of the letter, of that clause of the Constitution which declares that "no preference shall be given, by any regulation of commerce or revenue, to the ports of one State over those of another."

Sir, upon this point I do not speak without the highest authority. In the very midst of the South Carolina nullification controversy, it was suggested, that in the recess of Congress, and without a law to govern him, the President, Andrew Jackson, meant to send down a fleet to Charleston and blockade the port. But the bare suggestion called forth the indignant protest of Daniel Webster, himself the arch enemy of nullification, and whose brightest laurels were won in the three years' conflict in the Senate Chamber, with its ablest champions. In an address, in October, 1832, at Worcester, Massachusetts, to a National Republican convention—it was before the birth, or christening, at least of the Whig party—the great expounder of the Constitution, said:

We are told, sir, that the President will immediately employ the military force, and at once blockade Charleston. A military remedy—a remedy by direct belligerent operation, has thus been suggested, and nothing else has been suggested, as the intended means of preserving the Union. Sir, there is no little reason to think that this suggestion is true. We can not be altogether unmindful of the past, and, therefore, we can not be altogether unapprehensive for the future. For one, sir, I raise my voice, beforehand, against the unauthorized employment of military power, and against superseding the authority of the laws, by an armed force, under pretense of putting down nullification. *The President has no authority to blockade Charleston.*

Jackson! Jackson, sir! the great Jackson! did not dare to do it without authority of Congress; but our Jackson of to-day, the little Jackson at the other end of the avenue, and the mimic Jacksons around him, do blockade, not only Charleston harbor, but the whole Southern coast, three thousand miles in extent, by a single stroke of the pen.

"The President has no authority to employ military force till he shall be duly required"—Mark the word: "*required* so to do by law and civil authorities. His duty is to cause the laws to be executed. His duty is to support *the civil authority.*"

As in the *Merryman* case, forsooth; but I shall recur to that hereafter:

His duty is, if the laws be resisted, to employ the military force of the country, if necessary, for their support and execution; *but to do all this in compliance only with law and with decisions of the tribunals.* If, by any ingenious devices, those who resist the laws escape from the reach of judicial authority, as it is now provided to be exercised, it is entirely competent to *Congress* to make such new provisions as the exigency of the case may demand.

Treason, sir, rank treason, all this to-day. And, yet, thirty years ago, it was true Union patriotism and sound constitutional law! Sir, I prefer the wisdom and stern fidelity to principle of the fathers. . . .

Next after the blockade, sir, in the catalogue of daring executive usurpations, comes the proclamation of the 3rd of May, and the orders of the War and Navy Departments in pursuance of it—a proclamation and usurpation which would have cost any English sovereign his head at any time within the last two hundred years. Sir, the Constitution not only

confines to Congress the right to declare war, but expressly provides that
"Congress (not the President) shall have power to raise and support
armies" and to "provide and maintain a navy." In pursuance of this authority, Congress, years ago, had fixed the number of officers, and of the regiments, of the different kinds of service; and also, the number of ships,
officers, marines, and seamen which should compose the navy. Not only
that, but Congress has repeatedly, within the last five years, refused to increase the regular army. More than that still: in February and March last,
the House, upon several test votes, repeatedly and expressly refused to au-
thorize the President to accept the service of volunteers for the very purpose of protecting the public property, enforcing the laws, and collecting
the revenue. And, yet, the President, of his own mere will and authority,
and without the shadow of right, has proceeded to increase, and has increased, the standing army by twenty-five thousand men; the navy by
eighteen thousand; and has called for, and accepted the services of, forty
regiments of volunteers for three years, numbering forty-two thousand
men, and making thus a grand army, or military force, raised by executive
proclamation alone, without the sanction of Congress, without warrant of
law, and in direct violation of the Constitution, and of his oath of office, of
eighty-five thousand soldiers enlisted for three and five years, and already
in the field. And, yet, the President now asks us to support the army which
he has thus raised, to ratify his usurpations by a law *ex post facto,* and thus
to make ourselves parties to our own degradation, and to his infractions of
the Constitution. Meanwhile, however, he has taken good care not only to
enlist the men, organize the regiments, and muster them into service, but
to provide, in advance, for a horde of forlorn, worn-out, and broken-down
politicians of his own party, by appointing, either by himself, or through
the Governors of the States, major-generals, brigadier-generals, colonels,
lieutenant-colonels, majors, captains, lieutenants, adjutants, quarter-
masters, and surgeons, without any limit as to numbers, and without so
much as once saying to Congress, "By your leave, gentlemen."

Beginning with this wide breach of the Constitution, this enormous
usurpation of the most dangerous of all powers—the power of the

sword—other infractions and assumptions were easy; and after public liberty, private right soon fell. The privacy of the telegraph was invaded in the search after treason and traitors; although it turns out, significantly enough, that the only victim, so far, is one of the appointees and especial pets of the Administration. The telegraphic dispatches, preserved under every pledge of secrecy for the protection and safety of the telegraph companies, were seized and carried away without search warrant, without probable cause, without oath, and without description of the places to be searched, or of the things to be seized, and in plain violation of the right of the people to be secure in their houses, persons, *papers*, and effects, against unreasonable searches and seizures. One step more, sir, will bring upon us search and seizure of the public mails; and, finally, as in the worst days of English oppression—as in the times of the Russells and the Sydneys of English martyrdom—of the drawers and secretaries of the private citizen; though even then tyrants had the grace to look to the forms of the law, and the execution was judicial murder, not military slaughter. . . .

Sir, the rights of property having been thus wantonly violated, it needed but a little stretch of usurpation to invade the sanctity of the person; and a victim was not long wanting. A private citizen of Maryland, not subject to the rules and articles of war—not in a case arising in the land or naval forces, nor in the militia, when in actual service—is seized in his own house, in the dead hour of the night, not by any civil officer, nor upon any civil process, but by a band of armed soldiers, under the verbal orders of a military chief, and is ruthlessly torn from his wife and his children, and hurried off to a fortress of the United States—and that fortress, as if in mockery, the very one over whose ramparts had floated that star-spangled banner immortalized in song by the patriot prisoner, who, "by dawn's early light," saw its folds gleaming amid the wreck of battle, and invoked the blessings of heaven upon it, and prayed that it might long wave "o'er the *land of the free*, and the home of the brave."

And, sir, when the highest judicial officer of the land, the Chief Justice of the Supreme Court, upon whose shoulders, "when the judicial ermine fell, it touched nothing not as spotless as itself," the aged, the venerable, the gentle, and pure-minded Taney, who, but a little while before, had administered to the President the oath to support the *Constitution*, and to execute the laws, issued, as by law it was his sworn duty to issue, the high prerogative writ of *habeas corpus*—that great writ of right, that main bulwark of personal liberty, commanding the body of the accused to be brought before him, that justice and right might be done by due course of law, and without denial or delay, the gates of the fortress, its cannon turned towards, and in plain sight of the city, where the court sat, and frowning from its ramparts, were closed against the officer of the law, and the answer returned that the officer in command has, by the authority of the President, *suspended* the writ of *habeas corpus*. And thus it is, sir, that the accused has ever since been held a prisoner without due process of law; without bail; without presentment by a grand jury; without speedy, or public trial by a petit jury, of his own State or district, or any trial at all; without information of the nature and cause of the accusation; without being confronted with the witnesses against him; without compulsory process to obtain witnesses in his favor; and without the assistance of counsel for his defense. And this is our boasted American liberty? And thus it is, too, sir, that here, here in America, in the seventy-third year of the Republic, that great writ and security of personal freedom, which it cost the patriots and freemen of England six hundred years of labor and toil and blood to extort and to hold fast from venal judges and tyrant kings; written in the great charter of Runnymede by the iron barons, who made the simple Latin and uncouth words of the times, *nullus liber homo*, in the language of Chatham, worth all the classics; recovered and confirmed a hundred times afterward, as often as violated and stolen away, and finally, and firmly secured at last by the great act of Charles II, and transferred thence to our own Constitution and laws, has been wantonly and ruthlessly trampled in the dust. Ay, sir, that great writ, bearing, by a special command of Parliament, those other uncouth, but magic words, *per statutum tricessimo primo Caroli secundi regis*, which no English judge, no

English minister, no king or queen of England, dare disobey; that writ, brought over by our fathers, and cherished by them, as a priceless inheritance of liberty, an American President has contemptuously set at defiance. Nay, more, he has ordered his subordinate military chiefs to suspend it at their discretion! And, yet, after all this, he cooly comes before this House and the Senate and the country, and pleads that he is only preserving and protecting the Constitution; and demands and expects of this House and of the Senate and the country their thanks for his usurpations; while, outside of this capitol, his myrmidons are clamoring for impeachment of the Chief Justice, as engaged in a conspiracy to break down the Federal Government.

Sir, however much necessity—the tyrant's plea—may be urged in extenuation of the usurpations and infractions of the President in regard to public liberty, there can be no such apology or defense for his invasions of private right. What overruling necessity required the violation of the sanctity of private property and private confidence? What great public danger demanded the arrest and imprisonment, without trial by common law, of one single private citizen, for an act done weeks before, openly, and by authority of his State? If guilty of treason, was not the judicial power ample enough and strong enough for his conviction and punishment? What, then, was needed in his case, but the precedent under which other men, in other places, might become the victims of executive suspicion and displeasure?

As to the pretense, sir, that the President has the Constitutional right to suspend the writ of *habeas corpus,* I will not waste time in arguing it. The case is as plain as words can make it. It is a legislative power; it is found only in the legislative article; it belongs to Congress only to do it. . . .

I have finished now, Mr. Chairman, what I proposed to say at this time upon the message of the President. As to my own position in regard to this most unhappy civil war, I have only to say that I stand to-day just where I stood upon the 4th of March last; where the whole Democratic party, and the whole Constitutional Union party, and a vast majority, as I believe, of the people of the United States stood too. I am for *peace,* speedy, immediate, honorable *peace,* with all its blessings. . . .

Do Not Serve as a Chaplain

ALFRED H. LOVE

In this letter dated August 22, 1861, peace activist Alfred H. Love urges a friend not to become a military chaplain in the Civil War. In his private business dealings Love, who would found the Universal Peace Union in 1866, chose not to sell goods to the army as a matter of conscience. A biographer says that this decision "caused the dissolution of the firm with which he was connected, and brought him great pecuniary loss as well as persecution."

I was, indeed, astonished at the announcement of thy abandoning thy peace principles for the present, owing to the peculiar demands of the war for the government and the Union, and accepting a position as chaplain of a body of soldiers. . . .

Acknowledging war a horrible evil, and yet accepting it on account of the cause, seemingly so just, is not calculated to lessen its enormity, nor elevate thee in the estimation of those poor, unfortunate people who so readily spring to arms at the least provocation. Nor can the evils be mitigated by saying "there are some more horrible." The proposition, "of two evils choose the lesser," is fallacious. The moment we recognize the evils, we presuppose the right; therefore of two evils choose neither—choose the right, for it admits of no comparative degree—no alternative. The positive admission of its being an evil, should, therefore, deter thee from taking any part, or encouraging others to do so. It seems almost unnecessary to weigh war in the scale of horrible evils. Where is the evil that is parent to more sin and crime than this, and more fully super-induces a transgression of every one of the ten commandments; in short, the portentousness of the evil to every one's estimate, sufficient it certainly is, that it is an evil—then reject it! Although a pure nonresistance by carnal weapons politically considered, may seem at this time impracticable, yet as Christians, we must know nothing of expediency, for that presupposes a palliation of evil; we must know nothing of compromises, for that mediates an agreement with wickedness; we must know nothing of majorities or minorities, for that engenders fear, and a reliance upon others, rather than ourselves. All we should know is our duty guided by the conscientious and revealed right. . . .

Mark the effect of thy encouraging war, *this or any other.* Those who look up to thee—follow. Becoming absorbed in the enthusiasm of the hour, we float along on the swelling tide, forgetful that popular movements always should be carefully watched, often even doubted. Let us heed that we do not become driftwood. The rushing tide has overleaped its banks, driftwood will not dam it—will not control it—rock masonry will. Stay this flood of waters, and it will deepen and compose; and its great powers, instead of dashing along uncontrolled, to waste, devastating all in its course, may be used to turn the glorious machinery of the world, the grist mills and the sawmills—the wheels of thought and action, of utility and morality! . . .

Patriotism used to mean love of country, and was then a virtue; but now it seems to be a love to have our own way, in our country, and is now ambition. The true patriot is one who loves to develop the highest excellence of his Father's bounty-land, and comprehends soil, institutions and his fellow men, untrammeled by geographical or genealogical lines. We forget that God is above country, and while the latter may do to live by, he alone will do to die by. Love of liberty, of life, family and home, are all virtues; but we must be watchful that the means used to protect them subserve the highest moral authority. The patriotism which says, I do not know how to fight—I will not learn—I would not fight if I knew how, nor aid others in doing so—a patriotism which elevates the spiritual above the animal nature; which regards the slaveholder less an enemy than an unfortunate, misguided and erring brother, who requires even more love and solicitude; which does not call him brute or savage, though facts might justify such expression; that metes out, the more he errs, kindness and goodness, with an earnest vindication of all the rights of humanity, an advanced civilization and the love of the whole country, with the love of its countrymen—such patriotism opens up the duties of the true citizen and patriot, and fears no peril to self or nation.

This sword is presented for the church, and for the past services therein of the recipient. Art thou not, on the one hand, desecrating the spirit of the church, and he, on the other, proving recreant to its teachings?

Why ask him to accept this sword "to be drawn in the defense of our holy religion"? A religion that needs the defense of the sword is not holy, nor worth defending. The moment it demands such protection, it ceases to be acceptable to our Father, who taught a religion in the example of his beloved Son, of meekness with firmness, submission with persuasion, martyrdom with resurrection. . . .

"But I should be a traitor to my country were I to refuse to take part in this contest." Is there but one way to take part? Is the spirit of nonresistance by force of arms such a cushioned-pew, easy rocking-chair or feather-bed existence that it demands no action; and are all who decline to join the army, or aid others in doing so, traitors? No! The work that opens to the nonresistant at this time is immense. It consists in arguing and appealing, petitioning and protesting, in demanding and prayerfully desiring—using the great levers of an enlightened age; these moral forces of action and example that are truly difficult, yet invincible. No! Thou wouldst be far from traitor by grasping with these difficulties on the purest peace basis, with a view to develop the highest claims of morality, by a long, anxious, unremitted, even if unpopular, effort. By testimonies that would bear trial and even martyrdom; and all for the love of our country, our fellow men, and our Creator.

"Under our national government the oppressed and down-trodden of every land on earth have found and may find a safe refuge." Forget not the African and the Indian! Thou dost not seem to forget the former, but alludes to the 4,000,000 enslaved, and yet this boastful North is verily guilty of the curse to a very great extent. I know thy sympathies are deeply moved in their behalf, but should we be so well satisfied that this war is the "death blow to slavery"? I mean slavery in its widest sense. There may open opportunities when slaves will be liberated, and how eager some will be to shield their war doctrines by proclaiming it the good work of war; unwilling to give credit, where it properly belongs, to the long, anxious and earnest efforts, of the purest *moral forces*, rather than the direct agency of the sword.

Should the glorious results, however, be accomplished, by other means than the pressure of moral sentiment, beware that it does not give a significance to war that will react; and hereafter, when any object is desired, this power will be adopted with the word: Oh! It achieved victories for the government and the slave, in days gone by, *we* will use it now, for our purposes. Thus we will be under the oppression of military power—standing armies—the slavery of the sword! Then, too, we may fear the slavery of caste—the exclusion of a portion of God's children from equal rights, because of some imagined disqualification of color. Be careful then and do not use *wicked* means even to free the slave!. . .

What a sublime spectacle it would be to find a people willing to relinquish their artificial claims of country for the sake of peace and carrying out the great principles of Christ. There never has been a nation willing to relinquish a single inch of territory. Why not part with discordant members for the sake of Union, which means harmony; why not be willing to retreat and retire into such a domain as would be harmonious, and where the rights of all of God's creatures would be recognized? This would, indeed, be an example of purity and morality challenging respect, and worthy of imitation. As there was free will in the formation of the Union, for mutual benefit, let it be maintained upon this free-will policy, which has been the admiration of the world. . . .

Gross, Shameless, Transparent Cheats

LYSANDER SPOONER

Lysander Spooner (1808–1887) was a radical abolitionist and libertarian. His opposition to government power included a belief in the right of peaceful secession, so he opposed slavery while supporting the Southern states' right to depart from the Union without violence. This excerpt is taken from Spooner's No Treason: The Constitution of No Authority *(1867).*

Lenders of blood money had, for a long series of years previous to the war, been the willing accomplices of the slave-holders in perverting the government from the purposes of liberty and justice, to the greatest of crimes. They had been such accomplices *for a purely pecuniary consideration,* to wit, a control of the markets in the South; in other words, the privilege of holding the slave-holders themselves in industrial and commercial subjection to the manufacturers and merchants of the North (who afterwards furnished the money for the war). And these Northern merchants and manufacturers, these lenders of blood-money, were willing to continue to be the accomplices of the slave-holders in the future, for the same pecuniary considerations. But the slave-holders, either doubting the fidelity of their Northern allies, or feeling themselves strong enough to keep their slaves in subjection without Northern assistance, would no longer pay the price which these Northern men demanded. And it was to enforce this price in the future—that is, to monopolize the Southern markets, to maintain their industrial and commercial control over the South—that these Northern manufacturers and merchants lent some of the profits of their former monopolies for the war, in order to secure to themselves the same, or greater, monopolies in the future. These—and not any love of liberty or justice—were the motives on which the money for the war was lent by the North. In short, the North said to the slave-holders: If you will not pay us our price (give us control of your markets) for our assistance against your slaves, we will secure the same price (keep control of your markets) by helping your slaves against you, and using them as our tools for maintaining dominion over you; for the control of your markets we will have, whether the tools we use for that purpose be black or white, and be the cost, in blood and money, what it may.

On this principle, and from this motive, and not from any love of liberty, or justice, the money was lent in enormous amounts, and at enormous rates of interest. And it was only by means of these loans that the objects of the war were accomplished.

And now these lenders of blood-money demand their pay; and the government, so called, becomes their tool, their servile, slavish, villainous tool, to extort it from the labor of the enslaved people both of the North and South. It is to be extorted by every form of direct, and indirect, and unequal taxation. Not only the nominal debt and interest—enormous as the latter was—are to be paid in full; but these holders of the debt are to be paid still further—and perhaps doubly, triply, or quadruply paid—by such tariffs on imports as will enable our home manufacturers to realize enormous prices for their commodities; also by such monopolies in banking as will enable them to keep control of, and thus enslave and plunder, the industry and trade of the great body of the Northern people themselves. In short, the industrial and commercial slavery of the great body of the people, North and South, black and white, is the price which these lenders of blood money demand, and insist upon, and are determined to secure, in return for the money lent for the war.

This program having been fully arranged and systematized, they put their sword into the hands of the chief murderer of the war, and charge him to carry their scheme into effect. And now he, speaking as their organ, says, "*Let us have peace.*"

The meaning of this is: Submit quietly to all the robbery and slavery we have arranged for you, and you can have "peace." But in case you resist, the same lenders of blood-money, who furnished the means to subdue the South, will furnish the means again to subdue you.

These are the terms on which alone this government, or, with few exceptions, any other, ever gives "peace" to its people.

The whole affair, on the part of those who furnished the money, has been, and now is, a deliberate scheme of robbery and murder; not merely to monopolize the markets of the South, but also to monopolize the currency, and thus control the industry and trade, and thus plunder and enslave the laborers, of both North and South. And Congress and the president are today the merest tools for these purposes. They are obliged to be, for they know that their own power, as rulers, so-called, is at an end, the moment their credit with the blood-money loan-mongers fails. They are like a bankrupt in the hands of an extortioner. They dare not say nay to any demand made upon them. And to hide at once, if possible, both their servility and crimes, they attempt to divert public attention, by crying out that they have "Abolished Slavery!" That they have "Saved the Country!" That they have "Preserved our Glorious Union!" and that, in now paying the "National Debt," as they call it (as if the people themselves, *all of them who are to be taxed for its payment*, had really and voluntarily joined in contracting it), they are simply "Maintaining the National Honor!"

By "maintaining the national honor," they mean simply that they themselves, open robbers and murderers, assume to be the nation, and will keep faith with those who lend them the money necessary to enable them to crush the great body of the people under their feet; and will faithfully appropriate, from the proceeds of their future robberies and murders, enough to pay all their loans, principal and interest.

The pretense that the "abolition of slavery" was either a motive or justification for the war, is a fraud of the same character with that of "maintaining the national honor." Who, but such usurpers, robbers, and murderers as they, ever established slavery? Or what government, except one resting upon the sword, like the one we now have, was ever capable of maintaining slavery? And why did these men abolish slavery? Not from any love of liberty in general—not as an act of justice to the black man himself, but only "as a war measure," and because they wanted his assistance, and that of his friends, in carrying on the war they had undertaken for maintaining and intensifying that political, commercial, and industrial slavery, to which they have subjected the great body of the people, both black and white. And yet these imposters now cry out that they have abolished the chattel slavery of the black man—although that was not the motive of the war—as if they thought they could thereby conceal, atone for, or justify that other slavery which they were fighting to perpetuate, and to render more rigorous and inexorable than it ever was before. There was no difference of principle—but only of degree—between the slavery they boast they have abolished, and the slavery they were fighting to preserve; for all restraints upon men's natural liberty, not necessary for the simple maintenance of justice, are of the nature of slavery, and differ from each other only in degree.

If their object had really been to abolish slavery, or maintain liberty or justice generally, they had only to say: All, whether white or black, who want the protection of this government, shall have it; and all who do not want it, will be left in peace, so long as they leave us in peace. Had they said this, slavery would necessarily have been abolished at once; the war would have been saved; and a thousand times nobler union than we have ever had would have been the result. It would have been a voluntary union of free men; such a union as will one day exist among all men, the world over, if the several nations, so called, shall ever get rid of the usurpers, robbers, and murderers, called governments, that now plunder, enslave, and destroy them.

Still another of the frauds of these men is that they are now establishing, and that the war was designed to establish, "a government of consent." The only idea they have ever manifested as to what is a government of consent, is this—that it is one to which everybody must consent, or be shot. This idea was the dominant one on which the war was carried on; and it is the dominant one, now that we have got what is called "peace."

Their pretenses that they have "Saved the Country," and "Preserved our Glorious Union," are frauds like all the rest of their pretenses. By them they mean simply that they have subjugated, and maintained their power over, an unwilling people. This they call "Saving the Country"; as if an enslaved and subjugated people—or as if any people kept in subjection by the sword (as it is intended that all of us shall be hereafter)—could be said to have any country. This, too, they call "Preserving our Glorious Union"; as if there could be said to be any Union, glorious or inglorious, that was not voluntary. Or as if there could be said to be any union between masters and slaves; between those who conquer, and those who are subjugated. All these cries of having "abolished slavery," of having "saved the country," of having "preserved the union," of establishing "a government of consent," and of "maintaining the national honor," are all gross, shameless, transparent cheats—so transparent that they ought to deceive no one—when uttered as justifications for the war, or for the government that has succeeded the war, or for now compelling the people to pay the cost of the war, or for compelling anybody to support a government that he does not want.

The lesson taught by all these facts is this: As long as mankind continue to pay "National Debts," so-called—that is, so long as they are such dupes and cowards as to pay for being cheated, plundered, enslaved, and murdered—so long there will be enough to lend the money for those purposes; and with that money a plenty of tools, called soldiers, can be hired to keep them in subjection. But when they refuse any longer to pay for being thus cheated, plundered, enslaved, and murdered, they will cease to have cheats, and usurpers, and robbers, and murderers and blood-money loan-mongers for masters.

4

The Spanish-American and Philippine-American Wars

We earnestly condemn the policy of the present National Administration in the Philippines. It seeks to extinguish the spirit of 1776 in those islands. We deplore the sacrifice of our soldiers and sailors, whose bravery deserves admiration even in an unjust war. We deplore the slaughter of the Filipinos as a needless horror.

—from the 1899 platform of the American Anti-Imperialist League

In April 1898 the United States went to war with Spain for the stated purpose of liberating Cuba from Spanish control. Although Spanish brutalities were undeniable, yellow journalism had made the details of the conflict in Cuba between the government and the rebels seem simpler than they really were.

Several months later, when the war had ended, Cuba had been transformed into an American protectorate, and Puerto Rico, Guam, and the Philippines had become American possessions. When the U.S. government decided not to grant independence to the Philippines, Filipino rebels led by Emilio Aguinaldo determined to resist American occupying forces. The result was a brutal guerrilla war that stretched on for years. Some 200,000 Filipinos lost their lives, either directly from the fighting or as a result of a cholera epidemic traceable to the war.

That American forces were engaged in a colonial war to suppress another people's independence provoked much soul-searching among important American thinkers, writers, and journalists. What eventually became the American Anti-Imperialist League began at a June 1898 meeting at Boston's Faneuil Hall, where people concerned about the colonial policy that the U.S. government may choose to adopt in the wake of the war gathered to speak out against the transformation of the United States into an imperial power. The League was formally established that November, dedicating its energies to propagating the anti-imperialist message by means of lectures, public meetings, and the printed word.

Those who later became anti-imperialists could be found among both supporters and opponents of the Spanish-American War of 1898: whatever the merits of that war, the anti-imperialists were agreed that America would betray her very soul were she to become an imperial power like all the rest.

Anti-imperialists were appalled at their government's practices in the Philippines, and focused on discovering and disseminating the truth about the fate of the Filipinos under American occupation. The *Nation*'s E. L. Godkin, for instance, declared that the U.S. government had substituted "keen effective slaughter for Spanish old-fashioned, clumsy slaughter." William James was astonished that his country could "puke up its ancient soul . . . in five minutes." Andrew Carnegie wrote to a friend who favored expansion: "It is a matter of congratulation . . . that you have about finished your work of civilizing the Fillipinos [sic]. It is thought that about 8,000 of them have been completely civilized and sent to Heaven. I hope you like it." ·

Carnegie even went so far as to offer to purchase the independence of the Philippines with a check for $20 million—the amount the U.S. government had paid Spain for the islands. (The government never took him up on it.)

That both the industrialist Andrew Carnegie and labor leader Samuel Gompers belonged to the League said something about the diversity that marked anti-imperialist sentiment. Conservatives and libertarians like Grover Cleveland and William Graham Sumner joined hands with prominent public figures like Jane Addams and William James.

It remains to be seen whether such a cross-ideological movement against empire can succeed today, but it has never been more urgently needed.

A Peace Appeal to Labor

BOLTON HALL

This statement was presented before the Central Labor Union of New York City on April 17, 1898. Bolton Hall was treasurer of the American Longshoremen's Union. His appeal was endorsed by William Dean Howells, Charles Frederick Adams, John S. Crosby, Josephine Shaw Lowell, Bishop Henry Codman Potter, and Ernest H. Crosby.

To the Workers of America:

We desire to call attention to the manifest folly of contributing even in the slightest degree to the warlike feeling so prevalent in the country. We admit fully the unjust character of the Spanish administration of Cuba, but we deny that war between Spain and the United States can be in any way conducive to the best interests of mankind.

(1) With reference to the destruction of the *Maine,* as a simple question of fact, there never was an issue more precisely adapted to arbitration than the one raised by this disaster. While we accept the findings of the naval board as conclusive upon ourselves, we cannot expect foreign countries to be satisfied with a one-sided proceeding. We understand that Spain has offered to submit this matter to arbitration, and we insist that there is no other honorable course for the country to pursue than to accept this proposal.

(2) The inhuman conditions which exist in Cuba have been primarily produced by that greed which gets in its work wherever man has the power to oppress his fellows. The cruelty exhibited in Cuba is no peculiarity of the Spanish race; within the last few weeks instances of cruelty to negroes have occurred in this country which equal, if they do not surpass, anything which has occurred in Cuba. Honesty compels us to acknowledge that it is not the Spanish race especially, but the human race at large, that is cruel, and that our crusade in this matter should begin at home. We see every day the vast injustice prevailing in our own land, the hopeless toil, the wretched poverty, the armies of unemployed, and until we remove these beams from our own eyes should not presume to take the mote from our brother's.

(3) But even if we were in a position in which we could without hypocrisy attempt to establish justice in a neighboring land, we protest that interference with the army and navy is of all the least effectual. We at once add sufferings to those already incurred; we put an end to such efforts as are now being made to relieve misery in Cuba, and we fill Spain and also America with mourning. The real evil, which is hatred between men, we extend all over our own land, and we hand down to our children a legacy of hate against people who differ in nowise from ourselves. We are in a position in which, by moral interference, we can insist on justice for the oppressed Cubans. Spain is ready to

yield everything but her nominal sovereignty, and we have no business to fight a foreign country for a mere sentimental question of nominal independence.

(4) If it is true that some thousands of Spanish speculators and office-holders have oppressed the Cubans, how in the name of common sense can that justify American workmen in shooting down Spanish workmen? A war will put all social improvements among us back ten years, and the Cuban workmen with us. The political freedom for which they are fighting is of no importance in comparison with the economic freedom which we are striving for. Could anything be more foolish than to drop the great fight and take up the smaller one? If there is a war, you will furnish the corpses and the taxes, and others will get all the glory. Speculators will make money out of it—that is, out of you. Men will get high prices for inferior supplies, leaky boats, for shoddy clothes and pasteboard shoes, and you will have to pay the bill, and the only satisfaction you will get is the privilege of hating your Spanish fellow-workmen, who are really your brothers and who have had as little to do with the wrongs of Cuba as you have.

(5) Finally, we believe that all questions should be settled by reason; and, as man is the only creature endowed with reason, the reasonable way is the manly way. Now, how can a war settle questions reasonably? To hold that such issues can be determined by physical force is as ridiculous as the superstitions of our ancestors who made prisoners walk over hot irons to prove their innocence. We have given up the duel in private life; why should we have recourse to it as a nation? It is only a way of saying that might is right, that the biggest must prevail, and that the feeble have no rights which strength is obliged to respect. If labor men adopt these principles they might as well give up their movement. If might be right, long live the strong monopolist! Let us bow down before him. But if, on the other hand, reason is to rule, let us appeal to that and not to brutal force.

War Is Kind

STEPHEN CRANE

Stephen Crane, best known for The Red Badge of Courage, *wrote the poem from which the selection below is excerpted for his 1899 collection* War Is Kind and Other Lines.

Do not weep, maiden, for war is kind.
Because your lover threw wild hands toward the sky
And the affrighted steed ran on alone,
Do not weep.
War is kind.

Hoarse, booming drums of the regiment
Little souls who thirst for fight,
These men were born to drill and die
The unexplained glory flies above them
Great is the battle-god, great, and his kingdom—
A field where a thousand corpses lie.

Do not weep, babe, for war is kind.
Because your father tumbled in the yellow trenches,
Raged at his breast, gulped and died,
Do not weep.
War is kind.

Swift, blazing flag of the regiment
Eagle with crest of red and gold,
These men were born to drill and die
Point for them the virtue of slaughter
Make plain to them the excellence of killing
And a field where a thousand corpses lie.

Mother whose heart hung humble as a button
On the bright splendid shroud of your son,
Do not weep.
War is kind.

The Conquest of the United States by Spain

WILLIAM GRAHAM SUMNER

William Graham Sumner (1840–1910), Yale professor and polymath, and a supporter of laissez-faire *in economics, argued in this 1899 essay that imperialism was leading the United States to adopt the same philosophy of imperial Spain, which Americans had just defeated in war.*

During the last year the public has been familiarized with descriptions of Spain and of Spanish methods of doing things until the name of Spain has become a symbol for a certain well-defined set of notions and policies. On the other hand, the name of the United States has always been, for all of us, a symbol for a state of things, a set of ideas and traditions, a group of views about social and political affairs. Spain was the first, for a long time the greatest, of the modern imperialistic states. The United States, by its historical origin, its traditions, and its principles, is the chief representative of the revolt and reaction against that kind of a state. I intend to show that, by the line of action now proposed to us, which we call expansion and imperialism, we are throwing away some of the most important elements of the American symbol and are adopting some of the most important elements of the Spanish symbol. We have beaten Spain in a military conflict, but we are submitting to be conquered by her on the field of ideas and policies.

Expansionism and imperialism are nothing but the old philosophies of national prosperity which have brought Spain to where she now is.

Those philosophies appeal to national vanity and national cupidity. They are seductive, especially upon the first view and the most superficial judgment, and therefore it cannot be denied that they are very strong for popular effect. They are delusions, and they will lead us to ruin unless we are hard-headed enough to resist them. In any case the year 1898 is a great landmark in the history of the United States. The consequences will not be all good or all bad, for such is not the nature of societal influences. They are always mixed of good and ill, and so it will be in this case. Fifty years from now the historian, looking back to 1898, will no doubt see, in the course which things will have taken, consequences of the proceedings of that year and of this present one which will not all be bad, but you will observe that that is not a justification for a happy-go-lucky policy; that does not affect our duty to-day in all that we do to seek wisdom and prudence and to determine our actions by the best judgment which we can form. . . .

The original and prime cause of the war was that it was a move of partisan tactics in the strife of parties at Washington. As soon as it seemed resolved upon, a number of interests began to see their advantage in it and hastened to further it. It was necessary to make appeals to the public which would bring quite other motives to the support of the enterprise and win the consent of classes who would never consent to either financial or political jobbery. Such appeals were found in sensational assertions which we had no means to verify, in phrases of alleged patriotism, in statements about Cuba and the Cubans which we now know to have been entirely untrue. . . .

There is another observation, however, about the war which is of far greater importance: that is, that it was a gross violation of self-government. We boast that we are a self-governing people, and in this respect, particularly, we compare ourselves with pride with older nations. What is the difference after all? The Russians, whom we always think of as standing at the opposite pole of political institutions, have self-government, if you mean by it acquiescence in what a little group of people at the head of the government agree to do. The war with Spain was precipitated upon us headlong, without reflection or deliberation, and without any due formulation of public opinion. Whenever a voice was raised in behalf of deliberation and the recognized maxims of statesmanship, it was howled down in a storm of vituperation and cant. Everything was done to make us throw away sobriety of thought and calmness of judgment and to inflate all expressions with sensational epithets and turgid phrases. It cannot be denied that everything in regard to the war has been treated in an exalted strain of sentiment and rhetoric very unfavorable to the truth. At present the whole periodical press of the country seems to be occupied in tickling the national vanity to the utmost by representations about the war which are extravagant and fantastic. There will be a penalty to be paid for all this. Nervous and sensational newspapers are just as corrupting, especially to young people, as nervous and sensational novels. The habit of expecting that all mental pabulum shall be highly spiced, and the corresponding loathing for whatever is soberly truthful, undermines character as much as any other vice. Patriotism is being prostituted into a nervous intoxication which is fatal to an apprehension of truth. It builds around us a fool's paradise, and it will lead us into errors about our position and relations just like those which we have been ridiculing in the case of Spain. . . .

. . . There is not a civilized nation which does not talk about its civilizing mission just as grandly as we do. The English, who really have more to boast of in this respect than anybody else, talk least about it, but the Phariseeism with which they correct and instruct other people has made them hated all over the globe. The French believe themselves the guardians of the highest and purest culture, and that the eyes of all mankind are fixed on Paris, whence they expect oracles of thought and taste. The Germans regard themselves as charged with a mission, especially to us Americans, to save us from egoism and materialism. The Russians, in their books and newspapers, talk about the civilizing mission of Russia in language that might be translated from some of the finest paragraphs in our imperialistic newspapers. . . . The point is that each of them repudiates the standards of the others, and the outlying nations, which are to be civilized, hate all the standards of civilized men. We assume that what we like and practice, and what we think better, must come as a welcome blessing to Spanish-Americans and Filipinos. This is grossly and obviously untrue. They hate our ways. They are hostile to our ideas. Our religion, language, institutions, and manners offend them. They like their own ways, and if we appear amongst them as rulers, there will be social discord in all the great departments of social interest. The most important thing which we shall inherit from the Spaniards will be the task of suppressing rebellions. If the United States takes out of the hands of Spain her mission, on the ground that Spain is not executing it well, and if this nation in its turn attempts to be school-mistress to others, it will shrivel up into the same vanity and self-conceit of which Spain now presents an example. To read our current literature one would think that we were already well on the way to it. Now, the great reason why all these enterprises which begin by saying to somebody else, We know what is good for you better than you know yourself and we are going to make you do it, are false and wrong is that they violate liberty; or, to turn the same statement into other words, the reason why liberty, of which we Americans talk so much, is a good thing is that it means leaving people to live out their own lives in their own way, while we do the same. If we believe in liberty, as an American principle, why do we not stand by it? Why are we going to throw it away to enter upon a Spanish policy of dominion and regulation? . . .

My patriotism is of the kind which is outraged by the notion that the United States never was a great nation until in a petty three months' campaign [the Spanish-American War] it knocked to pieces a poor, decrepit, bankrupt old state like Spain. To hold such an opinion as that is to abandon all American standards, to put shame and scorn on all that our ancestors tried to build up here, and to go over to the standards of which Spain is a representative.

A Lament from Kentucky

A MOTHER

This letter to the editor of Woman's Journal, *dated February 25, 1899, was signed simply, "A Mother, Lexington, Ky."*

Weary with fruitless effort to see any comfort in what seems to me an irreparable wrong done by our beloved country, an ineffaceable stain upon the flag four generations of Americans have held aloft as the emblem, not of conquest, but of liberty, I turn to the faithful, patriotic "H. B. B." [another letter writer] to ask if he can speak a word of comfort and encouragement, can show me how the great wrong done, when we had hoped to see great wrong made right, can ever be undone?

In what does our treatment of the Filipinos differ from Spain's treatment of the Cubans? How can the country that has bathed the land in the blood of the best of her sons to wash away the sin of slavery, have a right to buy ten millions of men, and butcher them by the thousand because they will not kiss the hand of their new masters? I cannot let my little grandson, who has gloried in the victory over Spain, that Cuba might be free, repeat the Declaration of Independence, as he wants to do on Washington's birthday, because it is such mockery to say all men have equal right to "life, liberty, and the pursuit of happiness," when we take life from the Filipinos because they will not give up their "liberty and pursuit of happiness." My boys must not say of Old Glory, "There's no blur on the brightness, / No stain on the bars," when its light is dimmed by the smoke of the burning homes of the men who have died in defense of them. Are not the Filipinos as truly patriots as any other men who fight for their freedom from any yoke, no matter how it is wreathed with garlands of the wealth and culture and higher civilization of the conquerors?

Oh, where is truth, honor, courage, generosity, justice, in the behavior of our great rich country to the poor, weak, helpless islands we had solemnly promised ourselves and the world to protect, and help them to be free? Oh, true friend of mothers, tell us what to teach our sons? "My country, right or wrong?" Is that all? Is that the best the sons of those who have four times fought for their country can teach us? Oh, that my eyes were fountains of tears, that I might weep "for the lost honor of my beloved country, and for the wasted lives of those who died to save what the wickedness of men in high places" has thrown away!

The Pesky Anti-Imperialist

WENDELL PHILLIPS GARRISON

Wendell Phillips Garrison, son of abolitionist William Lloyd Garrison, wrote this editorial for the May 8, 1902, issue of the Nation.

It is most provoking, we know, for Anti-Imperialists to pretend that they are still alive. They have been killed so often. After 1899 we were to hear no more of them. In 1900 they were again pronounced dead, although, like the obstinate Irishman, they continued to protest that, if they were dead, they were not conscious of it. Last year the slain were slaughtered once more, and that time buried as well, with all due ceremony. Yet the impudent creatures have resumed activity during the past few months just as if their epitaphs had not been composed again and again.

And the worst of it is that they seem to have acquired a strange power over the public and over Government. What the lonely and ridiculous Anti-Imperialist was whispering in the closet, a year ago, thousands are now shouting from the housetops. The impossible measures which the absurd fellow was demanding have been adopted by the President of the United States, and have even compelled the approval of Congress. When Gen. [Frederick] Funston [who served in the Philippine War], for example, began his blethering, it was the foolish Anti-

Imperialists who said that the President ought to reprimand and silence him, and how the jeers arose! That was just like the silly old impracticables—attacking a popular hero. But presently the said hero had a gag forcibly inserted between his teeth by Executive order, just as if the Anti-Imperialists had been right about it from the beginning. It is not necessary to recall the triumphs of the mistaken beings in the whole matter of the Philippine investigation and of courts-martial for the implicated officers. Enough to say that, in the entire affair, the Administration and Congress have acted on the demand and as if by the advice of that handful of out-of-date and laughable persons, the Anti-Imperialists.

The phenomenon occasions much scratching of the Imperialist head. How to account for it? Imperialist editors and statesmen are puzzled. Their despised and helpless opponents are actually swaying the policy of the Government! It is absurd, of course, really quite preposterous, but there stands the fact. It is all very fine, and it's lots of fun, to make merry at the expense of wrong-headed people who get in the way of national progress, and hope to turn back the dial of evolution, but how if they succeed? Prodigiously unreasonable, it goes without saying, and truly disgusting to the well-ordered mind of the Imperialist; but what is the explanation?

Very simple, cocksure brothers of the Empire, we assure you. All you have to do is to remember that Anti-Imperialism is only another name for old-fashioned Americanism, and all will be clear to you. An American who has a settled body of convictions, as to which he is ready to speak out at a moment's notice, and which he is ready to apply promptly and sharply to every fresh set of circumstances that turns up; who with his inherited ideas has an inherited courage, an inherited love of equality and justice; who has also a sense of humor which cannot be imposed upon by Uncle Sam masquerading in Louis Quatorze garments—why, he is a natural born Anti-Imperialist, and it is simply his Americanism that makes him think and act as he does.

We have had some beautiful illustrations of this truth in the weeks last past. What is the true American way of dealing with a rampant military banqueter like Funston? Or with news from the Philippines that makes the blood curdle? It is to say on the spot what you think, is it not? Well, that is exactly what the Anti-Imperialists did. It was the other sort who looked at each other in wild surmise, wondered if they dared say anything at all, kept still until shame finally drove them into mumbling speech, and acted in all ways as if they were the terrified and hunted minority afraid to say their souls were their own. Is that Imperialism? We do not know. We only know that it is not Americanism, and that in this case, as so many times before, the citizens who first found their voices, who first spoke out their honest indignation and made their righteous demands, were the ones to move public opinion and to influence official action, while the palterers and the apologizers had to come shamefacedly after.

And it is, too, the "ancient humor," as well as the elder staunchness, of true Americanism that has been coming to its own in the recent successes of the Anti-Imperialist cause. What are our anxious and solemn Imperialists thinking of when they imagine that Uncle Sam has forgotten how to take a joke? They gather about the old gentleman with attentive flatteries, and keep serious faces when he nervously asks them how his ermine hangs, and if his crown is on straight. All the while he would much prefer to have them laugh at him openly and tell him not to be a durn fool. Mark Twain is showing us to-day how true is his descent in the right line of American humor by his continued satires on the airs and graces of our Imperialists. He speaks in the very voice, if not in the numbers, of Hosea Biglow, and with all his sarcasm at the expense of the high and mighty ones who think to arrange all matters of statesmanship and of national policy without consulting the inquisitive democrat of field and shop—"Wal, it's a marcy we've got folks to tell us / The rights an' the wrongs o' these matters, I vow."

This, in a word, is what makes the Anti-Imperialist so pesky—he is American to the core. He has fed on his country's tradition. With him, as with Gov. Andrew and with Lincoln, justice does not depend upon the color of a man's skin. He cannot distinguish between the flag and the principles which first set the flag flying. With John Quincy Adams he believes that the Declaration of Independence is the very Alcoran of American political doctrine. And he does not in the least mind being in a minority. He remembers that the history of success is the history of minorities. Sneers and jeers are alike indifferent to him, and when the Red Slayer thinks to have made an end of him, he turns and passes and comes again. He is content to bide his time, knowing that the road of popular persuasion is a long one, though sure in the end, and that republics cannot march to their goal with "the decisiveness and consistency of despotism." Withal, he knows how to shoot a dart of ridicule at Imperialist folly as it flies, and drives amusement as well as hope from Uncle Sam's humorous appreciation of his present plight. This might well be caricatured to-day, as we have heard it suggested, by a picture of your Uncle ruefully contemplating his Philippine extremities, enormously swollen by ulcers and boils, and saying with whimsical melancholy, "And they call this expansion!"

The Paralyzing Influence of Imperialism

WILLIAM JENNINGS BRYAN

William Jennings Bryan delivered these remarks at the Democratic National Convention in 1900. Bryan had supported the Spanish-American War but objected to the occupation of the Philippines that followed. War continued to be a central issue in his career: Bryan would later resign as secretary of state to Woodrow Wilson following the 1915 sinking of the Lusitania, *convinced that Wilson and his advisers were neither truly impartial in their judgment of the conflict nor committed to avoiding American involvement in the war.*

If it is right for the United States to hold the Philippine Islands permanently and imitate European empires in the government of colonies, the Republican Party ought to state its position and defend it, but it must expect the subject races to protest against such a policy and to resist to the extent of their ability.

The Filipinos do not need any encouragement from Americans now living. Our whole history has been an encouragement, not only to the Filipinos but to all who are denied a voice in their own government. If the Republicans are prepared to censure all who have used language calculated to make the Filipinos hate foreign domination, let them condemn the speech of Patrick Henry. When he uttered that passionate appeal, "Give me liberty or give me death," he expressed a sentiment which still echoes in the hearts of men.

Let them censure Jefferson; of all the statesmen of history none have used words so offensive to those who would hold their fellows in political bondage. Let them censure Washington, who declared that the colonists must choose between liberty and slavery. Or, if the statute of limitations has run against the sins of Henry and Jefferson and Washington, let them censure Lincoln, whose Gettysburg speech will be quoted in defense of popular government when the present advocates of force and conquest are forgotten.

Someone has said that a truth once spoken can never be recalled. It goes on and on, and no one can set a limit to its ever widening influence. But if it were possible to obliterate every word written or spoken in defense of the principles set forth in the Declaration of Independence, a war of conquest would still leave its legacy of perpetual hatred, for it was God Himself who placed in every human heart the love of liberty. He never made a race of people so low in the scale of civilization or intelligence that it would welcome a foreign master.

Those who would have this nation enter upon a career of empire must consider not only the effect of imperialism on the Filipinos but they must also calculate its effects upon our own nation. We cannot repudiate the principle of self-government in the Philippines without weakening that principle here. . . .

If we have an imperial policy we must have a great standing army as its natural and necessary complement. The spirit which will justify the forcible annexation of the Philippine Islands will justify the seizure of other islands and the domination of other people, and with wars of conquest we can expect a certain, if not rapid, growth of our military establishment.

That a large permanent increase in our regular army is intended by Republican leaders is not a matter of conjecture but a matter of fact. In his message of December 5, 1898, the President [William McKinley] asked for authority to increase the standing army to 100,000. In 1896 the army contained about 25,000. Within two years the President asked for four times that many, and a Republican House of Representatives complied with the request after the Spanish treaty had been signed, and when no country was at war with the United States.

If such an army is demanded when an imperial policy is contemplated but not openly avowed, what may be expected if the people encourage the Republican Party by endorsing its policy at the polls?

A large standing army is not only a pecuniary burden to the people and, if accompanied by compulsory service, a constant source of irritation but it is even a menace to a republican form of government. The army is the personification of force, and militarism will inevitably change the ideals of the people and turn the thoughts of our young men from the arts of peace to the science of war. The government which relies for its defense upon its citizens is more likely to be just than one which has at call a large body of professional soldiers.

A small standing army and a well-equipped and well-disciplined state militia are sufficient at ordinary times, and in an emergency the nation should in the future as in the past place its dependence upon the volunteers who come from all occupations at their country's call and return to productive labor when their services are no longer required—

men who fight when the country needs fighters and work when the country needs workers. . . .

There is no place in our system of government for the deposit of arbitrary and irresistible power. That the leaders of a great party should claim for any President or Congress the right to treat millions of people as mere "possessions" and deal with them unrestrained by the Constitution or the Bill of Rights shows how far we have already departed from the ancient landmarks and indicates what may be expected if this nation deliberately enters upon a career of empire.

The territorial form of government is temporary and preparatory, and the chief security a citizen of a territory has is found in the fact that he enjoys the same constitutional guarantees and is subject to the same general laws as the citizen of a state. Take away this security and his rights will be violated and his interests sacrificed at the demand of those who have political influence. This is the evil of the colonial system, no matter by what nation it is applied. . . .

Some argue that American rule in the Philippine Islands will result in the better education of the Filipinos. Be not deceived. If we expect to maintain a colonial policy, we shall not find it to our advantage to educate the people. The educated Filipinos are now in revolt against us, and the most ignorant ones have made the least resistance to our domination. If we are to govern them without their consent and give them no voice in determining the taxes which they must pay, we dare not educate them lest they learn to read the Declaration of Independence and the Constitution of the United States and mock us for our inconsistency.

The principal arguments, however, advanced by those who enter upon a defense of imperialism are:

First, that we must improve the present opportunity to become a world power and enter into international politics.

Second, that our commercial interests in the Philippine Islands and in the Orient make it necessary for us to hold the islands permanently.

Third, that the spread of the Christian religion will be facilitated by
a colonial policy.

Fourth, that there is no honorable retreat from the position which
the nation has taken.

The first argument is addressed to the nation's pride and the second
to the nation's pocketbook. The third is intended for the church member and the fourth for the partisan.

It is sufficient answer to the first argument to say that for more than
a century this nation has been a world power. For ten decades it has
been the most potent influence in the world. Not only has it been a
world power but it has done more to affect the policies of the human
race than all the other nations of the world combined. Because our
Declaration of Independence was promulgated, others have been promulgated. Because the patriots of 1776 fought for liberty, others have
fought for it. Because our Constitution was adopted, other constitutions
have been adopted.

The growth of the principle of self-government, planted on American soil, has been the overshadowing political fact of the nineteenth
century. It has made this nation conspicuous among the nations and
given it a place in history, such as no other nation has ever enjoyed.
Nothing has been able to check the onward march of this idea. I am not
willing that this nation shall cast aside the omnipotent weapon of truth
to seize again the weapons of physical warfare. I would not exchange
the glory of this republic for the glory of all the empires that have risen
and fallen since time began.

The permanent chairman of the last Republican National Convention presented the pecuniary argument in all its baldness when he said:

We make no hypocritical pretense of being interested in the Philippines solely on account of others. While we regard the welfare of those
people as a sacred trust, we regard the welfare of the American people
first. We see our duty to ourselves as well as to others. We believe in

trade expansion. By every legitimate means within the province of government and constitution we mean to stimulate the expansion of our trade and open new markets.

This is the commercial argument. It is based upon the theory that war can be rightly waged for pecuniary advantage and that it is profitable to purchase trade by force and violence. . . . The Democratic Party is in favor of the expansion of trade. It would extend our trade by every legitimate and peaceful means; but it is not willing to make merchandise of human blood.

But a war of conquest is as unwise as it is unrighteous. A harbor and coaling station in the Philippines would answer every trade and military necessity and such a concession could have been secured at any time without difficulty. It is not necessary to own people in order to trade with them. We carry on trade today with every part of the world, and our commerce has expanded more rapidly than the commerce of any European empire. We do not own Japan or China, but we trade with their people. We have not absorbed the republics of Central and South America, but we trade with them. Trade cannot be permanently profitable unless it is voluntary.

When trade is secured by force, the cost of securing it and retaining it must be taken out of the profits, and the profits are never large enough to cover the expense. Such a system would never be defended but for the fact that the expense is borne by all the people while the profits are enjoyed by a few.

Imperialism would be profitable to the Army contractors; it would be profitable to the shipowners, who would carry live soldiers to the Philippines and bring dead soldiers back; it would be profitable to those who would seize upon the franchises, and it would be profitable to the officials whose salaries would be fixed here and paid over there; but to the farmer, to the laboring man, and to the vast majority of those engaged in other occupations, it would bring expenditure without return and risk without reward. . . .

The pecuniary argument, though more effective with certain classes, is not likely to be used so often or presented with so much enthusiasm as the religious argument. If what has been termed the "gunpowder gospel" were urged against the Filipinos only, it would be a sufficient answer to say that a majority of the Filipinos are now members of one branch of the Christian Church; but the principle involved is one of much wider application and challenges serious consideration.

The religious argument varies in positiveness from a passive belief that Providence delivered the Filipinos into our hands for their good and our glory to the exultation of the minister who said that we ought to "thrash the natives (Filipinos) until they understand who we are," and that "every bullet sent, every cannon shot, and every flag waved means righteousness."

We cannot approve of this doctrine in one place unless we are willing to apply it everywhere. If there is poison in the blood of the hand, it will ultimately reach the heart. It is equally true that forcible Christianity, if planted under the American flag in the far-away Orient, will sooner or later be transplanted upon American soil. . . . The shedding of American blood in the Philippine Islands does not make it imperative that we should retain possession forever; American blood was shed at San Juan Hill and El Caney, and yet the President has promised the Cubans independence. The fact that the American flag floats over Manila does not compel us to exercise perpetual sovereignty over the islands; the American flag waves over Havana today, but the President has promised to haul it down when the flag of the Cuban republic is ready to rise in its place. Better a thousand times that our flag in the Orient give way to a flag representing the idea of self-government than that the flag of this republic should become the flag of an empire.

There is an easy, honest, honorable solution of the Philippine question. It is set forth in the Democratic platform and it is submitted with confidence to the American people. This plan I unreservedly endorse. If elected, I will convene Congress in extraordinary session as soon as inaugurated and recommend an immediate declaration of the nation's purpose: first, to establish a stable form of government in the Philippine Islands, just as we are now establishing a stable form of government in Cuba; second, to give independence to the Cubans; third, to protect the Filipinos from outside interference while they work out their destiny, just as we have protected the republics of Central and South America, and are, by the Monroe Doctrine, pledged to protect Cuba. . . .

When our opponents are unable to defend their position by argument, they fall back upon the assertion that it is destiny and insist that we must submit to it no matter how much it violates our moral precepts and our principles of government. This is a complacent philosophy. It obliterates the distinction between right and wrong and makes individuals and nations the helpless victims of circumstances. Destiny is the subterfuge of the invertebrate, who, lacking the courage to oppose error, seeks some plausible excuse for supporting it. Washington said that the destiny of the republican form of government was deeply, if not finally, staked on the experiment entrusted to the American people. . . .

I can conceive of a national destiny surpassing the glories of the present and the past—a destiny which meets the responsibilities of today and measures up to the possibilities of the future. Behold a republic, resting securely upon the foundation stones quarried by revolutionary patriots from the mountain of eternal truth—a republic applying in practice and proclaiming to the world the self-evident proposition that all men are created equal; that they are endowed with inalienable rights; that governments are instituted among men to secure these rights, and that governments derive their just powers from the consent of the governed.

Behold a republic in which civil and religious liberty stimulate all to earnest endeavor and in which the law restrains every hand uplifted for a neighbor's injury—a republic in which every citizen is a sovereign, but in which no one cares to wear a crown. Behold a republic standing erect while empires all around are bowed beneath the weight of their own armaments—a republic whose flag is loved while other flags are only feared. Behold a republic increasing in population, in wealth, in strength, and in influence, solving the problems of civilization and hastening the coming of a universal brotherhood—a republic which shakes thrones and dissolves aristocracies by its silent example and gives light and inspiration to those who sit in darkness. Behold a republic gradually but surely becoming a supreme moral factor in the world's progress and the accepted arbiter of the world's disputes—a republic whose history, like the path of the just, "is as the shining light that shineth more and more unto the perfect day."

The American Birthright and the Philippine Pottage

HENRY VAN DYKE

Following his tenure as pastor of New York City's Brick Presbyterian Church from 1883 until 1899, Henry Van Dyke served as a vice president of the Anti-Imperialist League of New York, a member of the Philippine Independence Committee, and a vice president of the Filipino Progress Association. He delivered this sermon on Thanksgiving Day, 1898.

Are the United States to continue as a peaceful republic, or are they to become a conquering empire? Is the result of the war with Spain to be the banishment of European tyranny from the Western Hemisphere, or is it to be the entanglement of the Western republic in the rivalries of European kingdoms? Have we set the Cubans free, or have we lost our own faith in freedom? Are we still loyal to the principles of our forefathers, as expressed in the Declaration of Independence, or are we now ready to sell the American birthright for a mess of pottage in the Philippines?

Nine months ago no one dreamed of such a question. Not one American in five hundred could have told you what or where the Philippines were; if any one thought of their possession as a possible result of the war, he kept the thought carefully concealed.

Six months ago, while Admiral Dewey's triumphant fleet was resting in Cavite Bay, there were not fifty people in the country who regarded his victory as the first step in a career of imperial conquest in the Far East: the question of reversing a whole national policy and extending our dominion at one stroke of the sword over a vast and populous group of islands in the China Sea was utterly unconsidered.

Without warning, without deliberation, and apparently without clear intention, it has been made the burning question of the day. Never has fate sprung a more trying surprise upon an unsuspecting and ingenuous people. Never has the most difficult problem of a great republic been met so hastily, so lightly or with such inconsiderate confidence. And, as if to add to the irony of the situation, political leaders assure us not only that the question has been raised unintentionally, but also that it has been already settled involuntarily. Without any adequate discussion, without any popular vote, without any intelligent and responsible leadership, by a mysterious and non-resident destiny, by the accident that a Spanish fleet destroyed on the first of May, 1898, was in the harbor of Manila instead of on the high seas, the future career of the American Republic has been changed irrevocably; the nation has been committed to a policy of colonial expansion, and the United States of America have been transformed into the "United States and Conquered Territories of America and the China Sea." Surely this is the veriest comedy of self-government, the most ridiculous blind-man's bluff of national development that ever a scorner of democracy dared to imagine. If it were true it would be a humorous commentary on the Declaration of Independence and a farcical finale of the American Revolution.

But, fortunately, it is not true. There is an old-fashioned document called the American Constitution which was expressly constructed to discourage the unconscious humor of such sudden changes. Before the die is cast the people must be taken fairly into the game; before the result is irrevocable the Supreme Court must pass upon the rules and the play. The question whether the American birthright is to be bartered for the Philippine pottage is still open. A brief, preliminary discussion of this question will not be out of place this morning. . . .

The proposal to annex, by force, or purchase, or forcible purchase, these distant, unwilling and semi-barbarous islands is hailed as a new and glorious departure in American history. A new word—imperialism—has been coined to define it. It is frankly confessed that it involves a departure from ancient traditions; it is openly boasted that it leaves the counsels of Washington and Jefferson far behind us forever. Because of this novelty, because of this separation from what we once counted a most precious heritage, I venture to ask whether this bargain offers any fit compensation for the loss of our American birthright? . . .

Nothing has yet been said or done which binds us to take permanent possession of these islands. Granting that the Philippines need a strong hand to set them in order, it has not been shown that ours is the only hand, nor that we must do it all alone. A protectorate for a limited time and with the purpose of building up a firm self-government would be one of the possible solutions of the difficulty. To pass this by and say that our only resort is to assume sovereignty of these yet unconquered islands is merely to beg the question. . . . It is the prospect of profit that makes those distant islands gleam before our fancy as desirable acquisitions. The argument drawn from the supposed need of creating and fortifying new outlets for our trade has the most practical force. It is the unconscious desire of rivaling England in her colonial wealth and power that allures us to the untried path of conquest; and this in spite of the fact that during the last seven years, England, with all her colonies, has lost five percent of her export trade, while the United States, without colonies, have gained eighteen percent. It is a secret discontent with the part of a peaceful, industrious, self-contained nation that urges us to take an armed hand in the partition of the East and exchange our birthright for a mess of pottage. . . . Every following step in the career of colonial imperialism will bring us into conflict with our own institutions, and necessitate constitutional change or insure practical failure. Our Government, with its checks and balances, with its prudent and conservative divisions of power, is the best in the world for peace and self-defense; but the worst in the world for what the President called, a few months ago, "criminal aggression." We cannot compete with monarchies and empires in the game of land-grabbing and vassal ruling. We have not the machinery; and we cannot get it, except by breaking up our present system of government and building a new fabric out of the pieces. Republics have not been successful as rulers of colonies. When they have entered that career they have changed quickly into monarchies or empires. . . . The swiftness of action, the secrecy, not to say slipperiness of policy, and the absolutism of control which are essential to success in territorial conquest and dominion are inconsistent with republicanism as America has interpreted it. Imperialism and democracy, militarism and self-government are contradictory terms. A government of the people, by the people, for the people is impregnable for defense, but impotent for conquest. When imperialism comes in at the door democracy flies out at the window. An imperialistic democracy is an impossible hybrid; we might as well speak of an atheistic religion, or a white blackness. To enter upon a career of colonial expansion with our present institutions is to court failure or to prepare for silent revolution. . . .

The cost of militarism comes out of the pockets of the people. So far as armies and navies are needed, their expense must be cheerfully borne. I am no advocate of parsimony in national defense; our American navy has been worth all that it has cost; and if our army has disappointed us in any way it is because we have not realized its importance, nor treated it with generosity and prudence. But to willfully increase our need of military force by an immense and unnecessary extension of our frontier of danger is to bind a heavy burden and lay it upon the unconscious backs of future generations of toiling men. If we enter the course of foreign conquest, the day is not far distant when we must spend in annual preparation for wars more than the $180,000,000 that we now spend every year in the education of our children for peace. . . .

Hear the unintentional warning of an interested friend! Colonial expansion means coming strife; the annexation of the Philippines means the annexation of a new danger to the world's peace. The acceptance of imperialism means that we must prepare to beat our ploughshares into swords and our pruning hooks into spears, and be ready to water distant lands and stain foreign seas with an ever increasing torrent of American blood. Is it for this that philanthropists and Christian preachers urge us to abandon our peaceful mission of enlightenment and thrust forward, sword in hand, into the arena of imperial conflict?

But the chief argument against the forcible extension of American sovereignty over the Philippines is that it certainly involves the surrender of our American birthright of glorious ideals. "This imitation of Old World methods," said *Outlook*, one of our most powerful journals, a few months ago, "by the New World appears to us to be based upon an entire disregard, not merely of American precedence, but of American principles.". . .

How can we pass by the solemn and majestic claim of our Declaration of Independence, that "Government derives its just powers from the consent of the governed"? How can we abandon the principle for which our fathers fought and died: "No taxation without representation"? . . .

Anonymous patriots have written to warn me that it is a dangerous task to call for this discussion. It imperils popularity. The cry of to-day is: "Wherever the American flag has been raised it never must be hauled down." The man who will not join that cry may be accused of disloyalty and called a Spaniard. So be it, then. If the price of popularity is the stifling of conviction, I want none of it. If the test of loyalty is to join in every thoughtless cry of the multitude, I decline it. I profess a higher loyalty—*allegiance to the flag, not for what it covers, but for what it means.*

There is one thing that can happen to the American flag worse than to be hauled down. That is to have its meaning and its message changed.

Hitherto it has meant freedom, and equality, and self-government, and battle only for the sake of peace. Pray God its message may never be altered.

May the luster of its equal stars never be dimmed by the shadow of the crowned imperial eagle. May its stripes of pure red and white never be crossed by the yellow bar-sinister of warfare for conquest. May it never advance save to bring liberty and self-government to all beneath its folds. May it never retreat save from a place where its presence would mean disloyalty to the American idea. May it float untarnished, and un-changed, save by the blossoming of new stars in its celestial field of blue. May all seas learn to welcome it, and all lands look to it as the emblem of the Great Republic: the mountain-peak of nations, lonely, if need be, till others have risen to her lofty standard.

God keep her from lowering her flag from that proud solitude of splendor to follow the fortunes of the conquering sword.

God save the birthright of the one country on earth whose ideal is not to subjugate the world but to enlighten it.

5

World War I

*And here let me emphasize the fact—and it cannot be re-
peated too often—that the working class who fight all the
battles, the working class who make the supreme sacrifices,
the working class who freely shed their blood and furnish the
corpses, have never yet had a voice in either declaring war
or making peace. It is the ruling class that invariably does
both. They alone declare war and they alone make peace.*

—EUGENE V. DEBS,
June 16, 1918, from the speech for which he
received a ten-year prison sentence

Until April 1917, when the United States declared war on Imperial
Germany, most Americans were hardly panting for war. The European
war, begun in 1914, was far away. Indeed, if asked why there had been
only sporadic conflicts but no general war in Europe since the Congress
of Vienna in 1814 most Americans might have replied, as did Lord
Palmerston when asked in Parliament about the mid-nineteenth-
century Schleswig-Holstein War, that "only three men in Europe have
ever understood it. One was Prince Albert, who is dead. The second was
a German professor who became mad. I am the third and I have forgotten all about it."

The European Great Powers were heavily armed, economic rivals, intertwined with entangling alliances, expansionist sentiments, and often populated with restive nationalities. The giants of the nineteenth century, Benjamin Disraeli and Otto von Bismarck, were gone, replaced by plodding, unimaginative leaders in seats of power in London, Paris, St. Petersburg, Berlin and Vienna. In the wake of the Austrian Archduke's murder by a Serbian nationalist, preventing the war may have been impossible. It is no wonder that Edward Grey, the British Foreign Minister, could dolefully announce on the eve of the war, "The lamps are going out all over Europe." Ahead lay enormous loss of human lives and property.

Enter Woodrow Wilson. A former Princeton University president and governor of New Jersey and the son of a Presbyterian minister, he was first elected in 1912 as a progressive reformer but with no real experience or interest in foreign affairs. His reelection slogan in 1916, two years after war had begun in Europe, was "He Kept Us Out of War" (though he had approved sending U.S. troops to intervene in Mexico's civil war).

To the American people he pledged neutrality. But as the war proceeded, it is quite possible that many in Washington and in corporate boardrooms began sensing far-reaching markets for American goods and sources of raw materials in the postwar world.

Despite large numbers of German Americans who either supported Germany or, in the case of the American Irish, detested England, there was in fact a greater sense of cultural and economic ties with England. Into that setting Wilson established George Creel's Committee on Public Information, whose task was to promote U.S. entry into the war. Using innovative public relations practices Creel set out to portray the Germans as brutal barbarians. Coupled with appeals to buy war bonds he helped arouse a fierce patriotism and support for the allies. The true aggressors, went the party line, were the Germans, who were solely responsible for the war, a view that underlay the future consequences of the harsh Versailles Treaty once Germany surrendered. No mention was made of competing European imperial ambitions.

Still, the job of bringing the nation into war was made easier by German blunders, such as its resort to unrestricted submarine warfare that led to the sinking of the British ship *Lusitania* on May 7, 1915. Nearly twelve hundred passengers, including 128 Americans, were killed when the ship was torpedoed. It was also carrying munitions of war, but whether or not she was a legitimate military target remains in dispute. The sinking, however, was yet another step in convincing many that the nation had to intervene militarily. Germany then pledged to end this kind of warfare but later reneged after the interception of the senseless Zimmerman Telegram. Sent by the German Ambassador to Mexico it urged Mexicans to join with Germany if the U.S. entered the war. Mexico could "reconquer the lost territory in Texas, New Mexico, and Arizona."

On April 6, 1917, after tense debate in Congress, the United States declared war. "I wanted to stand by my country," said Representative Jeannette Rankin of Montana, "but I could not vote for war." (She cast yet another no vote in December 1941.) Forty-nine other House members voted no, Civil War veterans among them. One representative, Claude Kitchin, the Democratic floor leader whose father had fought for the Confederacy, shouted that it didn't take much courage for politicians to send young men to fight a war.

Once involved in the war Wilson began trumpeting his newest theme: "The world must be made safe for democracy." Wilson's fantasy of democratic triumphs thanks to the war was aimed at the rest of the world, but not the United States, where among many of other violations of liberty and the freedom to dissent he backed the Espionage and Sedition Acts, which gave the federal government enormous power over its citizens. Wilson, the alleged symbol of democracy the world over— though he never expressed much empathy for the plight of black Americans—authorized censorship of the American press and cable transmissions. Draft resisters and conscientious objectors were threatened, harassed, and jailed. Seventeen men received death sentences, though all were eventually reprieved. Many other dissenters received harsh prison sentences. Most notably, the famous war critic and opponent of conscription Eugene V. Debs, the labor leader and socialist who had the temerity to tell an audience "you are fit for something better than slavery and cannon fodder," was shipped off to prison for ten years. Resisting appeals even after the killing had stopped in 1919, the inflexible Wilson refused to pardon Debs until Warren Harding, Wilson's successor, finally freed him. Some war resistors remained in prison until President Franklin Roosevelt finally pardoned them in 1933.

In 1919, at war's end, the European victors ignored Wilson's Fourteen Points and went instead after the spoils. The Versailles Treaty proclaimed Germany alone responsible for the war, a controversial claim at best, while the British and French divided Germany's empire and created artificial nations like Iraq. There is good reason to believe that their treatment of Germany may have been one of the reasons that a candidate named Hitler could in the early thirties receive a plurality of the German vote—and become what he became.

Nearly 120,000 Americans perished in the war. Many other veterans, suffering from a variety of mental and physical wounds, lived on. Wilson's illusion that war could lead to worldwide freedom and self-determination was, for the moment, effectively dashed.

Wealth's Terrible Mandate

SENATOR GEORGE W. NORRIS

Senator George W. Norris (R–NE) delivered this speech in opposition to American entry into World War I on the Senate floor on April 4, 1917.

While I am most emphatically and sincerely opposed to taking any step that will force our country into the useless and senseless war now being waged in Europe, yet, if this resolution passes, I shall not permit my feeling of opposition to its passage to interfere in any way with my duty either as a senator or as a citizen in bringing success and victory to American arms. I am bitterly opposed to my country entering the war, but if, notwithstanding my opposition, we do enter it, all of my energy and all of my power will be behind our flag in carrying it on to victory.

The resolution now before the Senate is a declaration of war. Before taking this momentous step, and while standing on the brink of this terrible vortex, we ought to pause and calmly and judiciously consider the terrible consequences of the step we are about to take. We ought to consider likewise the route we have recently traveled and ascertain whether we have reached our present position in a way that is compatible with the neutral position which we claimed to occupy at the beginning and through the various stages of this unholy and unrighteous war.

No close student of recent history will deny that both Great Britain and Germany have, on numerous occasions since the beginning of the war, flagrantly violated in the most serious manner the rights of neutral vessels and neutral nations under existing international law, as recognized up to the beginning of this war by the civilized world.

The reason given by the President in asking Congress to declare war against Germany is that the German government has declared certain war zones, within which, by the use of submarines, she sinks, without notice, American ships and destroys American lives. . . . The first war zone was declared by Great Britain. She gave us and the world notice of it on the fourth day of November, 1914. The zone became effective Nov. 5, 1914. . . . This zone so declared by Great Britain covered the whole of the North Sea. . . . The first German war zone was declared on the fourth day of February, 1915, just three months after the British war zone was declared. Germany gave fifteen days' notice of the establishment of her zone, which became effective on the 18th day of February, 1915. The German war zone covered the English Channel and the high seawaters around the British Isles. . . .

It is unnecessary to cite authority to show that both of these orders declaring military zones were illegal and contrary to international law. It is sufficient to say that our government has officially declared both of them to be illegal and has officially protested against both of them. The only difference is that in the case of Germany we have persisted in our protest, while in the case of England we have submitted.

What was our duty as a government and what were our rights when we were confronted with these extraordinary orders declaring these military zones? First, we could have defied both of them and could have gone to war against both of these nations for this violation of international law and interference with our neutral rights. Second, we had the technical right to defy one and to acquiesce in the other. Third, we could, while denouncing them both as illegal, have acquiesced in them both and thus remained neutral with both sides, although not agreeing with either as to the righteousness of their respective orders. We could have said to American shipowners that, while these orders are both contrary to international law and are both unjust, we do not believe that the provocation is sufficient to cause us to go to war for the defense of our rights as a neutral nation, and, therefore, American ships and American citizens will go into these zones at their own peril and risk.

Fourth, we might have declared an embargo against the shipping from American ports of any merchandise to either one of these governments that persisted in maintaining its military zone. We might have refused to permit the sailing of any ship from any American port to either of these military zones. In my judgment, if we had pursued this course, the zones would have been of short duration. England would have been compelled to take her mines out of the North Sea in order to get any supplies from our country. When her mines were taken out of the North Sea then the German ports upon the North Sea would have been accessible to American shipping and Germany would have been compelled to cease her submarine warfare in order to get any supplies from our nation into German North Sea ports.

There are a great many American citizens who feel that we owe it as a duty to humanity to take part in this war. Many instances of cruelty and inhumanity can be found on both sides. Men are often biased in their judgment on account of their sympathy and their interests. To my mind, what we ought to have maintained from the beginning was the strictest neutrality. If we had done this, I do not believe we would have been on the verge of war at the present time. We had a right as a nation, if we desired, to cease at any time to be neutral. We had a technical right to respect the English war zone and to disregard the German war zone, but we could not do that and be neutral. . . .

We have loaned many hundreds of millions of dollars to the Allies in this controversy. While such action was legal and countenanced by international law, there is no doubt in my mind but the enormous amount of money loaned to the Allies in this country has been instrumental in bringing about a public sentiment in favor of our country taking a course that would make every bond worth a hundred cents on the dollar and making the payment of every debt certain and sure. Through this instrumentality and also through the instrumentality of others who have not only made millions out of the war in the manufacture of munitions, etc., and who would expect to make millions more if our country can be drawn into the catastrophe, a large number of the great newspapers and news agencies of the country have been controlled and enlisted in the greatest propaganda that the world has ever known to manufacture sentiment in favor of war.

It is now demanded that the American citizens shall be used as insurance policies to guarantee the safe delivery of munitions of war to belligerent nations. The enormous profits of munition manufacturers, stockbrokers, and bond dealers must be still further increased by our entrance into the war. This has brought us to the present moment, when Congress, urged by the President and backed by the artificial sentiment, is about to declare war and engulf our country in the greatest holocaust that the world has ever known. . . .

To whom does war bring prosperity? Not to the soldier who for the munificent compensation of $16 per month shoulders his musket and goes into the trench, there to shed his blood and to die if necessary; not to the brokenhearted widow who waits for the return of the mangled body of her husband; not to the mother who weeps at the death of her brave boy; not to the little children who shiver with cold; not to the babe who suffers from hunger; nor to the millions of mothers and daughters who carry broken hearts to their graves. War brings no prosperity to the great mass of common and patriotic citizens. It increases the cost of living of those who toil and those who already must strain every effort to keep soul and body together. War brings prosperity to the stock gambler on Wall Street—to those who are already in possession of more wealth than can be realized or enjoyed. . . .

Their object in having war and in preparing for war is to make money. Human suffering and the sacrifice of human life are necessary, but Wall Street considers only the dollars and the cents. The men who do the fighting, the people who make the sacrifices are the ones who will not be counted in the measure of this great prosperity that he depicts. The stockbrokers would not, of course, go to war because the very object they have in bringing on the war is profit, and therefore they must remain in their Wall Street offices in order to share in that great prosperity which they say war will bring. The volunteer officer, even the drafting officer, will not find them. They will be concealed in their palatial offices on Wall Street, sitting behind mahogany desks, covered up with clipped coupons—coupons soiled with the sweat of honest toil, coupons stained with mothers' tears, coupons dyed in the lifeblood of their fellowmen.

We are taking a step today that is fraught with untold danger. We are going into war upon the command of gold. We are going to run the risk of sacrificing millions of our countrymen's lives in order that other countrymen may coin their lifeblood into money. And even if we do not cross the Atlantic and go into the trenches, we are going to pile up a debt that the toiling masses that shall come many generations after us will have to pay. Unborn millions will bend their backs in toil in order to pay for the terrible step we are now about to take.

We are about to do the bidding of wealth's terrible mandate. By our act we will make millions of our countrymen suffer, and the consequences of it may well be that millions of our brethren must shed their lifeblood, millions of brokenhearted women must weep, millions of children must suffer with cold, and millions of babes must die from hunger, and all because we want to preserve the commercial right of American citizens to deliver munitions of war to belligerent nations.

The People Do Not Want This War

ROBERT M. LA FOLLETTE

Senator Robert La Follette from Wisconsin was a prominent progressive who opposed American entry into World War I. He delivered these remarks on April 4, 1917, two days after Woodrow Wilson's appeal for war.

A minority in one Congress—mayhap a small minority in one Congress—protesting, exercising the rights which the Constitution confers upon a minority, may really be representing the majority opinion of the country, and if, exercising the right that the Constitution gives them, they succeed in defeating for the time being the will of the majority, they are but carrying out what was in the mind of the framers of the Constitution; that you may have from time to time in a legislative body a majority in numbers that really does not represent the principle of democracy; and that if the question could be deferred and carried to the people it would be found that a minority was the real representative of the public opinion. So, Mr. President, it was that they wrote into the Constitution that a President—that one man—may put his judgment against the will of a majority, not only in one branch of the Congress but in both branches of the Congress; that he may defeat the measure that they have agreed upon and may set his one single judgment above the majority judgment of the Congress. That seems, when you look at it nakedly, to be in violation of the principle that the majority shall rule; and so it is. Why is that power given? It is one of those checks provided by the wisdom of the fathers to prevent the majority from abusing the

ANTI-ENLISTMENT LEAGUE

Working Men and Women of the United States:

Your brothers in Europe are destroying each other; the militarists in this country may soon try to send you to the trenches. They will do so in the name of "Defense of Home" or "National Honor," the reasons given to the people of every one of the twelve nations now at war.

But **DO NOT ENLIST.** Think for yourselves. The Workers of the World are YOUR BROTHERS; their wrongs are your wrongs; their good is your good. War stops Trade, and makes vast armies of Unemployed.

DO NOT ENLIST. The time for Defense by Armies is over. Belgium, Germany and Great Britain have defended themselves with the mightiest of fortresses, armies or navies; and today each country suffers untold misery. War can avenge, punish and destroy; but war can NO LONGER defend.

DO NOT ENLIST. Your country needs you for PEACE; to do good and USEFUL work; to destroy POVERTY and bring in INDUSTRIAL JUSTICE.

WOMEN, REFUSE your consent to the enlistment of your men; the TRUE COURAGE is to STAND FOR THE RIGHT and REFUSE TO KILL.

PEACE IS THE DUTY—NOT WAR
MIGHT IS NOT RIGHT
USE YOUR LIGHT
DO NOT FIGHT

Join the ANTI-ENLISTMENT LEAGUE, 61 QUINCY ST., Brooklyn, N. Y.

(vertical text at left: WORK AND VOTE — AGAINST "PREPAREDNESS")

I, being over eighteen years of age, hereby pledge myself against enlistment as a volunteer for any military or naval service in international war, either offensive or defensive, and against giving my approval to such enlistment on the part of others.

Name...

Address...

Committee, JESSIE WALLACE HUGHAN, Secretary,
TRACY D. MYGATT.

Forward to the Anti-Enlistment League,
61 Quincy Street, Brooklyn, New York.

When World War I began, Jessie Wallace Hughan and three women formed the Anti-Enlistment League hoping to dissuade men from joining the military. She helped found the War Resisters League in 1923. A teacher, she wrote on her state loyalty oath, "This obedience being qualified always by dictates of conscience." In 1940 she formed the Pacifist Teachers League. During World War II she warned that without an end to the fighting, European Jews faced the prospect of mass slaughter.

power that they chance to have, when they do not reflect the real judgment, the opinion, the will of the majority of the people that constitute the sovereign power of the democracy. . . .

The poor, Sir, who are the ones called upon to rot in the trenches, have no organized power, have no press to voice their will upon this question of peace or war; but, oh, Mr. President, at some time they will be heard. I hope and I believe they will be heard in an orderly and a peaceful way. I think they may be heard from before long. I think, Sir, if we take this step, when the people today who are staggering under the burden of supporting families at the present prices of the necessaries of life find those prices multiplied, when they are raised 100 percent, or 200 percent, as they will be quickly, aye, sir, when beyond that those who pay taxes come to have their taxes doubled and again doubled to pay the interest on the nontaxable bonds held by Morgan and his combinations, which have been issued to meet this war, there will come an awakening; they will have their day and they will be heard. It will be as certain and as inevitable as the return of the tides, and as resistless, too. . . .

In his message of April 2, the President said:

We have no quarrel with the German people; it was not upon their impulse that their government acted in entering this war; it was not with their previous knowledge or approval.

Again he says:

We are, let me say again, sincere friends of the German people and shall desire nothing so much as the early reestablishment of intimate relations of mutual advantage between us.

At least, the German people, then, are not outlaws.

What is the thing the President asks us to do to these German people of whom he speaks so highly and whose sincere friend he declares us to be? Here is what he declares we shall do in this war. We shall undertake, he says—

> the utmost practicable cooperation in council and action with the governments now at war with Germany, and as an incident to that, the extension to those governments of the most liberal financial credits in order that our resources may, so far as possible, be added to theirs.

"Practicable cooperation!" Practicable cooperation with England and her allies in starving to death the old men and women, the children, the sick and the maimed of Germany. The thing we are asked to do is the thing I have stated. It is idle to talk of a war upon a government only. We are leagued in this war, or it is the President's proposition that we shall be so leagued, with the hereditary enemies of Germany. Any war with Germany, or any other country for that matter, would be bad enough, but there are not words strong enough to voice my protest against the proposed combination with the Entente Allies.

When we cooperate with those governments, we endorse their methods; we endorse the violations of international law by Great Britain; we endorse the shameful methods of warfare against which we have again and again protested in this war; we endorse her purpose to wreak upon the German people the animosities which for years her people have been taught to cherish against Germany; finally, when the end comes, whatever it may be, we find ourselves in cooperation with our ally, Great Britain, and if we cannot resist now the pressure she is exerting to carry us into the war, how can we hope to resist, then, the thousandfold greater pressure she will exert to bend us to her purposes and compel compliance with her demands?. . .

Sir, if we are to enter upon this war in the manner the President demands, let us throw pretense to the winds, let us be honest, let us admit that this is a ruthless war against not only Germany's Army and her Navy but against her civilian population as well, and frankly state that the purpose of Germany's hereditary European enemies has become our purpose. . . .

Just a word of comment more upon one of the points in the President's address. He says that this is a war "for the things which we have always carried nearest to our hearts—for democracy, for the right of those who submit to authority to have a voice in their own government." In many places throughout the address is this exalted sentiment given expression. It is a sentiment peculiarly calculated to appeal to American hearts and, when accompanied by acts consistent with it, is certain to receive our support; but in this same connection, and strangely enough, the President says that we have become convinced that the German government as it now exists—"Prussian autocracy" he calls it—can never again maintain friendly relations with us. His expression is that "Prussian autocracy was not and could never be our friend," and repeatedly throughout the address the suggestion is made that if the German people would overturn their government, it would probably be the way to peace. So true is this that the dispatches from London all hailed the message of the President as sounding the death knell of Germany's government.

But the President proposes alliance with Great Britain, which, however liberty-loving its people, is a hereditary monarchy, with a hereditary ruler, with a hereditary House of Lords, with a hereditary landed system, with a limited and restricted suffrage for one class and a multiplied suffrage power for another, and with grinding industrial conditions for all the wageworkers. The President has not suggested that we make our support of Great Britain conditional to her granting home rule to Ireland, or Egypt, or India. We rejoice in the establishment of a democracy in Russia, but it will hardly be contended that if Russia was still an autocratic government, we would not be asked to enter this alliance with her just the same.

Italy and the lesser powers of Europe, Japan in the Orient; in fact, all the countries with whom we are to enter into alliance, except France and newly revolutionized Russia, are still of the old order—and it will be generally conceded that no one of them has done as much for its people in the solution of municipal problems and in securing social and industrial reforms as Germany.

Is it not a remarkable democracy which leagues itself with allies already far overmatching in strength the German nation and holds out to such beleaguered nation the hope of peace only at the price of giving up their government? I am not talking now of the merits or demerits of any government, but I am speaking of a profession of democracy that is linked in action with the most brutal and domineering use of autocratic power. Are the people of this country being so well represented in this war movement that we need to go abroad to give other people control of their governments? Will the President and the supporters of this war bill submit it to a vote of the people before the declaration of war goes into effect? Until we are willing to do that, it ill-becomes us to offer as an excuse for our entry into the war the unsupported claim that this war was forced upon the German people by their government "without their previous knowledge or approval."

Who has registered the knowledge or approval of the American people of the course this Congress is called upon to take in declaring war upon Germany? Submit the question to the people, you who support it. You who support it dare not do it, for you know that by a vote of more than ten to one the American people as a body would register their declaration against it.

In the sense that this war is being forced upon our people without their knowing why and without their approval, and that wars are usually forced upon all peoples in the same way, there is some truth in the statement; but I venture to say that the response which the German people have made to the demands of this war shows that it has a degree of popular support which the war upon which we are entering has not and never will have among our people. The espionage bills, the conscription bills, and other forcible military measures which we understand are being ground out of the war machine in this country is the complete proof that those responsible for this war fear that it has no popular support and that armies sufficient to satisfy the demand of the Entente Allies cannot be recruited by voluntary enlistments. . . .

Now, I want to repeat: It was our absolute right as a neutral to ship food to the people of Germany. That is a position that we have fought for through all of our history. The correspondence of every secretary of state in the history of our government who has been called upon to deal with the rights of our neutral commerce as to foodstuffs is the position stated by Lord Salisbury. . . . He was in line with all of the precedents that we had originated and established for the maintenance of neutral rights upon this subject.

In the first days of the war with Germany, Great Britain set aside, so far as her own conduct was concerned, all these rules of civilized naval warfare.

According to the Declaration of London, as well as the rules of international law, there could have been no interference in trade between the United States and Holland or Scandinavia and other countries, except in the case of ships which could be proven to carry absolute contraband, like arms and ammunition, with ultimate German destination. There could have been no interference with the importation into Germany of any goods on the free list, such as cotton, rubber, and hides. There could have properly been no interference with our export to Germany of anything on the conditional contraband list, like flour, grain, and provisions, unless it could be proven by England that such shipments were intended for the use of the German Army. There could be no lawful interference with foodstuffs intended for the civilian population of Germany, and if those foodstuffs were shipped to other countries to be reshipped to Germany, no question could be raised that they were not intended for the use of the civilian population.

It is well to recall at this point our rights as declared by the Declaration of London and as declared without the Declaration of London by settled principles of international law, for we have during the present war become so used to having Great Britain utterly disregard our rights on the high seas that we have really forgotten that we have any, as far as Great Britain and her allies are concerned. . . .

It is not my purpose to go into detail into the violations of our neutrality by any of the belligerents. While Germany has again and again yielded to our protests, I do not recall a single instance in which a protest we have made to Great Britain has won for us the slightest consideration, except for a short time in the case of cotton. I will not stop to dwell upon the multitude of minor violations of our neutral rights, such as seizing our mails, violations of the neutral flag, seizing and appropriating our goods without the least warrant or authority in law, and impressing, seizing, and taking possession of our vessels and putting them into her own service. . . .

The only reason why we have not suffered the sacrifice of just as many ships and just as many lives from the violation of our rights by the war zone and the submarine mines of Great Britain as we have through the unlawful acts of Germany in making her war zone in violation of our neutral rights is simply because we have submitted to Great Britain's dictation. If our ships had been sent into her forbidden high-sea war zone as they have into the proscribed area Germany marked out on the high seas as a war zone, we would have had the same loss of life and property in the one case as in the other; but because we avoided doing that, in the case of England, and acquiesced in her violation of law, we have not only a legal but a moral responsibility for the position in which Germany has been placed by our collusion and cooperation with Great Britain. By suspending the rule with respect to neutral rights in Great Britain's case, we have been actively aiding her in starving the civil population of Germany. We have helped to drive Germany into a corner, her back to the wall to fight with what weapons she can lay her hands on to prevent the starving of her women and children, her old men and babes.

The flimsy claim which has sometimes been put forth that possibly the havoc in the North Sea was caused by German mines is too absurd for consideration. . . .

I find all the correspondence about the submarines of Germany; I find them arrayed; I find the note warning Germany that she would be held to a "strict accountability" for violation of our neutral rights; but you will search in vain these volumes for a copy of the British order in council mining the North Sea.

I am talking now about principles. You cannot distinguish between the principles which allowed England to mine a large area of the Atlantic Ocean and the North Sea in order to shut in Germany, and the principle on which Germany by her submarines seeks to destroy all shipping which enters the war zone which she has laid out around the British Isles.

The English mines are intended to destroy without warning every ship that enters the war zone she has proscribed, killing or drowning every passenger that cannot find some means of escape. It is neither more nor less than that which Germany tries to do with her submarines in her war zone. We acquiesced in England's action without protest. It is proposed that we now go to war with Germany for identically the same action upon her part. . . .

I say again that when two nations are at war any neutral nation, in order to preserve its character as a neutral nation, must exact the same conduct from both warring nations; both must equally obey the principles of international law. If a neutral nation fails in that, then its rights upon the high seas—to adopt the President's phrase—are relative and not absolute. There can be no greater violation of our neutrality than the requirement that one of two belligerents shall adhere to the settled principles of law and that the other shall have the advantage of not doing so. The respect that German naval authorities were required to pay to the rights of our people upon the high seas would depend upon the question whether we had exacted the same rights from Germany's enemies. If we had not done so, we lost our character as a neutral nation and our people unfortunately had lost the protection that belongs to neutrals. Our responsibility was joint in the sense that we must exact the same conduct from both belligerents. . . .

The failure to treat the belligerent nations of Europe alike, the failure to reject the unlawful "war zones" of both Germany and Great Britain is wholly accountable for our present dilemma. We should not seek to hide our blunder behind the smoke of battle, to inflame the mind of our people by half truths into the frenzy of war in order that they may never appreciate the real cause of it until it is too late. I do not believe that our national honor is served by such a course. The right way is the honorable way.

One alternative is to admit our initial blunder to enforce our rights against Great Britain as we have enforced our rights against Germany; demand that both those nations shall respect our neutral rights upon the high seas to the letter; and give notice that we will enforce those rights from that time forth against both belligerents and then live up to that notice. The other alternative is to withdraw our commerce from both. The mere suggestion that food supplies would be withheld from both sides impartially would compel belligerents to observe the principle of freedom of the seas for neutral commerce.

The State

RANDOLPH BOURNE

Randolph Bourne (1886–1918), a progressive writer, never finished this essay. He died young, in the flu epidemic that followed World War I. "War is the health of the state," Bourne's famous refrain in what follows, remains part of the American political lexicon.

The Government, with no mandate from the people, without consultation of the people, conducts all the negotiations, the backing and filling, the menaces and explanations, which slowly bring it into collision with some other Government, and gently and irresistibly slides the country into war. For the benefit of proud and haughty citizens, it is fortified with a list of the intolerable insults which have been hurled toward us by the other nations; for the benefit of the liberal and beneficent, it has a convincing set of moral purposes which our going to war will achieve; for the ambitious and aggressive classes, it can gently whisper of a bigger role in the destiny of the world. The result is that, even in those countries where the business of declaring war is theoretically in the hands of representatives of the people, no legislature has ever been known to decline the request of an Executive, which has conducted all foreign affairs in utter privacy and irresponsibility, that it order the nation into battle. Good democrats are wont to feel the crucial difference between a State in which the popular Parliament or Congress declares war, and the State in which an absolute monarch or ruling class declares war. But, put to the stern pragmatic test, the difference is not striking. In the freest of republics as well as in the most tyrannical of empires, all foreign policy, the diplomatic negotiations which produce or forestall war, are equally the private property of the Executive part of the Government, and are equally exposed to no check whatever from popular bodies, or the people voting as a mass themselves.

The moment war is declared, however, the mass of the people, through some spiritual alchemy, become convinced that they have willed and executed the deed themselves. They then, with the exception of a few malcontents, proceed to allow themselves to be regimented, coerced, deranged in all the environments of their lives, and turned into a solid manufactory of destruction toward whatever other people may have, in the appointed scheme of things, come within the range of the Government's disapprobation. The citizen throws off his contempt and indifference to Government, identifies himself with its purposes, revives all his military memories and symbols, and the State once more walks, an august presence, through the imaginations of men. Patriotism becomes the dominant feeling, and produces immediately that intense and hopeless confusion between the relations which the individual bears and should bear toward the society of which he is a part.

The patriot loses all sense of the distinction between State, nation, and government. . . . Country is a concept of peace, of tolerance, of living and letting live. But State is essentially a concept of power, of competition: it signifies a group in its aggressive aspects. And we have the misfortune of being born not only into a country but into a State, and as we grow up we learn to mingle the two feelings into a hopeless confusion.

. . . When a country acts as a whole in relation to another country, or in imposing laws on its own inhabitants, or in coercing or punishing individuals or minorities, it is acting as a State. The history of America as a country is quite different from that of America as a State. In one case it is the drama of the pioneering conquest of the land, of the growth of wealth and the ways in which it was used, of the enterprise of education, and the carrying out of spiritual ideals, of the struggle of economic classes. But as a State, its history is that of playing a part in the world, making war, obstructing international trade, preventing itself from being split to pieces, punishing those citizens whom society agrees are offensive, and collecting money to pay for all. . . .

Wartime brings the ideal of the State out into very clear relief, and reveals attitudes and tendencies that were hidden. In times of peace the sense of the State flags in a republic that is not militarized. For war is essentially the health of the State. The ideal of the State is that within its territory its power and influence should be universal. As the Church is the medium for the spiritual salvation of man, so the State is thought of as the medium for his political salvation. Its idealism is a rich blood flowing to all the members of the body politic. And it is precisely in war that the urgency for union seems greatest, and the necessity for universality seems most unquestioned. The State is the organization of the herd to act offensively or defensively against another herd similarly organized. The more terrifying the occasion for defense, the closer will become the organization and the more coercive the influence upon each member of the herd. War sends the current of purpose and activity flowing down to the lowest levels of the herd, and to its remote branches. All the activities of society are linked together as fast as possible to this central purpose of making a military offensive or military defense, and the State becomes what in peacetimes it has vainly struggled to become—the inexorable arbiter and determinant of men's businesses and attitudes and opinions. The slack is taken up, the crosscurrents fade out, and the nation moves lumberingly and slowly, but with ever accelerated speed and integration, towards the great end, towards that peacefulness of being at war, of which L. P. Jacks has spoken so unforgettably.

. . . Every individual citizen who in peacetimes had no living fragment of the State becomes an active amateur agent of the Government in reporting spies and disloyalists, in raising Government funds, or in propagating such measures as are considered necessary by officialdom. Minority opinion, which in times of peace was only irritating and could not be dealt with by law unless it was conjoined with actual crime, becomes with the outbreak of war, a case for outlawry. Criticism of the State, objections to war, lukewarm opinions concerning the necessity or the beauty of conscription, are made subject to ferocious penalties, far exceeding [in] severity those affixed to actual pragmatic crimes. Public opinion, as expressed in the newspapers, and the pulpits and the schools, becomes one solid block. . . . The triumphant orthodoxy of the State is shown at its apex perhaps when Christian preachers lose their pulpits for taking in more or less literal terms the Sermon on the Mount, and Christian zealots are sent to prison for twenty years for distributing tracts which argue that war is unscriptural.

War is the health of the State. It automatically sets in motion throughout society those irresistible forces for uniformity, for passionate cooperation with the Government in coercing into obedience the minority groups and individuals which lack the larger herd sense. The machinery of government sets and enforces the drastic penalties. The minorities are either intimidated into silence, or brought slowly around by subtle process of persuasion which may seem to them really to be converting them. Of course, the ideal of perfect loyalty, perfect uniformity is never really attained. The classes upon whom the amateur work of co-ercion falls are unwearied in their zeal, but often their agitation, instead of converting merely serves to stiffen their resistance. Minorities are rendered sullen, and some intellectual opinion bitter and satirical. But in general, the nation in wartime attains a uniformity of feeling, a hierarchy of values culminating at the undisputed apex of the State ideal, which could not possibly be produced through any other agency than war. Other values such as artistic creation, knowledge, reason, beauty, the enhancement of life, are instantly and almost unanimously sacrificed, and the significant classes who have constituted themselves the amateur agents of the State, are engaged not only in sacrificing these values for themselves but in coercing all other persons into sacrificing them.

War—or at least modern war waged by a democratic republic against a powerful enemy—seems to achieve for a nation almost all that the most inflamed political idealist could desire. Citizens are no longer indifferent to their Government, but each cell of the body politic is brimming with life and activity. We are at last on the way to full realization of that collective community in which each individual somehow contains the virtue of the whole. In a nation at war, every citizen identifies himself with the whole and feels immensely strengthened in that identification. The purpose and desire of the collective community live in each person who throws himself whole-heartedly into the cause of war. The impeding distinction between society and the individual is almost blotted out. At war, the individual becomes almost identical with his society. He achieves a superb self-assurance, an intuition of the rightness of all his ideas and emotions, so that in the suppression of opponents or heretics he is invincibly strong; he feels behind him all the power of the collective community. The individual as social being in war seems to have achieved almost his apotheosis. . . .

For these secular goods, connected with the enhancement of life, the education of men and the use of the intelligence to realize reason and beauty in the nation's communal living, are alien to our traditional ideal of the State. The State is intimately connected with war, for it is the organization of the collective community when it acts in a political manner, and to act in a political manner towards a rival group has meant, throughout all history—war. . . .

On our entrance into the war there were many persons who predicted exactly this derangement of values, who feared lest democracy suffer more at home from an America at war than could be gained for democracy abroad. That fear has been amply justified. The question whether the American nation would act like an enlightened democracy going to war for the sake of high ideals, or like a State-obsessed herd, has been decisively answered. The record is written and cannot be erased. History will decide whether the terrorization of opinion, and the regimentation of life was justified under the most idealistic of democratic administrations. It will see that when the American nation had ostensibly a chance to conduct a gallant war, with scrupulous regard to the safety of democratic values at home, it chose rather to adopt all the most obnoxious and coercive techniques of the enemy and of the other countries at war, and to rival in intimidation and ferocity of punishment the worst governmental systems of the age. For its former unconsciousness and disrespect of the State ideal, the nation apparently paid the penalty in a violent swing to the other extreme. It acted so exactly like a herd in its irrational coercion of minorities that there is no artificiality in interpreting the progress of the war in terms of herd psychology. It unwittingly brought out into the strongest relief the true characteristics of the State and its intimate alliance with war. . . .

War cannot exist without a military establishment, and a military establishment cannot exist without a State organization. War has an immemorial tradition and heredity only because the State has a long tradition and heredity. But they are inseparably and functionally joined. We cannot crusade against war without crusading implicitly against the State. And we cannot expect, or take measures to ensure, that this war is a war to end war, unless at the same time we take measures to end the State in its traditional form. The State is not the nation, and the State can be modified and even abolished in its present form, without harming the nation. On the contrary, with the passing of the dominance of the State, the genuine life-enhancing forces of the nation will be liberated. If the State's chief function is war, then the State must suck out of the nation a large part of its energy for purely sterile purposes of defense and aggression. It devotes to waste or to actual destruction as much as it can of the vitality of the nation. No one will deny that war is a vast complex of life-destroying and life-crippling forces. If the State's chief function is war, then it is chiefly concerned with coordinating and developing the powers and techniques which make for destruction. And this means not only the actual and potential destruction of the enemy, but of the nation at home as well. For the very existence of a State in a system of States means that the nation lies always under a risk of war and invasion, and the calling away of energy into military pursuits means a crippling of the productive and life-enhancing process of the national life.

All this organizing of death-dealing energy and technique is not a natural but a very sophisticated process. Particularly in modern nations, but also all through the course of modern European history, it could never exist without the State. For it meets the demands of no other institution, it follows the desires of no religious, industrial, political group. If the demand for military organization and a military establishment seems to come not from the officers of the State but from the public, it is only that it comes from the State-obsessed portion of the public, those groups which feel most keenly the State ideal. And in this country we have had evidence all too indubitable about how powerless the pacifically minded officers of the State may be in the face of a State-obsession of the significant classes. If a powerful section of the significant classes feels more intensely the attitudes of the State, then they will most infallibly mold the Government in time to their wishes, bring it back to act as the embodiment of the State which it pretends to be. . . . That is why the referendum which was advocated by some people as a test of American sentiment in entering the war was considered even by thoughtful democrats to be something subtly improper. The die had been cast. Popular whim could derange and bungle monstrously the majestic march of State policy in its new crusade for the peace of the world. The irresistible State ideal got hold of the bowels of men. Whereas up to this time, it had been irreproachable to be neutral in word and deed, for the foreign policy of the State had so decided it, henceforth it became the most arrant crime to remain neutral. The Middle West, which had been soddenly pacifistic in our days of neutrality, became in a few months just as soddenly bellicose, and in its zeal for witch-burning and its scent for enemies within gave precedence to no section of the country. The herd-mind followed faithfully the State-mind and, the agitation for a referendum being soon forgotten, the country fell into the universal conclusion that, since its Congress had formally declared the war, the nation itself had in the most solemn and universal way devised and brought on the entire affair.

Oppression of minorities became justified on the plea that the latter were perversely resisting the rationally constructed and solemnly declared will of a majority of the nation. The herd coalescence of opinion which became inevitable the moment the State had set flowing the war attitudes became interpreted as a prewar popular decision, and disinclination to bow to the herd was treated as a monstrously antisocial act. So that the State, which had vigorously resisted the idea of a referendum and clung tenaciously and, of course, with entire success to its autocratic and absolute control of foreign policy, had the pleasure of seeing the country, within a few months, given over to the retrospective impression that a genuine referendum had taken place. When once a country has lapped up these State attitudes, its memory fades; it conceives itself not as merely accepting, but of having itself willed, the whole policy and technique of war. The significant classes, with their trailing satellites, identify themselves with the State, so that what the State, through the agency of the Government, has willed, this majority conceives itself to have willed.

All of which goes to show that the State represents all the autocratic, arbitrary, coercive, belligerent forces within a social group, it is a sort of complexus of everything most distasteful to the modern free creative spirit, the feeling for life, liberty, and the pursuit of happiness. War is the health of the State. Only when the State is at war does the modern society function with that unity of sentiment, simple uncritical patriotic devotion, cooperation of services, which have always been the ideal of the State lover. . . .

Strike Against War

HELEN KELLER

Well known for her inspiring story as a deaf and blind woman, Helen Keller was also involved in a great many progressive causes. A socialist, she opposed American entry into World War I. She delivered this speech before the Women's Peace Party of New York City on January 5, 1916.

The future of the world rests in the hands of America. The future of America rests on the backs of 80,000,000 working men and women and their children. We are facing a grave crisis in our national life. The few who profit from the labor of the masses want to organize the workers into an army which will protect the interests of the capitalists. You are urged to add to the heavy burdens you already bear the burden of a larger army and many additional warships. It is in your power to refuse to carry the artillery and the dreadnoughts and to shake off some of the burdens, too, such as limousines, steam yachts and country estates. You do not need to make a great noise about it. With the silence and the dignity of creators you can end wars and the system of selfishness and exploitation that causes wars. All you need to do to bring about this stupendous revolution is to straighten up and fold your arms.

    We are not preparing to defend our country. Even if we were as helpless as Congressman Gardner says we are, we have no enemies foolhardy enough to attempt to invade the United States. The talk about attack from Germany and Japan is absurd. Germany has its hands full and will be busy with its own affairs for some generations after the European war is over.

With full control of the Atlantic Ocean and the Mediterranean Sea, the allies failed to land enough men to defeat the Turks at Gallipoli; and then they failed again to land an army at Salonica in time to check the Bulgarian invasion of Serbia. The conquest of America by water is a nightmare confined exclusively to ignorant persons and members of the Navy League.

Yet, everywhere, we hear fear advanced as argument for armament. It reminds me of a fable I read. A certain man found a horseshoe. His neighbor began to weep and wail because, as he justly pointed out, the man who found the horseshoe might someday find a horse. Having found the shoe, he might shoe him. The neighbor's child might someday go so near the horse's heels as to be kicked, and die. Undoubtedly the two families would quarrel and fight, and several valuable lives would be lost through the finding of the horseshoe. You know the last war we had we quite accidentally picked up some islands in the Pacific Ocean which may some day be the cause of a quarrel between ourselves and Japan. I'd rather drop those islands right now and forget about them than go to war to keep them. Wouldn't you?

Congress is not preparing to defend the people of the United States. It is planning to protect the capital of American speculators and investors in Mexico, South America, China and the Philippine Islands. Incidentally this preparation will benefit the manufacturers of munitions and war machines.

Until recently there were uses in the United States for the money taken from the workers. But American labor is exploited almost to the limit now, and our national resources have all been appropriated. Still the profits keep piling up new capital. Our flourishing industry in implements of murder is filling the vaults of New York's banks with gold. And a dollar that is not being used to make a slave of some human being is not fulfilling its purpose in the capitalistic scheme. That dollar must be invested in South America, Mexico, China, or the Philippines.

It was no accident that the Navy League came into prominence at the same time that the National City Bank of New York established a branch in Buenos Aires. It is not a mere coincidence that six business associates of J. P. Morgan are officials of defense leagues. And chance did not dictate that [New York City] Mayor [John Purroy] Mitchel should appoint to his Committee of Safety a thousand men that represent a fifth of the wealth of the United States. These men want their foreign investments protected.

Every modern war has had its root in exploitation. The Civil War was fought to decide whether the slaveholders of the South or the capitalists of the North should exploit the West. The Spanish-American War decided that the United States should exploit Cuba and the Philippines. The South African War decided that the British should exploit the diamond mines. The Russo-Japanese War decided that Japan should exploit Korea. The present war is to decide who shall exploit the Balkans, Turkey, Persia, Egypt, India, China, Africa. And we are whetting our sword to scare the victors into sharing the spoils with us. Now, the workers are not interested in the spoils; they will not get any of them anyway.

The preparedness propagandists have still another object, and a very important one. They want to give the people something to think about besides their own unhappy condition. They know the cost of living is high, wages are low, employment is uncertain and will be much more so when the European call for munitions stops. No matter how hard and incessantly the people work, they often cannot afford the comforts of life; many cannot obtain the necessities.

Every few days we are given a new war scare to lend realism to their propaganda. They have had us on the verge of war over the *Lusitania*, the *Gulflight*, the *Ancona*, and now they want the workingmen to become excited over the sinking of the *Persia*. The workingman has no interest in any of these ships. The Germans might sink every vessel on the

Atlantic Ocean and the Mediterranean Sea, and kill Americans with every one—the American workingman would still have no reason to go to war.

All the machinery of the system has been set in motion. Above the complaint and din of the protest from the workers is heard the voice of authority.

"Friends," it says, "fellow workmen, patriots; your country is in danger! There are foes on all sides of us. There is nothing between us and our enemies except the Pacific Ocean and the Atlantic Ocean. Look at what has happened to Belgium. Consider the fate of Serbia. Will you murmur about low wages when your country, your very liberties, are in jeopardy? What are the miseries you endure compared to the humiliation of having a victorious German army sail up the East River? Quit your whining, get busy and prepare to defend your firesides and your flag. Get an army, get a navy; be ready to meet the invaders like the loyal-hearted freemen you are."

Will the workers walk into this trap? Will they be fooled again? I am afraid so. The people have always been amenable to oratory of this sort. The workers know they have no enemies except their masters. They know that their citizenship papers are no warrant for the safety of themselves or their wives and children. They know that honest sweat, persistent toil and years of struggle bring them nothing worth holding on to, worth fighting for. Yet, deep down in their foolish hearts they believe they have a country. Oh blind vanity of slaves!

The clever ones, up in the high places know how childish and silly the workers are. They know that if the government dresses them up in khaki and gives them a rifle and starts them off with a brass band and waving banners, they will go forth to fight valiantly for their own enemies. They are taught that brave men die for their country's honor. What a price to pay for an abstraction—the lives of millions of young men; other millions crippled and blinded for life; existence made hideous for still more millions of human beings; the achievement and inheritance of generations swept away in a moment—and nobody better off for all the misery! This terrible sacrifice would be comprehensible if the thing you die for and call country fed, clothed, housed and warmed you, educated and cherished your children. I think the workers are the most unselfish of the children of men; they toil and live and die for other people's country, other people's sentiments, other people's liberties and other people's happiness! The workers have no liberties of their own; they are not free when they are compelled to work twelve or ten or eight hours a day. They are not free when they are ill-paid for their exhausting toil. They are not free when their children must labor in mines, mills and factories or starve, and when their women may be driven by poverty to lives of shame. They are not free when they are clubbed and imprisoned because they go on strike for a raise of wages and for the elemental justice that is their right as human beings.

We are not free unless the men who frame and execute the laws represent the interests of the lives of the people and no other interest. The ballot does not make a free man out of a wage slave. There has never existed a truly free and democratic nation in the world. From time immemorial men have followed with blind loyalty the strong men who had the power of money and of armies. Even while battlefields were piled high with their own dead they have tilled the lands of the rulers and have been robbed of the fruits of their labor. They have built palaces and pyramids, temples and cathedrals that held no real shrine of liberty.

As civilization has grown more complex the workers have become more and more enslaved, until today they are little more than parts of the machines they operate. Daily they face the dangers of railroad, bridge, skyscraper, freight train, stokehold, stockyard, lumber raft and mine. Panting and straining at the docks, on the railroads and underground and on the seas, they move the traffic and pass from land to land the precious commodities that make it possible for us to live. And what is their reward? A scanty wage, often poverty, rents, taxes, tributes and war indemnities.

The kind of preparedness the workers want is reorganization and reconstruction of their whole life, such as has never been attempted by statesmen or governments. The Germans found out years ago that they could not raise good soldiers in the slums so they abolished the slums. They saw to it that all the people had at least a few of the essentials of civilization—decent lodging, clean streets, wholesome if scanty food, proper medical care and proper safeguards for the workers in their occupations. That is only a small part of what should be done, but what wonders that one step toward the right sort of preparedness has wrought for Germany! For eighteen months it has kept itself free from invasion while carrying on an extended war of conquest, and its armies are still pressing on with unabated vigor. It is your business to force these reforms on the Administration. Let there be no more talk about what a government can or cannot do. All these things have been done by all the belligerent nations in the hurly-burly of war. Every fundamental industry has been managed better by the governments than by private corporations.

It is your duty to insist upon still more radical measures. It is your business to see that no child is employed in an industrial establishment or mine or store, and that no worker is needlessly exposed to accident or disease. It is your business to make them give you clean cities, free from smoke, dirt and congestion. It is your business to make them pay you a living wage. It is your business to see that this kind of preparedness is carried into every department of the nation, until every one has a chance to be well born, well nourished, rightly educated, intelligent and serviceable to the country at all times.

Strike against all ordinances and laws and institutions that continue the slaughter of peace and the butcheries of war. Strike against war, for without you no battles can be fought. Strike against manufacturing shrapnel and gas bombs and all other tools of murder. Strike against preparedness that means death and misery to millions of human beings. Be not dumb, obedient slaves in an army of destruction. Be heroes in an army of construction.

Jane Addams was the first American woman honored with the Nobel Peace Prize. Here she is demonstrating with Mary McDowell against the United States' entry into World War I. Best known for cofounding (with Ellen Starr) Chicago's Hull House, which served the poor, she also helped form the Women's Peace Party in 1915 and in 1919 became the first president of the Women's International League for Peace and Freedom.

Courtesy of the Jane Addams Memorial Collection, University of Illinois at Chicago.

Disarm and Have Peace:
A Pacifist Plea to End War

JANE ADDAMS

The following originally appeared in Liberty, *March 12, 1932.*

The chief skepticism pacifism meets comes from a widely accepted conviction that war is a necessary and inevitable factor in human affairs. Let us consider that in light of one example.

In 1812 America and England were at war. Six years later representatives of the two governments agreed by treaty that the Canadian frontier should be unfortified. Neighbors along a frontier of almost four thousand miles, two people have lived during one hundred and fourteen years enjoying a sense of security neither treaties nor armaments can give.

By 1913, in each thousand men in Europe, one hundred and twenty were soldiers! Then came the crisis in 1914. We have wished to "forget the war." But I should like to recall it briefly.

At the end of it Europe was confronted by a crisis unequaled since the Great Plague, or the famine accompanying the Thirty Years War, when a third of the population of Europe perished.

And yet, in spite of this lesson, a decade after the treaty was signed six million men were under arms in fifty-two nations; ten million were receiving military training; twenty-seven million were enrolled in military reserves!

During the period immediately after the Great War closed, political leaders had turned to a more arrant and arrogant "nationalism" than that which had gone before.

We have reached a stage in the advancement of civilization when we are quite willing to concede that finance, industry, transportation, science, medicine, culture, and trade are not bounded by national frontiers, but must be international. Must our political thought alone remain insular and blindly "national"?

Surely, now that we begin to comprehend the moral, social, and economic consequences of the late war, we must examine openly the question of how to avoid another.

It seems necessary that two things be done:

First, that peaceful methods substituted for war in the settlement of international disputes should be increased and strengthened.

Second, that these peaceful methods should be given a fair chance invariably to succeed, even in grave crises, by the final *abolition* of armaments.

Ten or a dozen of these peaceful methods have been developed in an unprecedented degree during the past generation. The chief of these were the Hague Court of Arbitration, the League of Nations, the World Court, and the Kellogg Pact. Each of these has been used repeatedly—the first one many times; and whenever they have been resorted to they invariably have succeeded.

But in a half dozen crises of the past generation, including the Chinese-Japanese crisis of today, they have been brushed aside and a resort has been made to armed force.

At the Geneva arms conference, which at this writing is about to open, a *principle* should be agreed upon and rigidly applied. The nations should pledge themselves—in another Kellogg Pact—never again to resort to armaments in their dealings with one another. The next step would be to agree upon methods of securing total disarmament. Experts now conceive of the warfare of the future as *bound to involve whole populations.*

At the last Women's International League Congress a report on disarmament was read which stated: "Defensive warfare will have no meaning, as nothing can any longer be defended; for modern war will inevitably be an attack on the civil population."

The history of one nation after another shows that it was the mothers who first protested that their children should no longer be slain as living sacrifices upon the altars of tribal gods. Women rebelled against the waste of the life they had nurtured.

I should like to see the women of civilization rebel against the senseless wholesale human sacrifice of warfare. I am convinced that many thousands of women throughout the world would gladly rise to this challenge. . . .

The Subject Class Always Fights the Battles

EUGENE V. DEBS

This speech by perennial socialist presidential candidate Eugene V. Debs resulted in a ten-year prison sentence under the Espionage Act of 1917. The Supreme Court upheld the sentence in Debs v. U.S. *(1919). Debs received a million votes in the 1920 presidential election even though he was still in prison. A campaign button featured Debs's face along with the words, FOR PRESIDENT: CONVICT NO. 9653. President Woodrow Wilson denied all*

Courtesy of the Debs Collection, Indiana State University.

Eugene V. Debs, trade-union and Socialist Party leader, is shown on his way to prison after receiving a ten-year sentence for opposing the draft and American participation in World War I.

appeals for Debs's release. It was his successor, Warren Harding—who, unlike Wilson himself, is despised by historians—who finally released Debs, in 1921. "I want him to eat his Christmas dinner with his wife," Harding said.

I realize that, in speaking to you this afternoon, there are certain limitations placed upon the right of free speech. I must be exceedingly careful, prudent, as to what I say, and even more careful and prudent as to how I say it. I may not be able to say all I think; but I am not going to say anything that I do not think. I would rather a thousand times be a free soul in jail than to be a sycophant and coward in the streets. They may put those boys in jail—and some of the rest of us in jail—but they can not put the Socialist movement in jail. Those prison bars separate their bodies from ours, but their souls are here this afternoon. They are simply paying the penalty that all men have paid in all the ages of history for standing erect, and for seeking to pave the way to better conditions for mankind....

There is but one thing you have to be concerned about, and that is that you keep foursquare with the principles of the international Socialist movement. It is only when you begin to compromise that trouble begins. So far as I am concerned, it does not matter what others may say, or think, or do, as long as I am sure that I am right with myself and the cause. There are so many who seek refuge in the popular side of a great question. As a Socialist, I have long since learned how to stand alone. For the last month I have been traveling over the Hoosier State; and, let me say to you, that, in all my connection with the Socialist movement, I have never seen such meetings, such enthusiasm, such unity of purpose; never have I seen such a promising outlook as there is today, notwithstanding the statement published repeatedly that our leaders have deserted us. Well, for myself, I never had much faith in leaders. I am willing to be charged with almost anything, rather than to be charged with being a leader. I am suspicious of leaders, and especially of the intellectual variety. Give me the rank and file every day in the week. If you go to the city of Washington, and you examine the pages of the Congressional Directory, you will find that almost all of those corporation lawyers and cowardly politicians, members of Congress, and misrepresentatives of the masses—you will find that almost all of them claim, in glowing terms, that they have risen from the ranks to places of eminence and distinction. I am very glad I cannot make that claim for myself. I would be ashamed to admit that I had risen from the ranks. When I rise it will be with the ranks, and not from the ranks. . . .

Are we opposed to Prussian militarism? Why, we have been fighting it since the day the Socialist movement was born; and we are going to continue to fight it, day and night, until it is wiped from the face of the earth. Between us there is no truce—no compromise.

But, before I proceed along this line, let me recall a little history, in which I think we are all interested.

In 1869 that grand old warrior of the social revolution, the elder Liebknecht, was arrested and sentenced to prison for three months, because of his war, as a Socialist, on the Kaiser and on the Junkers that rule Germany. In the meantime the Franco-Prussian war broke out. Liebknecht and Bebel were the Socialist members in the Reichstag.

They were the only two who had the courage to protest against taking Alsace-Lorraine from France and annexing it to Germany. And for this they were sentenced two years to a prison fortress charged with high treason; because, even in that early day, almost fifty years ago, these leaders, these forerunners of the international Socialist movement were fighting the Kaiser and fighting the Junkers of Germany. They have continued to fight them from that day to this. Multiplied thousands of Socialists have languished in the jails of Germany because of their heroic warfare upon the despotic ruling class of that country.

Let us come down the line a little farther. You remember that, at the close of Theodore Roosevelt's second term as President, he went over to Africa to make war on some of his ancestors. You remember that, at the close of his expedition, he visited the capitals of Europe; and that he was wined and dined, dignified and glorified by all the Kaisers and Czars and Emperors of the Old World. He visited Potsdam while the Kaiser was there; and, according to the accounts published in the American newspapers, he and the Kaiser were soon on the most familiar terms. They were hilariously intimate with each other, and slapped each other on the back. After Roosevelt had reviewed the Kaiser's troops, according to the same accounts, he became enthusiastic over the Kaiser's legions and said: "If I had that kind of an army, I could conquer the world." He knew the Kaiser then just as well as he knows him now. He knew that he was the Kaiser, the Beast of Berlin. And yet, he permitted himself to be entertained by that Beast of Berlin; had his feet under the mahogany of the Beast of Berlin; was cheek by jowl with the Beast of Berlin. And, while Roosevelt was being entertained royally by the German Kaiser, that same Kaiser was putting the leaders of the Socialist Party in jail for fighting the Kaiser and the Junkers of Germany. Roosevelt was the guest of honor in the white house of the Kaiser, while the Socialists were in the jails of the Kaiser for fighting the Kaiser. Who then was fighting for democracy? Roosevelt? Roosevelt, who was honored by the Kaiser, or the Socialists who were in jail by order of the Kaiser?

"Birds of a feather flock together."

. . . If Theodore Roosevelt is the great champion of democracy—
the arch-foe of autocracy, what business had he as the guest of honor of
the Prussian Kaiser? And when he met the Kaiser, and did honor to the
Kaiser, under the terms imputed to him, wasn't it pretty strong proof
that he himself was a Kaiser at heart? Now, after being the guest of Emperor Wilhelm, the Beast of Berlin, he comes back to this country, and
wants you to send ten million men over there to kill the Kaiser; to murder his former friend and pal. Rather queer, isn't it? And yet, he is the
patriot, and we are the traitors. I challenge you to find a Socialist anywhere on the face of the earth who was ever the guest of the Beast of
Berlin, except as an inmate of his prison. . . .

A little more history along the same line. In 1902 Prince Henry paid
a visit to this country. Do you remember him? I do, exceedingly well.
Prince Henry is the brother of Emperor Wilhelm. Prince Henry is another Beast of Berlin, an autocrat, an aristocrat, a Junker of Junkers—
very much despised by our American patriots. He came over here in
1902 as the representative of Kaiser Wilhelm; he was received by Congress and by several state legislatures—among others, by the state legislature of Massachusetts, then in session. He was invited there by the
capitalist captains of that so-called commonwealth. And when Prince
Henry arrived, there was one member of that body who kept his self-
respect, put on his hat, and as Henry, the Prince, walked in, that member of the body walked out. And that was James F. Carey, the Socialist
member of that body. All the rest—all the rest of the representatives in
the Massachusetts legislature—all, all of them—joined in doing honor,
in the most servile spirit, to the high representative of the autocracy of
Europe. And the only man who left that body, was a Socialist. And yet,
and yet they have the hardihood to claim that they are fighting autocracy and that we are in the service of the German government.

A little more history along the same line. I have a distinct recollec-
tion of it. It occurred fifteen years ago when Prince Henry came here.
All of our plutocracy, all of the wealthy representatives living along
Fifth Avenue—all, all of them—threw their palace doors wide open

and received Prince Henry with open arms. But they were not satisfied with this; they got down and groveled in the dust at his feet. Our plutocracy—women and men alike—vied with each other to lick the boots of Prince Henry, the brother and representative of the "Beast of Berlin." And still our plutocracy, our Junkers, would have us believe that all the Junkers are confined to Germany. It is precisely because we refuse to believe this that they brand us as disloyalists. They want our eyes focused on the Junkers in Berlin so that we will not see those within our own borders. . . .

Wars throughout history have been waged for conquest and plunder. In the Middle Ages when the feudal lords who inhabited the castles whose towers may still be seen along the Rhine concluded to enlarge their domains, to increase their power, their prestige and their wealth they declared war upon one another. But they themselves did not go to war any more than the modern feudal lords, the barons of Wall Street go to war. The feudal barons of the Middle Ages, the economic predecessors of the capitalists of our day, declared all wars. And their miserable serfs fought all the battles. The poor, ignorant serfs had been taught to revere their masters; to believe that when their masters declared war upon one another, it was their patriotic duty to fall upon one another and to cut one another's throats for the profit and glory of the lords and barons who held them in contempt. And that is war in a nutshell. The master class has always declared the wars; the subject class has always fought the battles. The master class has had all to gain and nothing to lose, while the subject class has had nothing to gain and all to lose—especially their lives.

They have always taught and trained you to believe it to be your patriotic duty to go to war and to have yourselves slaughtered at their command. But in all the history of the world you, the people, have never had a voice in declaring war, and strange as it certainly appears, no war by any nation in any age has ever been declared by the people.

And here let me emphasize the fact—and it cannot be repeated too often—that the working class who fight all the battles, the working class who make the supreme sacrifices, the working class who freely shed their blood and furnish the corpses, have never yet had a voice in either declaring war or making peace. It is the ruling class that invariably does both. They alone declare war and they alone make peace. . . .

Yours not to reason why;

Yours but to do and die.

If war is right let it be declared by the people. You who have your lives to lose, you certainly above all others have the right to decide the momentous issue of war or peace. . . .

It is the minorities who have made the history of this world. It is the few who have had the courage to take their places at the front; who have been true enough to themselves to speak the truth that was in them; who have dared oppose the established order of things; who have espoused the cause of the suffering, struggling poor; who have upheld without regard to personal consequences the cause of freedom and righteousness. It is they, the heroic, self-sacrificing few who have made the history of the race and who have paved the way from barbarism to civilization. The many prefer to remain upon the popular side. They lack the courage and vision to join a despised minority that stands for a principle; they have not the moral fiber that withstands, endures and finally conquers. They are to be pitied and not treated with contempt for they cannot help their cowardice. But, thank God, in every age and in every nation there have been the brave and self-reliant few, and they have been sufficient to their historic task; and we, who are here today, are under infinite obligations to them because they suffered, they sacrificed, they went to jail, they had their bones broken upon the wheel, they were burned at the stake and their ashes scattered to the winds by the hands of hate and revenge in their struggle to leave the world better for us than they found it for themselves. We are under eternal obligations to them because of what they did and what they suffered for us and the only way we can discharge that obligation is by doing the best we can for those who are to come after us. And this is the high purpose of every Socialist on earth. Everywhere they are animated by the same lofty principles; everywhere they have the same noble ideals; everywhere they are clasping hands across national boundary lines; everywhere they are calling one another Comrade, the blessed word that springs from the heart of unity and bursts into blossom upon the lips. Each passing day they are getting into closer touch all along the battle line, waging the holy war of the working class of the world against the ruling and exploiting class of the world. They make many mistakes and they profit by them all. They encounter numerous defeats, and grow stronger through them all. They never take a backward step. . . .

They are continually talking about your patriotic duty. It is not their but your patriotic duty that they are concerned about. There is a decided difference. Their patriotic duty never takes them to the firing line or chucks them into the trenches. . . .

If: A Mother to Her Daughter

FLORENCE GUERTIN TUTTLE

This poem, after Rudyard Kipling's "If," *appeared in* Four Lights *on July 28, 1917.*

If you can lose your head when all about you
Are losing theirs and saying false is true;
If you can feel that Might alone is Mighty—
Reverse your creed in all you say and do;
If you can cast aside your private ethics,
And claim another law holds for the pack;
If you can join in race annihilation
And never pause to question or look back;
If you can call yourself a Christ disciple
Yet incense burn before the God of war;

If you can chant with saints the sixth commandment,
Then plan to kill and kill—and kill some more;
If you can keep your tender woman's spirit
And dull the charge of murder on your soul,
If you can ease your conscience with a bandage
And daily sit and dumbly roll and roll;
If you can sing "My Country first" and never
Observe that lands melt freely into one;
If you can prove mankind is not united,
Led by one hope as by one rising sun;
If you can doubt that greed of State must perish,
And God, the King, One Sovereignty unfurl,
You'll be a "loyal patriot" my darling,
And which is more—a thing of stone, my girl.

Victory

MARION PATTON WALDRON

This poem appeared in Century, *July 1917.*

Many and many are weeping for their lovers;
For the shallow graves in Flanders they are weeping,
For the lovers heaped with earth who cannot come to them,
While I—I have my lover back again!
First, word that he lay upon a narrow bed
As in a grave without the grave's release.
Death had despoiled his body, claimed his soul;
Yet those who tended would not give him up
To the earth's rest, and I who waited could not.
By that brave magic which proves man a god
Only less cunning than a modern gun

The surgeons mended bit by broken bit;
Patiently blew to spark the reluctant ashes,
Built with their will upon his power of anguish,
While I compelled his spirit with my spirit
Monument by monument, holding, drawing him back.
They wrote at last that he was coming home!
It was at dusk they brought him back to me
And laid him gently down and covered him;
Lingered, wanting to speak, yet silent, troubled,
Till awkwardly they left me with my living.
He lay so still, so still beneath the covers,
It was as if they had said, "Your soldier's dead."
But when I laid my hand on him I felt
The warm blood beating, and he spoke. His voice—
His voice it was—and he was calling me!
All night I crouched with my head against his arm
To feel its warmth. It was as if I doubted
The miracle. I dared not lift his shroud,
But watched beside him as a wife beside
Her husband laid in death—a wife who, turning
As in old griefs to her old comforter,
Longing to cower against him, and yet fearing
Lest he should shut her from him, *he* be cold
When most she needs him, *he* be stone to her,
Suddenly hears his answers fill her silence,
Feeds the touch of the dead healing their pain.
Such was my miracle.
O lover's body with its man's grave beauty,
O lover's eyes in which I launched my soul!
I shall be hands and feet to him, and eyes!
And he can never see me if I falter;
No, and he cannot see me. God forgive me
If I shrink and sicken when I look at him

Before I learn to bear it! There will be years,

There will be years and years to learn. Even now

I can laugh when he makes jests about the fingers

He left to fight for him while he ran home!

Through the long, useless hours what are his thoughts?

What is he thinking all the idle days?

Sometimes he hides his marred face close against me

Like a tired child. That's easier, almost sweet,

Till I mind me of the old times when I teased him

Because he was so big, and called him little,

Half vexed, half pleased him calling him my baby,

He who planned always how he'd care for me

With his great strength, how he would always spare me.

My man, my man that's turned a poor stale joke;

But I can't think of any other now,

So I keep silent, thinking out my thoughts.

They say the lame child is his mother's dearest.

He is my child now, yes, *our* child, *our* child.

Not like the son we dreamed of long ago;

No, but the child of our renunciation,

Born of his beautiful body that went away,

Born of my spirit that sent him forth and waited.

What though the fruit of us be blighted and broken?

We have fought with death, the odds against us, and conquered!

(Hush! What was that echo of terrible laughter?

Who laughed? I fancied a far-off, cynical mocking.)

Many and many are weeping for their lovers;

For the shallow graves in Flanders they are weeping,

For the lovers heaped with earth who cannot come to them,

While I—I have my lover back again!

6

World War II

It is my opinion that the use of this barbarous [atomic] weapon at Hiroshima and Nagasaki was of no material assistance in our war against Japan. The Japanese were already defeated and ready to surrender because of the effective sea blockade and the successful bombing with conventional weapons. . . . My own feeling was that in being the first to use it, we had adopted an ethical standard common to the barbarians of the Dark Ages. I was not taught to make war in that fashion, and wars cannot be won by destroying women and children.

—Fleet Admiral William D. Leahy, chief of staff
to Franklin Roosevelt and Harry Truman

World War II was without a doubt the most popular in our nation's history. Regularly we are reminded of the heroism and sacrifices during that worldwide conflict—though rarely of the vital role played by Soviet armies. And while there was considerable opposition to entering the war, once Pearl Harbor was attacked and the savagery of Nazism and Japanese militarism became more evident, Americans of every class, race, and section rallied to the flag as never before or since. The quintessential "Good War" and the sacrifices of the "greatest generation" brought victory but also carried with them the seeds of vast changes at home and abroad, some positive (victory and a return to prosperity and the growth of a healthy middle class) and some problematic. For example, during the war innocent Americans of Japanese heritage were imprisoned without justification or trial (Italian Americans too), two Japanese cities were atom bombed and many millions of civilians became military targets. At home a fear of nuclear war emerged as the U.S.S.R. and the United States became locked in a fierce struggle highlighted by future proxy wars.

Following the end of World War I and the refusal of the U.S. Senate to join the League of Nations, Americans were said to have turned inward. It was called isolationism, but a more accurate description is opposition to military intervention in foreign wars. Cultural exchange flourished. The student exchange program got its start on the grounds that the better we know each other, the less likely that misunderstandings would lead to war. College courses began teaching the histories of countries Americans had hardly studied before.

It was war people wanted to avoid. In England, which had suffered grievously in World War I, a huge number of students accepted the Oxford Pledge, which repudiated service in war. Much the same occurred in the U.S., where left and right anti-interventionist, nationalist, and pacifist sentiments merged.

The leading antiwar group, the America First Committee (AFC), was founded in 1940 by Yale law students, among them Douglas Stuart, Jr., Gerald Ford, John F. Kennedy, Potter Stewart (later a Supreme Court justice) and Sargent Shriver, one of the founders of the Peace Corps. It had an estimated eight hundred thousand members, mainly centered in the Middle West, attracting supporters of diverse political positions, with the exception of communists who could act only upon instructions from Moscow. (The American Communist Party favored intervention until the infamous Nazi-Soviet Non-Aggression Pact of 1939 turned them isolationist and their slogan abruptly became "No, the Yanks Are Not Coming"—before switching to a pro-war position after Germany invaded the U.S.S.R. in 1941.) Other AFC members included conservative newspaper publishers Colonel Robert McCormick of the *Chicago Tribune* and Joseph M. Patterson of the *New York Daily News*, both of whom loathed the New Deal and Franklin D. Roosevelt. General Robert E. Woods, chief executive of Sears, Roebuck chaired the AFC and many businessmen followed his example. Still another member was the anti-Semitic Catholic radio priest Charles Coughlin. The AFC also included longtime progressive Senators Burton K. Wheeler, Gerald P. Nye, and Robert La Follette Jr. as well as Chester Bowles, William Saroyan, Frank Lloyd Wright, preeminent Socialist Party leader Norman Thomas, the poet E. E. Cummings, Walt Disney, Theodore Roosevelt's daughter Alice Longworth Roosevelt, Burton D. Wolfe (who later wrote a seminal denunciation of Lenin, Trotsky, and Stalin in *Three Who Made a Revolution*), and author Sinclair Lewis, whose novel *It Can't Happen Here* raised fears about demagogues like Huey Long. It also included Charles Lindbergh, the famous "Lone Eagle" whose speech in Des Moines on September 11, 1941, asserting that Jews were one of the groups behind the race to war with Germany was widely assailed as anti-Semitic. But before December 7, 1941, while Americans hotly debated whether America should or should not enter the war, the Japanese attack changed everything and Americans overwhelmingly supported war.

The major prointerventionist group, the Committee to Defend America by Aiding the Allies (CDA), was founded in 1940 after FDR spoke with William Allen White, the Republican editor of the *Emporia (Kansas) Gazette*, about the dangers inherent in an Axis victory. White took the lead in forming the CDA and was soon joined by J. P. Morgan's Thomas Lamont and, in time, Claude Pepper, Clark Eichelberger, Adlai Stevenson, and many others.

Neither the AFC nor the CDA was monolithic, and both had members and supporters with varying opinions. Some in the AFC emphasized concentration on hemispheric defense, while others opposed yet another "imperialist" war. Within the CDA, many backed "aid short of war," with others wanting the United States to enter the war sooner rather than later.

What is not debatable is that while the AFC prevented the U.S. from becoming even more involved in the European war for some two years, the evidence of Nazi savagery and fears arising from its sweeping military victories in Europe were becoming more vivid. Still, it was the bombing of Pearl Harbor that forced the AFC to disband four days after the attack and President Roosevelt's subsequent call for a congressional declaration of war against the Axis nations. "Our principles were right," read the final AFC statement. "Had they been followed, war could have been avoided." On the other hand, Hitler might have prevailed and the U.S. forced to confront a triumphant Germany alone. We shall never know.

World War II resulted in some sixty million deaths, mainly nonmilitary, death camps and the horrors of the Holocaust as well as the birth of the nuclear era. Five years after the surrender of Germany and Japan, American forces were fighting again in Korea, but this time came away with no more than a bloody draw in 1953 ("Die for a tie" was the cynical lament of some soldiers and journalists) with thirty-eight thousand Americans dead, many more wounded, and several million Koreans killed or uprooted.

Two Votes Against War: 1917 and 1941

JEANNETTE RANKIN

Montana's Jeannette Rankin was the first woman to be elected to the U.S. Congress. This essay appeared in Liberation *magazine in March 1958.*

As the first woman to sit in the legislature of any sovereign nation, I cast my first vote in April 1917 against the entry of the United States into World War I. As I said at the time, I wanted to stand by my country, but I could not vote for war. I look back with satisfaction to that momentous occasion.

I had been deeply involved in the preceding years in the struggle for woman suffrage. That struggle and the struggle against war were integrally related in my youthful thoughts and activities. After the World War had broken out and it had become increasingly clear that the United States was going to be drawn in, I was the angriest person you ever saw. I was in a rage because no one had ever seriously taught us about the nature of war itself or given us any inkling of the causes of this specific war. I was not so naïve as to think that war just started in a minute. Behind the scenes preparation had to be made and was made for such things. Now we seemed, in 1914, suddenly and inexplicably to be on the eve of war.

Deep down, I guess I had always felt strongly about war. I remember that in college, when I was assigned to read publicly a poem glorifying war and soldiers, I told the professor: "But this is hideous. I can't read it."

As we went about in Montana in 1914 campaigning for the vote, we would see long lines of people before the newspaper bulletin boards in every town and city. A large proportion of these people were foreign born, eagerly scanning the notices for war news that would give them some notion as to what was happening to relatives in their native countries. War was on everybody's mind. So we talked about suffrage in relation to war. I argued that women should get the vote because they would help keep the country out of war. It was a persuasive argument at that stage.

I do not want to give the impression that anti-war talk was universally popular. In a speech in Butte, Montana, I happened to suggest that, instead of sending youth into war, the old men ought to fight the wars. The papers picked up this suggestion and made a big thing of it. Then speeches began to be made and letters written to the papers on how presumptuous and shocking it was for an unmarried woman to consider herself competent to discuss such matters.

Representative Jeannette Rankin (R-MT) was the first woman elected to the House of Representatives. After President Wilson asked for a declaration of war in 1917, Rankin, a staunch opponent of all wars, told Congress, "I want to stand by my country, but I cannot vote for war. I vote no." And following the Japanese attack on Pearl Harbor, she was the only House member to again vote no. Senator Gerald P. Nye (R-ND) was a progressive senator and a member of the Senate Military Affairs Committee, which in 1934 cast much of the blame for the decision to join World War I on munitions makers and bankers. After the attack on Pearl Harbor, he voted for war, saying he preferred wartime unity rather than partisanship.

Courtesy of the Montana Historical Society, Helena, Montana.

I recall one curious incident that made a great impression on me during a suffrage campaign. It illustrates how we never know what will evoke our deepest feelings. Minnie J. Reynolds of New Jersey, a prominent suffrage campaigner, and I were walking down a street in Seattle. We passed a window full of baby chicks. Minnie stopped, pointed to them and talked passionately for some minutes about the loveliness and helplessness of those little chicks and how everyone would be outraged if someone were to start wantonly to torture them. She then went on to talk about men, women, old people, children all over the world, and men in war going out to kill them.

In the fall of 1916, I was elected Congresswoman-at-large from Montana. The women's vote helped. It was an additional advantage that the state was not divided into Congressional districts, because candidates who stand for something are likely to have a better chance under this set-up, especially women. Everyone could vote for both a man and a woman. It is harder to manipulate and control the voters of a whole state than those of a single district. Also people were not subjected to a radio and TV barrage and we could go from town to town, speaking on the street corners and in the homes.

Several women ran for Congress in various states that year, but I was the only one who really had a chance, and I was elected. Under the procedures in effect at that time, the outgoing Congress carried over until the first Tuesday in March of the following year and the newly elected Congress would not convene in session until autumn. I had plans made for an extensive, and, I hoped, remunerative lecture tour on woman suffrage and peace, capitalizing on the curiosity about a "female" Representative. But Woodrow Wilson, who had been elected on the slogan that he would keep us out of war, had decided that it was the duty of all, and especially of good liberals and idealists, to support intervention. He called a special session of Congress early in April, read his famous war message, and appealed to the newly elected Congress to declare war.

That time it took a week of tense debate to bring the matter to a vote, and in the House I was not the only one to vote "No." Forty-nine men in the House voted against entry. Among them were all the veterans of the Civil War who were in Congress. Claude Kitchin, the floor leader of the Democratic majority, voted "No" and wept unashamedly as he cried out: "It takes neither moral nor physical courage to declare a war for others to fight." It is one token of how the situation has deteriorated since that time that Kitchin was retained in the leadership in spite of this vote and the fact that he remained unenthusiastic about war measures. Champ Clark, the Speaker of the House, refrained from voting on this crucial measure. In the Senate, the elder Robert M. La Follette made his brilliant and courageous speech and cast his negative vote, as did five other Senators.

I am sorry to have to say that the attitude of most of the leaders of the woman suffrage movement was far from sympathetic to my stand. They thought that the "cause" would have been much better off if I had taken what they considered to be a patriotic stand. They brought a good deal of pressure to bear on me. As a matter of fact, the war advanced the movement to give women the vote and undermined opposition to it, and there is no reason to suppose that my vote on the war declaration had any appreciable effect on this issue.

It did have an effect on my own career. Running for reelection to the House of Representatives in 1918 was out of the question. In the period between the two world wars, I devoted a great deal of time to the effort to achieve the object for which the war had ostensibly been fought—the permanent abolition of war. . . .

In 1939, I began to think of running for Congress again the following year. The first move I made was to write a letter to all the high school principals in Montana, informing each that I would be at his school on such and such a date and available to address the students. I did not give a return address, lest some should reply that it would be inconvenient to have me. So I addressed virtually all of the high school assemblies in the state on the subject of war. I explained the futility of the war method as a means of settling disputes between nations. I never directly attacked the Army or Navy; I just made fun of some of their doings. Thus, in discussing the talk about the Japanese coming to attack San Francisco, I would remark that the distance from San Francisco to Tokyo was exactly the same as from Tokyo to San Francisco. I told the children to write President Roosevelt letters about their ideas on war, but not to write the letters until they had talked it over with their parents. In this way, I made sure that a lot of voters in Montana heard my name and heard something about my ideas on war. I also told the children not to say how old they were—that I never did. . . .

Once again, the nation was moving toward war. In November 1941, and early December, many people assumed that we would go in any day. As late as Saturday evening, December 6, I still felt that the country was not ready and that therefore entry would be put off. I was scheduled to speak in Detroit at an important meeting on Monday. On Sunday, though the attack on Pearl Harbor had occurred, I left Washington for Pittsburgh, en route to Detroit. I took it for granted that Congress would debate the declaration of war for a week, as it had in 1917, or at any rate for several days. But on arrival in Pittsburgh, I learned that we were living in another time and that Congress was going to vote on Monday. I hurried back to Washington. I secluded myself. I did not want to talk with anyone. I was much more upset than I had been in 1917. Then I had been sad. But this time I was grieved at seeing the men who were as opposed to going into the war as I was slipping away from their position at the critical moment. There were some important Republicans who wished to have all the Republicans vote against entry, partly from conviction, partly, I suppose, to embarrass Roosevelt. Nothing came of it.

This time I stood alone. It was a good deal more difficult than it had been the time before. Yet I think the men in Congress all sensed that I would vote "No" again. If I had done otherwise, I do not think I could have faced the remaining days in Congress. Even the men who were most convinced that we had to get into the war would have lost respect for me if I had betrayed my convictions.

When the first anniversary of that vote came around, on December 8, 1942, I extended remarks in the record in which I brought out some points which may well be recalled at the present critical moment. I referred, for one thing, to a book by an English author, Sidney Rogerson, entitled *Propaganda in the Next War.* It had been published in London in 1938 but banned from export to the United States by the British censorship in 1939. Rogerson had stated in his book that it would be much more difficult to bring the United States into the war than it had been in World War I. "The position," said Rogerson, "will naturally be considerably improved if Japan were to be involved. . . . At any rate, it would be a natural and obvious object of our propaganda to achieve this, just as during the Great War they succeeded in embroiling the United States with Germany."

I next reminded the Congress of Henry Luce's historic reference in *Life* magazine for July 20, 1942, to "the Chinese for whom the *U.S. had delivered the ultimatum that brought on Pearl Harbor.*" I introduced evidence that at the Atlantic Conference, August 12, 1941, Winston

Churchill had sought, and Roosevelt had given, assurances that the United States would bring economic pressure to bear on Japan. I cited the State Department Bulletin of December 20, 1941, which revealed that on September 3 a communication had been sent to Japan demanding that it accept the principle of "nondisturbance of the status quo in the Pacific," which amounted to demanding guarantees of the inviolateness of the white empires in the Orient.

On the subject of economic pressure on Japan, I had sought data from both the State and Commerce Departments. I had received from both an identical response: "Because of a special Executive Order, statistics on trade with Japan beginning with April 1941 are not being given out." There was, however, plenty of material from other sources to show that, in line with Roosevelt's assurances to Churchill, the Economic Defense Board, under Henry Wallace's chairmanship, had gotten economic sanctions under way less than a week after the Atlantic Conference. On December 2, 1941, the *New York Times* reported that Japan had been "cut off from about 75% of her normal trade by the Allied blockade."

In this connection, I recalled a statement made on April 4, 1942, by a member of Roosevelt's own party, Hatton W. Summers of Texas, chairman of the House Judiciary Committee: "This blaming the Pearl Harbor tragedy on the treachery of the Japs is like the fellow who had been tickling the hind leg of a mule trying to explain his bungled-up condition by blaming the mule for having violated his confidence."

There was one other development preceding Pearl Harbor, of which I reminded the House, namely the statement of Lieutenant Clarence E. Dickinson, U.S.N., in a *Saturday Evening Post* article, October 10, 1942, to the effect that, on November 28, 1941, Vice Admiral William F. Halsey, Jr., had given instructions to him and others to "shoot down anything we saw in the sky and to bomb anything we saw on the sea. In that way there could be no leak to the Japs." Such orders could hardly have been issued without Presidential sanction. I raise now, as I did on that first anniversary of Pearl Harbor, the question whether Roosevelt had not, at least nine days before the Japanese attacked Pearl Harbor without a declaration of war, authorized an identical attack upon the Japanese—also without a declaration of war.

And how much do the people and even the members of Congress know about the moves now being made by our government or other governments which may lead to another war? Our being kept in ignorance arouses my apprehensions today as it did more than forty years ago when World War I burst upon my world.

Assumptions about War

STUART CHASE

Economist Stuart Chase wrote the pamphlet "Four Assumptions about War," from which the excerpt below is taken, for the Chicago America First Committee in January 1941.

Our relative stability is compounded of many factors—our continental size, our natural resources, our geographical isolation, our dominating position in the hemisphere, our democratic habits practiced by generations of pioneer ancestors. As a result of these factors we have few wars in the hemisphere, fewer armed revolts, no fortified frontiers, and good neighbors north and south. Our standards of living are higher than anywhere else in the world today. This does not mean that living standards are adequate for all classes of people; only that they are unchallenged elsewhere and are, in most areas, well above the line of starvation, despair and revolt.

In the United States, citizens elect their leaders and have wide latitudes in the exercise of free speech, free press, free assembly, free worship, and freedom from being pushed around by autocrats, landowners, gentlemen in colored shirts, and the secret police. They are not immune from being pushed around—witness the Negroes and the Okies—but relative to Old World citizens, they are free men. Even in Britain, Sweden, Switzerland today, one has to do what the authorities tell one to do, or else.

A major test of stability was the Great Depression of 1929, which presently caused Europe to fall apart, but only rocked without shattering the Americas. We have found a sound culture bed. From this base, rough as it is, great developments are clearly visible—the abolition of poverty, unprecedented improvements in health and energy, a towering renaissance in the arts; an architecture and an engineering to challenge the gods. Towards these ends we are groping, with firm ground under our feet. We are the New World. We are the hope of mankind. Our culture is not burdened with the terrible dead weights which the Old World must carry.

Countries in the Old World do not have this stability. Just because they are old they are vulnerable to the impact of high technology. Their instability hardly needs documentation. Look at any edition of any newspaper: Britain fighting heroically for her life, as customs centuries old are melted down beneath the bombs. The British Empire swaying on the brink. The obliteration of France in a shadow so black we almost forget it is there at all. The frozen communities of Belgium, Holland, Scandinavia, Switzerland. The murderous tension in the Balkans, with boundary lines snapping in all directions. The gutted shell of Spain. The Mediterranean as the new Dead Sea. The gory deadlock in China. Terror in Iran, Africa and the East Indies. A precarious stability depending on one man's will in Germany, Russia, Italy.

Even in the best of times, Old World communities carry a load of unstable elements, largely lacking in the Americas. Consider the fractures implicit on a continent with twenty-five or more languages, tariff walls and currencies; with inadequate natural resources, with class divisions, violent ideologies, violent politics, bloody historical feuds. These cleavages were bad enough in the handicraft age. In the power age they make the culture unworkable. How many years, decades, will it take to steam-roller these differences into a stable pattern which can guarantee both goods and freedom? Power age communities need to be continental in scope to fit an expanding technology. Hitler now announces a new order in Europe. God knows Europe needs it, but one wonders if Hitler can do more than set up a kind of vineyard on Vesuvius. It looks as if the choice in Europe was to give up either nationalism or technology. Crusades to restore the rights of small nations will crash into the technological imperative, and vice versa. Can anyone resolve this crazy quilt but the people of Europe themselves? The British have not even suggested what they propose to do about it if they win.

The United States cannot solve the political and economic problems of Europe, Asia, Africa, and the Indies by armed assault on their totalitarian leaders. Consider what is involved. First, a military adventure—and we cannot possibly equip ourselves for military adventures overseas before 1944 at the earliest—in which America takes on Germany, Italy, and Japan with their smaller allies, and before the show is over perhaps Russia, Spain, and France as well. Britain might be more of a liability than an asset in this adventure because of the extreme vulnerability of the British Isles. Pledged to defend this outpost, now flanked by enemy bases and ringed on the west by fleets of submarines, we should be severely handicapped in our efforts to make a frontal assault on the European, African, or Asiatic mainland. If we confined our military effort solely to the defense of Britain, we might save the British Isles, and we might now. It would, I suspect, be a full-time job, and leave us little energy for the reduction of Berlin, Rome, Tokyo, Madrid, and Moscow.

On the fantastic assumption that all these capitals were in our hands, what then? Our work would have just begun. Then we should have to find a social framework to fit some 1.5 billion people, burdened with the cleavages just mentioned, and say to them: "Take this and like it." We can be quite sure that many of them, perhaps most of them, won't like it. So then we might try to make them like it. One way would be to keep a few million American boys, armed to the teeth, in constant attendance to see that they like it. Another would be concentration camps. Another would be puppet governments with strings pulled from Washington.

How long would this educational program take? How long should we be in establishing our new order in Europe, Asia, Africa and the Indies? And what if the blueprint turned out to be no good? Would the pattern we impose fit the revolutionary changes that are already far gone in those parts? Whom, by the way, would you nominate to prepare the blueprints—Mr. Walter Lippmann, Mr. Jesse Jones, Mr. Hoover? When people say we ought to go and help Britain knock out Hitler and restore democracy, the free market, and the little nations, they apparently have no conception of what such a crusade entails. Their imaginations go riotously to the shooting of Hitler, and there they stop. I grant it is a satisfying picture, but unfortunately the removal of Hitler would be only a preliminary incident in the total task before us.

Americans are fine, upstanding, enterprising folks. They could probably organize and defend the whole Western Hemisphere by giving their entire attention to the job. Or they might possibly win a stalemate peace for Britain which would preserve her shattered island and her honor. I do not see how they can do what I have indicated above. Giving Britain her island and her honor, furthermore, settles nothing, with Europe and Asia still in totalitarian hands.

If Americans attempt this program, whether they knock out the dictators or not, they will most assuredly wreck their own New World pattern. As I said, we are an enterprising people. When we start a thing we like to finish it. We have never lost a war yet. With war once declared, or acts of war committed, there would be no end except victory or defeat—unless it were the utter exhaustion of both sides.

The consequences to our culture of an all-out war abroad are simply told—. . . the liquidation of political democracy, of Congress, the Supreme Court, private enterprise, the banks, free press and free speech; the persecution of German-Americans and Italian-Americans, witch hunts, forced labor, fixed prices, rationing, astronomical debts, and the rest. We would become as a people tough, cruel and vindictive. Scientific research would go to pot. With the whole world on our hands, draining our life blood overseas, we would have no time and no desire to plan for the America of the future. Our pattern would be smashed beyond repair.

Why We Refused to Register

DONALD BENEDICT, ET AL.

The following statement was presented to the court by eight students at Union Theological Seminary, who elected in October 1940 not to register for the draft. It was published under the auspices of numerous antiwar groups, such as the Fellowship of Reconciliation and the Keep America Out of War Congress.

It is impossible for us to think of the conscription law without at the same time thinking of the whole war system, because it is clear to us that conscription is definitely a part of the institution of war. . . .

To us, the war system is an evil part of our social order, and we declare that we cannot cooperate with it in any way. War is an evil because it is in violation of the Way of Love as seen in God through Christ. It is a concentration and accentuation of all the evils of our society. War consists of mass murder, deliberate starvation, vandalism, and similar evils. Physical destruction and moral disintegration are the inevitable result. The war method perpetuates and compounds the evils it purports to overcome. It is impossible, as history reveals, to overcome evil with evil. The last World War is a notorious case of the failure of the war system, and there is no evidence to believe that this war will be any different. It is our positive proclamation as followers of Jesus Christ that we must overcome evil with good. We seek in our daily living to reconcile that separation of man from man and man from God which produces war.

We have also been led to our conclusion on the conscription law in the light of its totalitarian nature. It is a totalitarian move when our government insists that the manpower of the nation take a year of military training. It is a totalitarian move for the President of the nation to be able to conscript industry to produce certain materials which are deemed necessary for national defense without considering the actual physical needs of the people. We believe, therefore, that by opposing the Selective Service law, we will be striking at the heart of totalitarianism as well as war. . . .

We feel a deep bond of unity with those who decide to register as conscientious objectors, but our own decision must be different for the following reasons:

If we register under the act, even as conscientious objectors, we are becoming part of the act. The fact that we as conscientious objectors may gain personal exemption from the most crassly un-Christian requirements of the act does not compensate for the fact that we are complying with it and accepting its protection. If a policeman (or a group of vigilantes) stops us on the street, our possessions of the government's card shows that we are "all right"—we have complied with the act for the militarization of America. If that does not hurt our Christian consciences, what will? If we try to rationalize on the theory that we must go along with the act in order to fight the fascism and militarism of which it is a part, it seems to us that we are doing that very thing which all pacifist Christians abhor: we are consciously employing bad means on the theory that to do so will contribute to a good end. . . .

In similar vein, it is urged that great concessions have been won for religious pacifists and that we endanger these by our refusal to accept them. Fascism, as it gradually supplanted democracy in Germany, was aided by the decision of Christians and leftists to accept a partial fascism rather than to endanger those democratic concessions which still remained. It is not alone for our own exemption from fighting that we work—it is for freedom of the American people from fascism and militarism.

Partial exemption of conscientious objectors has come about partly through the work of influential pacifists and partly through the open-mindedness of certain non-pacifists. But it has also been granted because of the fear of the government that, without such a provision, public opposition to war would be too great to handle. In particular, it seems to us that one of the reasons the government has granted exemption to ministers and theological students is to gain a religious sanction for its diabolical war. Where actual support could not be gained, it hoped to soothe their consciences so that they could provide no real opposition.

We do not contend that the American people maliciously choose the vicious instrument of war. In a very perplexing situation, they lack the imagination, the religious faith, and the precedents to respond in a different manner. This makes it all the more urgent to build in this country and throughout the world a group trained in the techniques of non-violent opposition to the encroachments of militarism and fascism. Until we build such a movement, it will be impossible to stall the war machine at home. When we do build such a movement, we will have forged the only weapon which can ever give effective answer to foreign invasion. Thus in learning to fight American Hitlerism we will show an increasing group of war-disillusioned Americans how to resist foreign Hitlers as well.

For these reasons we hereby register our refusal to comply in any way with the Selective Training and Service Act. We do not expect to stem the war forces today; but we are helping to build the movement that will conquer in the future.

Why I Refused to Register in the October 1940 Draft and a Little of What It Led To

DAVID DELLINGER

David Dellinger was a pacifist who believed in nonviolent civil disobedience on behalf of social change. During the Depression, Dellinger, who came from a wealthy background, left Yale in order to live and work among the poor in Newark. He was one of the Chicago Seven, a group of people charged with conspiracy and inciting to riot in Chicago during the 1968 Democratic National Convention. He was convicted, but his conviction was later overturned by an appellate court.

One of my most vivid memories is of the widespread rejoicing I observed—and felt—when World War I came to an end in November 1918, about three months after my third birthday. "Now no one will have to kill other people," is the way my father put it at the time. When I was thirteen, a German officer from that war was invited to speak in our Wakefield, Massachusetts, town hall in a celebration of the tenth anniversary of the ending of the war. Many people spoke out against allowing an "enemy" to speak, but my father and I went to hear him. I was profoundly moved by the German's appeal for the people of the world to work across national boundaries to solve their differences rather than going to war and doing the terrible things that he had done. And it was an early lesson on the gains to be made by following one's own common sense and conscience, rather than being intimidated by self-styled patriots.

Sometime during college I read a book that contained a moving account of something that happened during the Christmas season among soldiers in rival trenches. One night the Germans, as I remember it, started singing Christmas carols. After a while the British also began singing carols. Soon a few soldiers started climbing out of their trenches and singing on the strip of land that separated them. Others joined in and together they shared the Christmas spirit. When dawn came they climbed back into their trenches. I don't remember if the story relates whether or when they resumed shooting at one another. But soldiers in many wars often shoot over the heads of their enemies when they receive orders to fire. My guess is that that's what most of those soldiers did.

Harry Rudin, a history teacher at Yale, participated in that war. He was the first person who told me that quite a few disillusioned soldiers made a point of firing over the heads of opponents rather than trying to kill them. He didn't do this at first, but he soon became horrified enough by the senseless slaughter to start doing so. Though I had no courses with Rudin, we became good friends and he strengthened my determination never to support war. He also had a historical perspective that supported my early anti-Nazism.

An even more inspiring example to me than Gandhi (who offered military support to the British during World War I) was Eugene Victor Debs, the charismatic labor leader who was sentenced to ten years in federal prison for his antiwar speeches. In the end he served only three years because the country had begun to realize that entering the war had been a terrible mistake. Even Woodrow Wilson, the president who had demanded U.S. participation in "A War to Make the World Safe for Democracy," reached a point of utter disillusionment when he said, "Is there any man, woman or child in America—let me repeat, is there any child—who does not know that this was an industrial and commercial war?"

I knew those words by heart long before the United States came close to entering what is known as the Second World War. And I also knew the words of Debs which told me that going to prison could have desirable spiritual consequences. At the time of his sentencing he said, "While there is a lower class I am in it; while there is a criminal element I am of it; while there is a soul in prison I am not free." Debs also said something that encouraged me long before World War II to develop my own conscience and to follow it rather than becoming a follower of role models: "I would not be a Moses to lead you into the Promised Land, because if I could lead you into it someone else could lead you out of it." This became especially relevant when most of the peace leaders from whom I had learned valuable lessons tried to persuade me to register for the 1940 draft.

Even Roger Baldwin, the head of the American Civil Liberties Union who had been jailed in the earlier war, appealed to me to register. Otherwise, he said, I would embarrass the peace organizations that had secured passage of a special nonmilitary assignment for draftees whose religious training forbade them to kill. Primarily the exemption was for Quakers, Mennonites, and Brethren, the so-called "peace churches." And indeed, the head of the American Friends Service Committee, whom I had long admired, tried to persuade me to register so that I could become the director of one of the camps for such draftees. Under my leadership, he argued, it could become a worldwide example of the importance of nonviolence. But I was working with youth gangs in a racially conflicted inner city, and to leave that to supervise nonviolent religionists raking leaves in an isolated geographical area wasn't the kind of nonviolence I believed in. To make it even worse, the rules were set by Gen. Lewis B. Hershey, and he forbade the residents to use their weekends or other spare time to go where other people lived and speak against the war. For a final example, Reinhold Niebuhr, who had inspired me at Yale with his brilliant, deeply religious, anti-imperialist pacifist sermons, went through a subsequent spiritual crisis. He became obsessed with the sinfulness of human beings, including himself, and condemned sinful "addiction" to nonviolence . . . as "arrogant utopianism." The day that I and seven other students at Union were carted off to prison, he preached a sermon in the chapel saying that his greatest failure as a Christian had been his inability to educate us as to the true nature of Christianity. . . .

When I graduated from Yale in 1936, I had won a graduate fellowship to study at Oxford University for two or three years. Before I entered Oxford, I made two trips to Nazi Germany, with a visit to Spain and Italy in between. . . .

Between Spain and Germany I spent a week or more tracing one of the routes of Francis of Assisi through southern Italy, stopping to spend solitary time in each of the little chapels identified with him. Like me, Francis was the son of a rich man but became committed to nonviolence, justice, and sharing. Of course, he went much further than I have in sharing worldly goods with the poor. But after Spain, and from what I had already learned about the challenge of being an anti-Nazi in Germany, I wanted to absorb as much as I could of Francis's spirit before going back for a second visit. . . .

The thirties was a time when the nonviolent Gandhian movement against the British occupation and rule in India was heavily publicized in the U.S. media. In part this was because the revolt was against the British rather than against U.S. imperialism in Cuba, Puerto Rico, Central America, and the Philippines. Also, the rulers of the United States were already aiming to replace British colonialism in much of the world by "more enlightened, more democratic" American imperialism, which was the underlying reason they entered both world wars. In any event, I got more extensive details of the spirit, methods, defeats, and triumphs of the Gandhian campaign than today's media ever prints about nonviolent campaigns for justice within the United States or its territories. In addition, there were radical visitors from the United States to India who supplied additional information that I savored. . . . So, whereas U.S. Communist party members were thrilled to "know" (despite evidence to the contrary) that the Soviet Union was a shining example of Leninist successes, I was thrilled to know that a creative and powerful nonviolent movement for justice and equality existed in India, even if it had not yet achieved most of its objectives. And soon the radical intentional pacifist community that I was a part of in the inner city of Newark was sharing experiences with the Non-violent Ashram . . . in Harlem and with the communitarians in Yellow Springs, Ohio. . . .

Finally, during every April since 1934, there was a day whose growing list of sponsors called for a National Student Strike Against War. Originally it was in response to the Oxford Pledge, in which a large number of students at Oxford pledged that they would never take part in an international war. Soon the pledge and the day of observance grew in this country and became very powerful. I can't remember whether I began to observe this strike in my sophomore year at Yale or slightly later. But for many years before the draft law was passed, many of my friends and I stayed away from classes on that day, holding a variety of public vigils, rallies, and demonstrations. And of course we did this in prison in April 1940. . . .

We eight Union Seminary students spent the first week of our imprisonment in New York City's West Street jail. There we mingled with Louis Lepke, the head of the Mafia, and several of his adjutants. To our surprise, they were friendly to us while saying to me such things as "I am in jail for killing people but you are here for refusing to kill anyone. It doesn't make sense." Or, "I just gave my lawyer a few thousand dollars to lessen my sentence, but all you guys had to do was to sign a paper that wouldn't have required you to do anything, and yet you refused. WOW!" Later, after one of my arrests, I stepped between another Mafioso and a guard who was roughing him up. He thanked me and said something like this: "Like us, you know that the system is based on stealing as much as you can from anyone you can, but unlike us you are trying to work out a better way of living.". . .

After West Street, we were transferred to the Federal Correctional Institution at Danbury, Connecticut. None of the top officials there showed any interest in making it a genuine correctional institution. I walked into the first Saturday night movie with a black man with whom I had been talking. The guard pointed to the white section for me and the black section for him, but I sat next to my friend in the black section. It was not a planned protest, just the instinctive, natural thing to do. Soon I was carried out and placed in a solitary cell in the maximum-security "troublemakers" cell block. Later, war objectors organized a number of protests against racial segregation, both at Danbury and in other prisons, including Lewisburg Penitentiary, where I did two years. When we took such actions, or did other things that I thought were in accord with the best teachings of Jesus and the Jewish prophets, we never received any support or understanding from the Christian chaplains at either Danbury or Lewisburg. But I developed a fruitful relationship with the rabbi [Jerome Malino] at Danbury, who stimulated me spiritually and encouraged me to be true to what I saw as the prophetic heritage. . . .

But at my arrival at the New Jersey jail, the officials had concluded that I must be "yellow," since I was refusing to defend my country militarily. Saying this to my face and to the prisoners in my assigned cell, they asked the prisoners to "take care of this unpatriotic guy." The men they said this to were in a small, overcrowded cell where the most violent prisoners were kept. Later, when I was leaving on my own recognizance, a slightly nicer guard said that he hadn't approved of where I had been put but hoped that I had learned how evil prisoners and Nazis can be and had given up my ideas that nonviolence is a practical way of combating them. Despite all this, I was clearly saved from what might have happened to me—not by my own efforts, but because this was the prison where, on my arrival, I had intervened when a Mafioso was being roughed up by a guard. Word of what had happened came rather quickly to the "worthless, evil" prisoners in the cell where I had been assigned and, step by step, several of them became my friends.

Not long after I arrived at Lewisburg, five of us conducted a long hunger strike for abolishing "the Hole," and eliminating the censorship of mail, books, and magazines. Winning the issue on censorship and feeling that the issue of the Hole had reached a fairly wide audience on the outside through prison visitors and progressive publicity, we stopped the strike on the sixty-fifth day (after a month of force feeding). The next day I was put in the "f— up dorm," which had a high percentage of southern military prisoners who had committed violent crimes. One of the two guards who took me there addressed the prisoners as follows: "This guy is one of those phonies who says he's too good to be in a regular prison with you." This was a total lie. Unlike a few war objectors, I had always opposed special classification and treatment as a political prisoner. "He's a nigger-lover who says that you guys should eat and sleep with the niggers and use the same toilets and showers as niggers do." True. "And he's a Nazi who spits on the flag and refuses to fight for our country." And, after a pause, as if to let his words sink in, "We're leaving now so that you guys can take care of him." Just before they closed the door, the other guard spoke for the first time: "When we come back, we hope you give him to us with his head in his hands.". . . .

I survived, though there were times . . . when I didn't expect to. . . .

This was only one of several times in Lewisburg when prisoners were asked to "take care of Dellinger," sometimes with the offer of parole if they did. But this was the most difficult occasion for me to handle because of my exhaustion from the long hunger strike. A few years later I wasn't surprised at something Dorothy Day, the co-founder of the Catholic Worker movement, said when she visited me and Elizabeth [Dellinger's wife] at our international pacifist community. It was the day after William Remington, a former commerce department official who was a victim of the McCarthy era, had been killed at Lewisburg. "You don't believe the official version, do you?" she asked. "That he was killed by a prisoner who was stealing his cigarettes when Remington came back to his cell and caught him?" Based on our similar prison experiences, we agreed that officials had asked some prisoners to kill him, probably saying something like, "He's a dirty Communist, so why don't you get rid of him. If you do, we'll reward you with parole, or time off your long sentence."

Is it any wonder that in my resume I include under "Education" the following:

Three years' imprisonment at Danbury, Connecticut, Federal Correctional Institution (1940–41) and Lewisburg, Pennsylvania, Federal Penitentiary (1942–45) [for refusal to register for the draft, even though I was militarily exempt as a divinity student]. Occasional refresher courses in other jails. Yale University B.A., magna cum laude, 1936; Henry Fellow to New College, Oxford, 1936–37; year and a half of courses at Yale Divinity School and Union Theological Seminary (1937–39).

I Think I'll Sit This One Out

MILTON S. MAYER

Milton Mayer was born in 1908 to a German Jewish father and an English-born mother. In the early 1950s he became a member of the Society of Friends, or Quakers. An author and journalist who opposed war and championed civil liberties, Mayer wrote the article that appears here for the Saturday Evening Post, *October 7, 1939.*

When I was in college, ten years ago, the bright young men were taking the [antiwar] Oxford oath. I was one of the bright young men, but I didn't take the Oxford oath. Of course I wasn't going to fight in any more imperialist wars, but something told me that the rest of the boys were. Something told me that these peacetime pacifists were bad company. Something told me that they wouldn't fight in any more imperialist wars except the next one. So I didn't take the Oxford oath.

Sure enough, I'm all alone now, as I was then. Of a dozen college friends, all of them the noisiest kind of slackers back in 1929, only one of them isn't itching to get his hands on a gun. He says he's going underground when we enter the war, and he's going to work for the revolution, and he wants to know if I'm with him. No, I'm against him, and it isn't because I've fallen for the democracy bunk again. It's because I haven't fallen for the democracy bunk or the revolution bunk either. I'm going to sit this one out for reasons all my own.

I think I know what brought the rest of the peacetime pacifists around, and I'm not sure that another batch of Hun atrocities—beg pardon, Nazi atrocities—won't bring me around. I'm afraid that when the bands start playing I'll get in line. I'm afraid that when the heat is on me, when the finger points, when "America calls," I'll grab a gun, and the girls will throw roses and the home folks will say, "There's Mayer; right there in the front."

To Fight or Not to Fight

I can make my decision now, to go or not to go, and, as in any prejudg-
ment, take the chance of having decided wrong. Or I can postpone my
decision as events move closer and closer. Today I have the prudence essential to making a choice. Will I have it tomorrow, a month from now,
six months from now, as the war fever rises around me? I know, of
course, that I can't really make a choice until I meet the problem face to
face. But I know, too, that as the war fever rises, as the emotional sweep
of events rolls up, there comes a time when I can no longer exercise the
prudence that enables me to choose. When that time comes I may still
think I am choosing, but my choice will be dictated by my hysteria.

I do not face this problem, now or when we enter the war, by thanking God that I am overage or flat-footed. I do not face this problem by
announcing that because of religious or conscientious scruples I will
sing psalms or empty bedpans behind the lines. I do not face this problem by getting a bombproof job in Washington while the goofs go out
and stop the bullets. There is only one way to face this problem, and
that is to face it. I have to decide, now or when we enter the war, to
stand up and fight or to stand up and oppose the war.

And so I exercise such prudence as the unpredictable future permits
and I make my decision now. I make my decision to oppose this war, to
oppose it now and when America enters it, and I make that decision despite my horror of "the Berchtesgaden maniac" and my disinclination to
set myself up as martyr to my ideals. I oppose the current war for three
reasons. I think it will destroy democracy. I think it will bring no peace.
And I think it will degrade humanity. And after I have explained what
I mean, I shall try to answer the arguments of the peacetime pacifists.

Let me imagine that, as an average citizen of Massachusetts Bay
Colony, I went to war, one fine day in 1755, in defense of home and
fireside against the French and Indians. I subsequently learn that I
fought and bled for the capricious benefit of a couple of kings, for the
profit of traders and pirates, and against some innocent dispossessed

red men. In 1763 I declare, with finality, that I will sit the next one out. Then, one day in July, 1776, I read a poster on the door of the town hall: "When, in the course of human events, it becomes necessary—" Do I stick by my decision of a few years before? Am I swept off my feet by patriot passion? Or have I prudence sufficient to decide that this war is just?

Today I am sure that the second world war is no more just than the first. Conditions may change tomorrow, a month from now, six months from now, to make it a just war. But I doubt that they will, and I have to decide on the basis of doubt or postpone my decision until I no longer know how to decide.

This is not an easy problem. If it were, it would not be worth arguing. I suppose there are just wars—wars which save more human lives than they destroy. But this war is like the last one, and the last one was not one of them. I suppose there are times when men must bestialize themselves in one last desperate effort to preserve their liberty. But this is not one of them. I see no justice in saving Poland's ghetto benches from Hitler. If I did, I would not wait for "my country's call"; I would get out and fight today.

This war is being fought, we are told, to save the world for democracy, or, if that expression is a little too reminiscent, simply to save democracy.

In 1917, Mr. Wilson and the elder statesmen assured us we were going to war for democracy. But while the air of the United States Senate grew fetid and fervent with the praise of democracy on the afternoon of April 4, 1917, the country's most ingenuous statesman pulled himself to his feet. "I am not voting for war in the name of democracy," said Warren Gamaliel Harding, "but for the maintenance of just American rights." Senator Harding's remarks were not widely quoted in the patriotic meetings of the next two years.

There was another speech in the Senate that day that was not widely quoted in respectable company afterward. Six men voted against the declaration of war. They were not typical elder statesmen, and their spokesman was the least typical of all. "I think, sir," said Robert Marion La Follette, "if we take this step, when the people today who are staggering under the burden of supporting families find prices multiplied, when those who pay taxes come to have their taxes doubled . . . there will come an awakening." Twenty years later, three fourths of the American people, according to the Gallup poll, had awakened to the fact that La Follette, Gronna, Lane, Stone, Vardaman and Norris voted right.

Democracy? Democracy made strange bedfellows in 1917. There was, for example, the leadership of the democrats at home. Mr. Samuel Insull, who lived to announce his preference for Fascist Italy and Nazi Germany to "a state whose policies were at the mercy of an uninformed rabble," was chairman of the Defense Committee of my state. Then there was the alliance with the democrats abroad—with the Romanoffs of Russia, the Savoys of Italy and the Mikado of Japan, to name a few. We may compare the map of the world today with the map of 1914 and see at a glance just how much of the world was saved for democracy, and how much lost. And if we conclude that the first World War destroyed Hohenzollern only to give us Hitler, we must consider it at least an even probability that the second will give us a Hitler as much worse than Hitler as Hitler is worse than Hohenzollern.

Just how much different, from the standpoint of democracy, is the second war from the first? It is a broad but suggestive exaggeration that if the Axis, after Munich, had only left England's imperial interests alone, Mr. Chamberlain would have been back in Munich in a month offering Hitler France. If we call the roll of our prospective allies in the current war for democracy, we find that the tyrant Stalin has lately departed us; but with us still, in the war for democracy, are the tyrant Smigly-Rydz [Poland], the tyrant Metaxas [Greece], the tyrant Carol [Romania], the tyranny of the French in Syria and the tyranny of the British in India and the Straits Settlements. Domestically we shall certainly have with us numerous individuals and institutions whose devotion to democracy is debatable.

I do not want Hitler to rule the world, and if he wins this war he will. The trouble is that if we win it he will rule the world anyway. "Autocracy" and "Prussianism" were crushed twenty years ago with the lives of millions of men and the money that reduced the world to poverty. And the map of the world today shows us how well they were crushed.

Of course it won't be Hitler twenty years from now. Hitler will have retired to Doorn. But Hitlerism, Prussianism, or whatever you want to call it, will be as much closer to ruling the world of 1960 as it is closer today than in 1920.

I am trying to keep my eye on the ball in spite of my hatred of a man called Hitler. Who is this Hitler, anyway? A man, like the rest of us, a man capable, like the rest of us, of acting like a man; but a man brutalized, as the rest of us may be, by war and the poverty of war and the animal degradation of war—a man, in short, behaving like an animal. Fascism is animalism. The wolves are Fascists; the bees have the perfect Fascist state. It is not Hitler I must fight, but Fascism. And I know, from philosophy and from science, from the Bible and from Freud, that it is not the sinner I must exorcise, but the sin. If I want to beat Fascism, I cannot beat it at its own game. War is at once the essence and the apotheosis, the beginning and the triumph, of Fascism, and when I go to war I join "Hitler's" popular front against the man in men. I cannot fight animals their way without turning animal myself.

The Shackles of War

I believe that this war, if we enter it, will destroy the democracy we have as a nation. When a nation goes to war—not just sends an expeditionary force, but really goes—everything physical and spiritual in that nation must necessarily be placed at the service of the state. And however eloquent and elegant the slogans, that is Fascism. For as democracy, in its simplest statement, is an order in which the state exists for men, so Fascism is an order in which men exist for the state. And in no condition to which men submit do they exist for the state so completely as in war.

Let me cite here the first World War and its effect on the American democratic system. Our war veterans—and only about one fourth of them saw actual service—are not distinguished for tolerance, that hallmark of democracy. Our civilians—and only a handful of them saw more than Sugarless Sundays and Liberty Loans—endorsed and engaged in an orgy of repression. The disappearance of human rights during that period—like Lincoln's suspension of habeas corpus—is forgotten because the war closed before the machinery of repression was more than beginning to operate. The postwar terrorism of Attorney General Palmer may likewise be forgotten by this time, along with the announcement of the national commander of the American Legion that "the Fascisti are to Italy what the American Legion is to the United States.". . .

The Law of the Pack

If the experience of war taught us anything except war, our veterans would be the most pacifistic of men. The difficulty with planning an equitable peace before entering the war is that war makes men incapable of writing an equitable peace. When men fight well, they fight like wolves, and the only equity among wolves, when the fight is over, is "winner takes all."

Equity rests on reason, not on force. Man is man, not because he possesses the animal power of force but because he also possesses the human power of reason. That power is always in contest with the animal power of force. The man in whom reason holds sway, in private and civil life we call a reasonable man; we honor and envy him and look to him for leadership. The man in whom force holds sway we call a brute and, unless we cherish a brutal society, we lock him up. Because we know that all men have brute in them, we write laws to restrain the brute in all of us. Reason is its own governor, and governor of the brute in all of us besides.

Democracy rests on the ability of men to govern themselves. The word "govern" is the key to the relative places of reason and force in democracy. It is not reason that has to be governed in men, but force. And the only man who can govern himself is the man who can govern his animal passions. Men under Fascism have their animal passions governed, not by themselves and the reason they possess, but by the animal passions of others.

I cannot see how we can have, or save, democratic states without democratic men, without men in whom reason governs. War, like Fascism, teaches men two things: How to be governed by the force of others; and how, the force of others permitting, to be governed by the force within themselves. If the worst thing that can happen to men is to come under the rule of the tooth and the claw, I cannot see why men should come under that rule voluntarily by going to war.

"But you can't argue with a madman." No, you can't. You have to use force, and your victory depends on your superior force. But war makes "madmen" of us all, and no balance of power that was ever devised remained in balance very long. For the victor grows fat and the vanquished grow lean, and the time comes when the vanquished have to fight and see their chance. Carl Sandburg's line might well be engraved above the doors of every foreign ministry in the world: "There are not nails enough to nail down victory."

The Problem of Persecution

Last winter the Nazis unleashed a terrible pogrom against the Jews. Of course, I was horrified—horrified at each new and horrible denial of the inalienable dignity of human beings. But these denials are as old as man himself. They did not begin with the Hohenzollerns or the Hitlers, or even with the Caesars or the Pharaohs, and they have not ended with Mayor Hague. . . .

Still, hardened as I am, I was moved by something that happened in a suburb of Berlin one day last February. I think the incident, reported in a few lines by the Associated Press, had something to do with my present decision. A crowd of children had driven an old Jew from his candy store and were carrying out great sacks of candy while their parents stood around cheering them. An old man walked up, an "Aryan." He watched the proceedings with a troubled look, and then he turned to the cheering parents and said to them: "You think you are hurting the Jew. You do not know what you are doing. You are teaching your children to steal." And the old man walked away.

That is my case against war, my peacetime pacifists. Let me hear your case for this one. The first thing you tell me is that I may be right in a vacuum, but "we've got to fight to save our skins. Self-preservation is the first law of Nature." All right; let's look at that one. All of you will agree with me that our skins are not our most valuable possessions. If they were, you wouldn't be so easily drawn into war. All of you will agree with me that dearer than life itself is liberty; and if, as we surely must, we have to lose our liberty when we lose our lives, we may still preserve our children's liberties. So it seems that saving our skins is not what we fight for. . . .

If I can be shown some way to stop Hitler, I'll go along. "We have no quarrel with the German people," said President Wilson in his War Message. But it was the German people whom we shot, and the forces with whom we really had a quarrel grew and festered, and festered and grew, until they flowered in Hitlerism. And now we are asked to shoot the German people again. Mr. Jay Gould is supposed to have said he could hire half the workers to shoot down the other half. When we enter this war we do Mr. Gould's work for him for free. . . .

Free Men or Brutes?

Some of my friends agree with me on some of these issues, but they all agree with one another that, as between war and neutrality in the present situation, war is the lesser of two evils. Just what does "the lesser of two evils" mean? It seems to me to mean that alternative choices are always narrowed to two—both of them, by definition, evil. It means that in choosing the lesser evil the world grows worse a little slower than if the greater evil is chosen. This is the essence of Greek tragedy, in which the central figure has so long postponed decision that he is left, in the end, with two choices, either of which is fatal.

I cannot concede that the world is condemned and that the only question is whether we shall enjoy a few years' or a century's stay of execution. I cannot concede that our civilization is through, that we have to risk collapse now or certainly get it later. And it is not because I am mystical. It is because I know who makes these wars that pull down civilizations. It is not stones, or fences, or clouds. It is men. And unless we acknowledge our responsibility, along with our rights, as men, I cannot see how we can claim our rights. If we are only animals, as incapable of solving our central problem as other animals, why, then, Hitler has justice with him when he treats men like animals. For the only justice among animals is the justice of the strong.

The question ultimately is whether we are free men or brutes. The house of a man, like the house of a nation, cannot stand divided against itself. If we are men with reason and free will, we have to choose and act upon our choice. Hobbes defines the state of nature as a state of war, and peace in the state of nature as "when there is no war." I may hold too high an opinion of myself and all other men, but I cannot concede that peace in the state of society must, like peace in the state of nature, rest upon accident. I cannot concede that men must live in that state in which life, in Hobbes' words, is "nasty, brutish, and short.". . . I think I can rise above the state of nature, and if I can, so can all men.

The choice is not between the lesser of two evils. The choice is among two evils and an alternative good. The evils, less and greater, fluctuate. The good remains the same, everywhere and in every age, and no matter whether there is war or peace. The human good is the good of reason and free will, and I cannot be persuaded, contrarily, that force is the answer to force, that hate is the antidote for hate, and that war will save the world from war. "For all they that take the sword," said a very wise man two thousand years ago, "shall perish with the sword," and according to my exegesis "all" means "all."

"But," says one of the reformed slackers, "that's the way the world is. I know it's bad, but that's the way it is, and we have to make the best of it." The best of a bad world is not very good. The real victories of men have been won by cultivating, not the world that is, but the world that should be. Must we admit, despite all our fine talk of human liberty, that we have to do as the Hitlers do? Someday, somewhere, some generation will have to say: "Oh, no. All the other holy wars were phony, and this one looks too much like them."

What Will Save Us

If the world is bad the way it is, we can start building a better one. And we can't postpone the building for just one more war any more than the drunkard can postpone the cure for just one more drink. The Pax Romana is the peace of a tired world, a world too tired and sore to build. This building of a better world is a long pull. It has taken us five thousand years to build the poor world we have; it may take us a few hundred, or a few thousand, years to build a better one. I have simply decided, a little egotistically perhaps, that I want to start now, to give my children and their children something to build on. They cannot build on the wreck and ruin of this war and, what is more, they won't even want to.

If I believed that force would ever build a better world, I would be a Marxist revolutionary. But I have no more faith in poor men's animalism than in rich men's. And I want no proletarian revolution until the proletariat has demonstrated a devotion to reason which the rich, with their larger opportunities to cultivate that virtue, have so universally failed to achieve. I favor the underdog against the upperdog, but I favor something better than a dog above both of them.

Socialism may be all right when men are fit to be Socialists. The way may be hard and slow, but until we take it we shall find that the so-called Socialist state degenerates into Fascism as rapidly as the pacifists with warm hearts degenerate into militarists with fevered brows.

Marxism, like Fascism and capitalism, is materialism. The love of material goods above all others is as animal as the love of war. The love of justice above material goods must save us in the end, if saved we may be.

Justice alone knows liberty, equality, and fraternity, and justice is a human virtue arising from man's human capacity to reason. We cannot make sense out of justice by looking at the moon or taking dope or building battleships. We can make sense out of justice by using our reason to discover why justice, like wisdom, is better than rubies.

It is a sensible military tactic to recognize the enemy before you shoot. The common enemy is the animality in man, and not the men here and there who are behaving like animals at the moment. Neither science nor prayer nor force will save us. What will save us is the reason that enables men, in ancient Israel or modern America, to choose between guns and butter, and to choose well. When we have produced men of reason, we shall have a world of reason, and the Hitlers will disappear. As long as we produce men of force we shall have a world of force, and the Hitlers, whoever wins the wars, will carry the day.

Society may make many demands on me, as long as it keeps me out of the cave. It may take my property. It may take my life. But when it puts me back into the cave I must say, politely but firmly, to hell with society. My ancestors were cannibals without benefit of parliaments.

My friends conclude that I can't be "reasoned with," and they agree to gang up on me with one last ad hominem appeal. "What good can you do in jail?" they ask. "A Debs, yes. But whoever heard of Mayer? Who cares if Mayer opposes the war?" And my answer is that Mayer is indeed inconsequential, but a thousand Mayers, a million Mayers, ten million Mayers, may prove to be too many to ignore. And if there are only a hundred Mayers this time, their example may produce a thousand Mayers next time. That will mean a lot of wars until the Mayers are heard, but I can wait.

And if there is only one Mayer, his case against this war remains the same. That one Mayer will have to take his kicking around like the man he claims to be, and he may not get a chance to open his mouth, much less build a better world. But he will have taken his stand, not because he thinks God or the big battalions are with him but because he can take no other. And he will have to say, with William the Silent, that it is not necessary to hope in order to undertake, nor to succeed in order to persevere.

7

The Cold War

*Will . . . the threat of extermination continue? . . . Must chil-
dren receive the arms race from us as a necessary inheritance?*
                                            —Pope John Paul II

*Ours is a world of nuclear giants and ethical infants. We
know more about war than we know about peace, more
about killing than we know about living.*
                                            —General Omar Bradley

The policy of global interventionism that the U.S. government
adopted during the Cold War with the Soviet Union enjoyed wide
bipartisan support. What little opposition existed came from progressive Democrats and conservative Republicans. Congressman
Howard Buffett (R-NE), for example, complained on the House floor
that not a peep of opposition to the so-called Truman Doctrine
(which called for an ambitious program of global intervention) could
be heard among the political class, in the face of what he called "probably the most far-reaching change in American foreign policy in one
hundred years."

Many of its opponents contend it starts us on the road of militarism and imperialism. Whatever its consequences are, I rise to propound a solemn question. How, in the existing political framework of this Nation, can the people of America, if they so desire, effectively oppose this policy? The policy is sponsored by the Democratic Party and collaborated in by the Republican leadership. If the people disapprove of this adventure, as many polls indicate, what recourse is left them when neither party provides the vehicle for effective opposition? When the Republican leadership, without consulting the people, does a "me too" on decisive issues, what method do the people then have to effectively influence governmental policies? Under this situation it would appear that the people are losing the all-important right to approve or reject decisive policies at the ballot box. For, as matters now stand, neither party affords the people the opportunity to effectively oppose this global program.

Buffett concluded with an appeal to Republican leaders: "I respectfully urge the Republican leaders responsible for this collaboration to explain this situation fairly and forthrightly to the American people. The people are entitled to a full explanation of a political performance which apparently deprives the people of an effective voice in determining America's future."

That, stripped to its essentials, was the true nature of America's much-heralded "bipartisan foreign policy": a foreign policy whose fundamentals were hardly ever questioned, and to which Americans were never presented with alternatives.

In the wake of the 1948 communist coup in Czechoslovakia, General Lucius Clay, commander in chief of U.S. forces in Europe, declared that war "may come with dramatic suddenness." Years later, when asked by his biographer what had led him to make those remarks, Clay confessed that policymakers in Washington had urged him to do so. "General [Stephen J.] Chamberlin . . . told me that the Army was having trouble getting the draft reinstituted and they needed a strong message from me that they could use in congressional testimony. So I wrote this cable."

That kind of hysteria was not exactly unusual. As we now know, Soviet capabilities were consistently exaggerated during the Cold War. When conservatives complained in the 1970s that the CIA was understating the Soviet threat, a group of outside experts (that included Paul Wolfowitz) known as Team B was established to render an independent judgment. As it turns out, not only were Team B's assessments grossly exaggerated, but even the CIA's supposedly low estimate had overstated true Soviet strength.

The Soviet Union may be long gone, but the military-industrial complex that got such a boost from the Cold War, and the interventionist thinking that came to dominate policymaking circles, are as strong as ever.

A Turning Point in American History

HENRY A. WALLACE

Henry A. Wallace was vice president of the United States from 1941 until 1945, when he became secretary of commerce. He also served as secretary of agriculture for much of the 1930s. As the 1948 presidential nominee of the Progressive Party, Wallace questioned the Cold War consensus and called for a less militaristic foreign policy.

Wallace delivered this speech on the Truman Doctrine on March 27, 1947.

March 12, 1947, marked a turning point in American history. It is not a Greek crisis that we face, it is an American crisis. It is a crisis in the American spirit. . . . Only the American people fully aroused and promptly acting can prevent disaster.

President Truman, in the name of democracy and humanitarianism, proposed a military lend-lease program. He proposed a loan of

$400,000,000 to Greece and Turkey as a down payment on an unlimited expenditure aimed at opposing Communist expansion. He proposed, in effect, that America police Russia's every border. There is no regime too reactionary for us provided it stands in Russia's expansionist path. There is no country too remote to serve as the scene of a contest which may widen until it becomes a world war.

President Truman calls for action to combat a crisis. What is this crisis that necessitates Truman going to Capitol Hill as though a Pearl Harbor has suddenly hit us? How many more of these Pearl Harbors will there be? How can they be foreseen? What will they cost?. . .

One year ago at Fulton, Missouri, Winston Churchill called for a diplomatic offensive against Soviet Russia. By sanctioning that speech, Truman committed us to a policy of combating Russia with British sources. That policy proved to be so bankrupt that Britain can no longer maintain it. Now President Truman proposes we take over Britain's hopeless task. Today Americans are asked to support the governments of Greece and Turkey. Tomorrow we shall be asked to support the governments of China and Argentina.

I say that this policy is utterly futile. No people can be bought. America cannot afford to spend billions and billions of dollars for unproductive purposes. The world is hungry and insecure, and the peoples of all lands demand change. President Truman cannot prevent change in the world any more than he can prevent the tide from coming in or the sun from setting. But once America stands for opposition to change, we are lost. America will become the most hated nation in the world.

Russia may be poor and unprepared for war, but she knows very well how to reply to Truman's declaration of economic and financial pressure. All over the world Russia and her ally, poverty, will increase the pressure against us. Who among us is ready to predict that in this struggle American dollars will outlast the grievances that lead to communism? I certainly don't want to see communism spread. I predict that Truman's policy will spread communism in Europe and Asia. You can't

Courtesy of the Fellowship of Reconciliation.

A young man receives a leaflet from one of fifty conscientious objectors staging a demonstration in 1948 in Los Angeles a few days before nationwide draft registration began.

fight something with nothing. When Truman offers unconditional aid to King George of Greece, he is acting as the best salesman communism ever had. In proposing this reckless adventure, Truman is betraying the great tradition of America and the leadership of the great American who preceded him. . . .

When President Truman proclaims the worldwide conflict between East and West, he is telling the Soviet leaders that we are preparing for eventual war. They will reply by measures to strengthen their position in the event of war. Then the task of keeping the world at peace will pass beyond the power of the common people everywhere who want peace. Certainly it will not be freedom that will be victorious in this struggle. Psychological and spiritual preparation for war will follow financial preparation; civil liberties will be restricted; standards of living will be forced downward; families will be divided against each other; none of the values that we hold worth fighting for will be secure. . . .

This is the time for an all-out worldwide reconstruction program for peace. This is America's opportunity. The peoples of all lands say to America: Send us plows for our fields instead of tanks and guns to be used against us. . . . The dollars that are spent will be spent for the production of goods and will come back to us in a thousand different ways. Our programs will be based on service instead of the outworn ideas of imperialism and power politics. It is a fundamental law of life that a strong idea is merely strengthened by persecution. The way to handle communism is by what William James called the replacing power of the higher affection. In other words, we give the common man all over the world something better than communism. I believe we have something better than communism here in America. But President Truman has not spoken for the American ideal. It is now the turn of the American people to speak.

Common sense is required of all of us in realizing that helping militarism never brings peace. Courage is required of all of us in carrying out a program that can bring peace. Courage and common sense are the qualities that made America great. Let's keep those qualities now.

===

The President Has No Right to Involve the United States in a Foreign War

SENATOR ROBERT A. TAFT

Senator Robert A. Taft, known in his day as "Mr. Republican," was the most prominent of the Republican noninterventionists who greeted Harry Truman's early Cold War policies with skepticism. Taft was critical of the Truman Doctrine and NATO, both of which he viewed as either unnecessarily provocative or ruinously expensive.

Then as now, voices of mainstream liberalism adopted the interventionist line against the heretic: Taft, wrote the prominent liberal columnist Richard Rovere, was an unsuitable presidential candidate in 1948 since the next president "should be an executive of the human race . . . who will boldly champion freedom before the world and for the world . . . [which] Taft simply could not do." Likewise, the Nation *called Taft and his allies in Congress "super-appeasers" whose policies "should set the bells ringing in the Kremlin."*

Here Taft speaks (on March 29, 1951) on the Senate floor against the war powers claimed by President Truman, who involved the United States in the Korean War without a declaration of war from Congress. The speech is actually a quite learned disquisition on the subject, from which we may provide only the barest excerpts. He refers to historian Henry Steele Commager, who—along with another liberal historian, Arthur Schlesinger, Jr.—tried to argue that his view of the president's war powers was historically indefensible and that the president had every right to deploy troops on his own authority. By the 1960s both historians admitted that they had been wrong, but their earlier denunciations of Taft reveal the bipartisan and cross-ideological nature of what some have called the War Party in America.

I desire this afternoon to discuss only the question of the power claimed by the President to send troops anywhere in the world and involve us in any war in the world and involve us in any war in which he chooses to involve us. I wish to assert the powers of Congress, and to point out that Congress has the power to prevent any such action by the President; that he has no such power under the Constitution; and that it is incumbent upon the Congress to assert clearly its own constitutional powers unless it desires to lose them. . . . We [in Congress] should state clearly the reasons why we believe the President has no such power as he claims.

In the long run, the question we must decide involves vitally, I think, not only the freedom of the people of the United States. More and more as the world grows smaller we are involved in problems of foreign

Senator Robert A. Taft (R-Ohio), son of William Howard Taft, a former U.S. president and Supreme Court justice, is pictured speaking at the National Press Club in Washington, D.C., in 1952. A conservative, and the most influential Republican of his era, he was dubbed Mr. Republican. He opposed most military interventions and uncontrolled domestic spending.

Courtesy of the Cincinnati Historical Society Library and the Cincinnati Museum Center.

policy. If in the great field of foreign policy the President has arbitrary and unlimited power, as he now claims, then there is an end to freedom in the United States in a great realm of domestic activity which affects, in the long run, every person in the United States.

If the President has unlimited power to involve us in war, war is more likely. History shows that when the people have the opportunity to speak, as a rule the people decide for peace. It shows that arbitrary rulers are more inclined to favor war than are the people, at any time. . . .

A document has been submitted to Congress entitled "Powers of the President to Send the Armed Forces Outside the United States." It is dated February 23, 1951. . . .

The document ends up with the most sweeping claims for power I have ever seen. It says on page 27:

As this discussion of the respective powers of the President and the Congress in this field has made clear, constitutional doctrine has been largely molded by practical necessities. Use of the congressional power to declare war, for example, has fallen into abeyance because wars are no longer declared in advance.

Those who prepared this document wipe out the power of Congress to declare war, and state in effect that the President can declare war whenever he so desires.

The constitutional power of the Commander in Chief—

has been exercised more often because the need for armed international action has grown more acute.

Apparently they claim that whenever the need for armed international action grows acute the President can undertake such action.

The long delays occasioned by the slowness of communications in the eighteenth century have given place to breath-taking rapidity in the tempo of history. Repelling aggression in Korea or Europe cannot wait upon congressional debate. However, while the need for speed and the growth in the size and complexity of the Armed Forces have enlarged the area in which the powers of the Commander in Chief are to be wielded, the magnitude of present-day military operations and international policies requires a degree of congressional support that was unnecessary in the days of the nineteenth century.

That is a very gracious concession to Congress. We no longer have any power to act; we are simply given the right to support the President after the President has acted.

Mr. President, I could not well permit this document to remain on the records of the Congress without asserting my belief that it presents an utterly false view of the Constitution of the United States; that most of the claims are wholly unsound; that the authorities cited do not support the conclusions which are reached; that there should be now a distinct repudiation by Congress, in its own action, of the claims made in this particular document. . . .

As soon as I made my first speech, the *New York Times* rushed to get Professor Commager to throw together in a day or two a superficial article, published in its Sunday magazine at that time, in which he asserts that the President has the right to start war whenever he sees fit to do so.

Time magazine makes the offhand statement that history books have listed more than 130 cases where United States Presidents sent United States armed troops into action "to defend the national interest.". . .

Mr. President, most of the cases which have been referred to . . . are cases where the use of our troops was limited to the protection of American citizens or to the protection of American property. . . .

I deny the conclusions of the documents presented by the President or by the executive department, and I would say that if the doctrines therein proclaimed prevailed, they would bring an end to government by the people, because our foreign interests are going gradually to predominate and require a larger and larger place in the field of the activities of our people.

When we add to this the danger which results from the wide powers given by treaties to international commissions to interfere in many American affairs, when we add the unlimited power of the President to fix the policy and the operations under the reciprocal-trade agreements, when we add the theory that the President can do anything by executive agreement without submitting such an executive agreement to the Senate for approval, as a treaty; when we reflect on the general ideas prevalent today of a planned economy for the world, I think it is fair to say that if we yield in this field of foreign policy we will find the President of the United States as arbitrary a dictator over the people of this country as were dictators in many other countries where they gradually gained power. . . .

Mr. President, there is one very definite limit—and I think it is admitted by every responsible authority who has discussed the problem—on the President's power to send troops abroad: He cannot send troops abroad if the sending of such troops amounts to the making of war. I think that has been frequently asserted; and whenever any broad statements have been made as to the President's power as Commander in Chief to send troops anywhere in the world, the point has been made that it is always subject to that particular condition. . . .

Dwight Eisenhower on the Military-Industrial Complex

On January 17, 1961, President Dwight Eisenhower delivered a farewell address to the nation that would be remembered for its warning about the dangers posed by the "military-industrial complex." The president acknowledged that the United States was faced with a new phenomenon in its history: a large military establishment combined with a large arms industry. These forces, and the friendly interaction between them, may influence American policy in ways that could damage the interests and well-being of the American people.

Eisenhower's statements proved prophetic, as a mountain of scholarship has since shown. The relationship between the military and the defense industry has grown much closer than Eisenhower could have imagined. "Upon retirement," explained economic historian Robert Higgs in 1995, "thousands of military officers found immediate employment with the [defense] contractors, while industry officials routinely occupied high-ranking positions in the Pentagon bureaucracy during leaves from their firms. It was easy to forget who worked for whom. As General James P. Mullins, former commander of the Air Force Logistics Command, remarked, the defense business 'is not business as usual among independent parties. This is a family affair among terribly interdependent parties.'"

The defense industry—or, more accurately, arms manufacture—has proven unusually profitable. When Higgs and Ruben Trevino investigated the top fifty defense contractors during the period 1970 to 1989, they found that those companies earned substantially higher profits than comparable

firms in other industries. One wonders: how many retired generals who call
for war on cable news channels are, in their retirement, consultants for some
defense firm—and why is their war advocacy not a clear conflict of interest?

By including this excerpt from Eisenhower's speech we wish to reveal
something about the evolution of our country over the past half century:
what was once treated as a serious danger against which a vigilant people
had to guard itself is now no longer even mentioned, much less made the
subject of a solemn warning, in either the mainstream media or the halls of
government—with the exception of a maverick like Ron Paul.

Our military organization today bears little relation to that known by
any of my predecessors in peacetime, or indeed by the fighting men of
World War II or Korea.

Until the latest of our world conflicts, the United States had no armaments industry. American makers of plowshares could, with time
and as required, make swords as well. But now we can no longer risk
emergency improvisation of national defense; we have been compelled
to create a permanent armaments industry of vast proportions. Added
to this, three and a half million men and women are directly engaged in
the defense establishment. We annually spend on military security more
than the net income of all United States corporations.

This conjunction of an immense military establishment and a large
arms industry is new in the American experience. The total influence—
economic, political, even spiritual—is felt in every city, every state
house, every office of the Federal government. We recognize the imperative need for this development. Yet we must not fail to comprehend its
grave implications. Our toil, resources and livelihood are all involved; so
is the very structure of our society.

In the councils of government, we must guard against the acquisition
of unwarranted influence, whether sought or unsought, by the military-
industrial complex. The potential for the disastrous rise of misplaced
power exists and will persist.

We must never let the weight of this combination endanger our liberties or democratic processes. We should take nothing for granted. Only an alert and knowledgeable citizenry can compel the proper meshing of the huge industrial and military machinery of defense with our peaceful methods and goals, so that security and liberty may prosper together. . . .

Those Who Protest: The Transformation of the Conservative Movement

ROBERT LEFEVRE

Robert LeFevre (1911–1986) was a businessman and radio personality, and the founder of the Freedom School in Colorado Springs, Colorado, whose purpose was to educate people from all walks of life in the libertarian intellectual tradition. Before it closed in 1968, it had featured among its rotating faculty Rose Wilder Lane, Milton Friedman, F. A. Harper, Frank Chodorov, Leonard Read, Gordon Tullock, G. Warren Nutter, Bruno Leoni, James J. Martin, and even Ludwig von Mises. He published the following as a leaflet in 1964.

We hear a great deal today about the "conservative movement." A brief review of its history may be in order.

Prior to the appearance of F. D. Roosevelt as president, the term was not used with any frequency to designate a particular group of persons. Rather, it was employed to signify an attitude, a point of reference which might relate to politics and equally might relate to science, religion, business, home life or a moral outlook.

Mr. Roosevelt's appearance as the major political figure of his time had an enormous effect upon the thinking of millions of Americans. Some were prone to accept him as the leader without a peer. Others were prone to oppose him and to recognize in his policies a turning away from the traditional stance of America as it related to citizens vis-à-vis their government.

It was at this juncture that the terms "conservative" and "liberal" took on other meanings than those classically employed. It was no longer sufficient to say of a person that he was a Republican or a Democrat.

These party labels began to slip into a hyphenated position. There were conservative-Republicans and conservative-Democrats. There were liberal-Republicans and liberal-Democrats. It became more important to know whether a person was a conservative or a liberal than to know what political party secured his allegiance.

The conservative position in the 1930s became the position of opposition to Roosevelt and his policies.

Roosevelt began to prepare for war. The conservatives opposed and branded his actions as interventionist, extravagant, outright un-American. They took the traditional stand of Americans, that this nation should mind its own business, stay out of European and Asiatic conflicts, and certainly stay out of war.

Roosevelt instituted Social Security, the NRA, and a host of governmental bureaus bloomed from an executive department of the government. Conservatives opposed, pointing out that this was enlarging the government, reducing the dignity and the importance of individuals, taxing everyone in a manner never before imagined.

Roosevelt instituted huge programs of relief and public welfare, and the conservatives branded these moves as socialistic, costly, unnecessary.

Thus, by the beginning of the 1940s, the lines were drawn. The conservative view was in favor of peace, individualism, lowered taxes, smaller government, independence, and self-reliance, and it contained a great love of the Constitution. The cry of the conservative was that we should "get back to the Constitution."

The "liberals," who rallied to Mr. Roosevelt's banner, proclaimed a new "deal" in which government would play an ever-larger role, taxes

A rare antiwar protest in Philadelphia during the Cold War 1950s.

would rise, governmental services would increase, America would intervene in all international affairs and assume a position of "world leadership."

Liberals branded conservatives as "isolationists," "reactionaries," "Cro-Magnon men," "diehards," and "me-too-ers." Conservatives branded liberals as "socialists," "interventionists," "war-makers," "social experimenters," "crooks," "thieves," and "opportunists."

The conservative cry of "Back to the Constitution" was met by all the liberals with their cry of "Forward to more social legislation and a brave new world."

This was the decisive moment. The lines were clearly drawn.

If you were a liberal, in the new meaning of the word, you were in favor of generous helpings of the taxpayers' money for all manner of governmental programs.

If you were a conservative, you favored independence, self-reliance, the right to private property, and a small and limited government.

Into this conservative-liberal stand-off was introduced a new note ... the threat of communism. Scholars, examining the Rooseveltian policies, discovered a strange parallel between the New Deal philosophy and the policies expounded by Karl Marx, Friedrich Engels and a host of socialist and pro-communist writers.

Could this parallel be circumstantial, inadvertent, a simple matter of political expediency?

Investigators turned up evidence that Russian spies, working in and out of various governmental offices, had stolen secrets, obtained restricted data, sometimes gotten hold of scarce and even rare material.

Russia was a communist country.

Suddenly, the whole thing seemed to fit together. It was a conspiracy, either of deliberate cooperation or one in which our own government people were the dupes of clever foreign operatives.

By the beginning of the 1950s the term "Communist" had been incontrovertibly linked with Russia. A "Communist" was presumed to be a Russian agent, a man working for the military takeover of this country by a foreign power. The conservatives became "patriots," those who sought to defend their nation from subversion at home or from military aggression abroad.

The attention of the American conservative shifted in emphasis. He became primarily concerned with foreign affairs. Russia was the new danger. It was no longer a matter of the rise of government and the displacement of individual rights, the erosion of property rights, the increase of taxes.

Instead, the conservative emphasis became known as anti-communism. And with this shift came a strange metamorphosis to the conservative objective.

For where it had served originally as the champion of peace, it now began to urge the line of "stand fast," "no compromise," "war if necessary."

And where it had originally championed the idea of smaller government, it began to clamor for larger bureaus to hunt down Communists. It called for expansion of the police powers, sought laws to arrest persons of non-conservative persuasion on the grounds that they were "traitors" and clamored for costly "investigations," all of which took more in the form of tax money.

Suddenly, it was not against high taxes per se, it was only against those taxes which were not to be used in anti-communist effort. All at once the government became the most important thing in the mind of the conservative. The government must be made strong. It must spend billions in missile and weapon research. It must develop "strong" men.

Gradually, the theory arose that the way to prevent a war with Russia was to start one. Russia was the head of the communist conspiracy. Russia was secretly planning for a military takeover of the world. The best defense was aggression.

Where conservatives had joined ranks in opposing the military draft of Roosevelt and in criticizing the draft of President Woodrow Wilson, they now joined hands in branding anyone who refused to be drafted as a "dupe" or an outright "red."

Those who saw in Civil Defense a massive new way for the government to obtain more power and more money, were suddenly the victims of conservative criticism. There was to be no limit on military preparedness. In the '30s such a move as C.D. would have been hooted down by conservatives. Now, moves to oppose massive new spending of this character were derided and vilified.

Those who had opposed Roosevelt's brand of interventionism now began to favor outright assistance to foreign countries which would oppose Russia. "Foreign aid," that biggest of all boondoggles, was seen to be a constructive thing if only it went to "non-communist" countries.

A Supreme Court justice who had consistently upheld the position of the government as it opposed the rights of individuals became the subject of praise if only the individual on trial was suspected or proved to be a Communist.

Still, within the framework of the "conservative movement" lived persons who objected to high taxes and the further advance of government. But the vigor of their opposition was blunted by their own cries to "make government strong."

This is the present status of the conservative movement. It is rent by conflicting philosophies. Its major "leaders" are beginning to hurl abuse at each other.

Most still favor lowered taxes. But at the same time they clamor for more power in the hands of government, more strict interpretation of law, more investigations, more crackdowns on those who disagree.

We believe that the original position of the conservative, that taken in the early days of Roosevelt's first term of office, is a proper and legitimate position. But, at the moment, the conservative, while still supporting this position to a degree, has tended to place all his emphasis in the anti-communist camp. And the anti-communist camp is sadly at variance within itself as to the things to be believed and the things to be done.

What we are beginning to see occur within the framework of conservative, is a new alliance between former "liberals" and latter-day "conservatives." The "liberal" of the '30s wanted larger government, principally in the area of social legislation, welfare and human experiment. The latter-day "conservatives" also want larger government. But they now want it in the police area of armies, navies, air forces and rocketry. They also want more trials, more rigid domestic policing.

But both the former liberal and the latter-day conservative desire larger government. And the end result of this combination is a bigger tax program, more spending on education (for defense), establishment of new bureaus (for patriotic reasons), and great emphasis upon national union.

The latter-day conservative, while still critical of the "welfare state" of the former liberal, lends his support to the formation of a military or a "police state" where things will be controlled at the top by a "strong man."

Meanwhile, another strange shift is occurring. For while some of the former liberals are intrigued by this turn of events and are now jumping on the bandwagon of "anti-communism," other liberals, in the nineteenth-century tradition of liberalism, are beginning to wonder about human liberty in the great sense, and are shifting over to oppose war-making, the draft, foreign intervention and even high taxes.

Thus, it appears that the liberal camp, as well as the conservative camp, is splitting. The traditional liberal of prior years is now aligning himself with the conservative of the '30s.

It seems to us that in times as confusing as these, only principles are safe and reliable. Only the truth is sure.

To try to find these principles, to try to discover truth should become each man's major concern. We cannot, any of us, afford to be wrong at this crucial juncture.

In times such as these, a re-anchoring to the basic concepts of America seems most urgent. To find these concepts, we can think of no better method than to turn to the Declaration of Independence, the basic document which sets forth the principles by means of which our forefathers sought to set down the motivating factors as they saw them. We believe they were valid then. We see no reason for supposing that they are not valid now.

The basic idea emphasized in the Declaration is the concept of freedom and individualism. There it was held that each man, by virtue of his creation, has certain unalienable rights. Among these rights are life, liberty and the pursuit of happiness.

Governments, it is clearly stated, are secondary in importance. They are tools devised by men for the preservation of their rights. Indeed, their importance is so meager that when men find themselves deprived of their rights, they have a right and a duty to throw off that government and to provide new methods, new guards for the preservation of those rights. It is the individual, not the government, who is the sovereign.

If this is true, and we believe it to be true, then the present position of both the latter-day conservative and the liberal of the '30s is in contravention of that truth. The rights of each individual man are supreme. Government, conceived either as a welfare agency or a police agent of aggressive potential, is invalid.

Nor does the threat of Russia change this truth. Nor does the threat of communism, socialism or welfare statism change it. What is paramount is freedom. What is of utmost value is the individual's right to be himself.

Any move to enlarge government is bound to be destructive of individual human rights in the long run. A "strong-man" government, even for the purpose of sustaining it, would dethrone human liberty.

We'll take our stand with the Declaration of Independence and the principles of individualism and human liberty.

Real Conservatives Don't Start Wars

BILL KAUFFMAN

Bill Kauffman wrote this essay for the May 1986 issue of Reason.

Back in the days when hippies roamed the earth, kids used to enjoy taunting their parents by speculating on the reception Jesus Christ would receive if he were to walk through the door of the local church. The joke was that the congregation would give him the heave-ho, long hair, sandals, and all, then return to their Christian worship.

Readers of a respected journal of foreign affairs were recently treated to a similar irony, albeit of a more temporal nature, courtesy of the provocative young foreign-policy analyst Christopher Layne. In the winter issue of the quarterly *Foreign Policy,* Layne strove valiantly to resurrect the noble but neglected conservative foreign policy of Ohio's Mr. Republican, Senator Robert Taft. Today's conservatives were none too pleased with this Second Coming, either.

Throughout the 1940s and early '50s, Taft led the opposition to the Cold War policies of the liberal Democrats. Taft and his conservative allies feared that the extensive foreign commitments America was making would strain our budget, imperil our liberties, and earn us the enmity of people around the world.

For their efforts these postwar conservatives were reviled and red-baited by eminent publications from the *New Republic* to the *New York Times*. Most all of these gallant old boys are dead now. Their collective epitaph, in light of J. Edgar Hoover, the Iranian hostages, and a $200-billion budget deficit, should be a giant WE TOLD YOU SO.

Layne tags Taft and his comrades "real conservatives" and contrasts them with the Reagan administration's neoconservatives. Real conservatives, explains Layne, believe that the primary purpose of our national defense should be to defend this nation and its vital interests. Ever mindful of the need for prudence in government expenditure, real conservatives desire to shift the cost of defending Europe and Japan from the hapless American taxpayer to the Europeans and the Japanese. And real conservatives, understanding that "vital American interests are not engaged in Afghanistan, Angola, Cambodia, and similar Third World hotspots," do not wish to entangle the United States in those peripheral conflicts.

Opposed to the real conservatives are the neoconservatives who run American foreign policy in the age of Reagan. Neoconservatives believe that the purpose of U.S. foreign policy is to wage a global war on communism. They are therefore willing to spend money hand over fist propping up anticommunist governments and insurgents and subsidizing the defenses of our NATO allies. America, in their view, is an imperial power with an almost limitless set of foreign obligations. The neoconservatives regard old-fashioned conservatism, with its caution and concern for preserving traditional American values, as a quaint but disturbing antique.

Nevertheless, Layne's essay hit a raw nerve among today's conservatives. Two of the right wing's leading lights—columnist cum TV

Dorothy Day and Peter Maurin cofounded the Catholic Worker movement, which reaches out to the hungry and homeless. Day, a devout Catholic as well as a pacifist, is seen here demonstrating on August 6, 1955, the tenth anniversary of the U.S. atomic bombing of Hiroshima. In their 1983 peace pastoral, *The Challenge of Peace*, the U.S. Catholic bishops affirmed Day's faith in nonviolence and conscientious objection as an alternative for Catholics.

Courtesy of the Marquette University Department of Special Collections and University Archive.

pontificator George Will and *New Republic* chin-puller Charles Krauthammer—moved quickly to snuff out this flame of heterodoxy.

Reaganite Will dismisses Layne as being "stuck in the 1940s." Interference in the Third World is necessary, Will argues, to roll back the Soviet Empire. If anything, U.S. foreign policy has been "too passive." It's not unfair to note that during America's futile crusade in Vietnam, Will served his country in the musty corners of graduate-school libraries.

Hawkish Democrat Krauthammer scarcely knows what to make of Layne's "extreme" isolationism. The United States is a superpower, he sagely observes. If all we care about is national security, then we require only "a minimal deterrent arsenal, a small navy, a border patrol, and hardly any foreign policy at all." This prospect strikes Krauthammer as ridiculous and undeserving of further comment. After all, what self-respecting superpower would mind its own business when there's a global crusade to be waged?

In fact, however, a foreign policy based on Layne's real conservatism offers us a peaceful and prosperous future. For starters, it'd take a huge chunk out of the enormous Reagan deficit. Approximately half of our $300-billion-plus defense budget goes toward defending Europe and Japan, which are certainly capable of building up their defenses to the point necessary to deter a Russian attack. A real conservative approach to defense would keep American dollars where they belong—in the hands of the folks who earn them.

It would also put to rest the nagging fear that American blood will be spilled in far-off lands in which we have no proper interest. If the Russians wish to don the imperialist mantle, let them. Imperialism is foreign to the American character; it corrupts us and enables the central government to build up its power at the expense of the liberties of the people. And it leads, ultimately, to the grisly sight of young American boys, stacked in military planes, coming home to parents and girlfriends in body bags.

Opposing U.S. interventionism from the right is a lonely business these days. Most of one's allies are likely to be pious, posturing leftists of the sort who throw wine and cheese parties for visiting Sandinistas. Not very pleasant company. But conservatives who are reluctant to challenge the wasteful and dangerous policies the Reagan administration is pursuing abroad are advised to remember the defiant words of Confederate statesman Alexander Stephens: "Times change and men often change with them, but principles never!"

War, Peace, and the State

MURRAY N. ROTHBARD

Murray N. Rothbard (1926–1995), prolific scholar and polymath, is considered the founder of the American libertarian movement. His book The Betrayal of the American Right, *which was finally published twelve years after his death, told the story of the transformation of the anti-state right-wing of the 1930s and 1940s—which included such figures as Albert Jay Nock, John T. Flynn, Garet Garrett, Rose Wilder Lane, and Isabel Paterson—into the heavily interventionist right-wing of Bill Buckley and* National Review. *Rothbard played a central role in making nonintervention into the official foreign-policy platform of the Libertarian Party. Here, in an essay first published in* The Standard *in 1963, and reprinted in his book* Egalitarianism as a Revolt Against Nature and Other Essays, *is Rothbard's derivation of noninterventionism from libertarian first principles, a message he delivered at a time when so many supporters of the free market were defending large-scale foreign intervention as the correct strategy against Communism. As the 1960s progressed, Rothbard began to collaborate with the New Left in a search for antiwar allies.*

The fundamental axiom of libertarian theory is that no one may threaten or commit violence ("aggress") against another man's person or property. Violence may be employed only against the man who commits such violence; that is, only defensively against the aggressive violence of another.

In short, no violence may be employed against a non-aggressor. Here is the fundamental rule from which can be deduced the entire corpus of libertarian theory.

Let us set aside the more complex problem of the State for awhile and consider simply relations between "private" individuals. Jones finds that he or his property is being invaded, aggressed against, by Smith. It is legitimate for Jones, as we have seen, to repel this invasion by defensive violence of his own. But now we come to a more knotty question: is it within the right of Jones to commit violence against innocent third parties as a corollary to his legitimate defense against Smith? To the libertarian, the answer must be clearly, no. Remember that the rule prohibiting violence against the persons or property of innocent men is absolute: it holds regardless of the subjective *motives* for the aggression. It is wrong and criminal to violate the property or person of another, even if one is a Robin Hood, or starving, or is doing it to save one's relatives, *or* is defending oneself against a third man's attack. We may understand and sympathize with the motives in many of these cases and extreme situations. We may later mitigate the guilt if the criminal comes to trial for punishment, but we cannot evade the judgment that this aggression is still a criminal act, and one which the victim has every right to repel, by violence if necessary. In short, A aggresses against B because C is threatening, or aggressing against, A. We may understand C's "higher" culpability in this whole procedure; but we must still label this aggression as a criminal act which B has the right to repel by violence.

To be more concrete, if Jones finds that his property is being stolen by Smith, he has the right to repel him and try to catch him; but he has *no* right to repel him by bombing a building and murdering innocent people or to catch him by spraying machine gun fire into an innocent crowd. If he does this, he is as much (or more of) a criminal aggressor as Smith is.

The application to problems of war and peace is already becoming evident. For while war in the narrower sense is a conflict between States, in the broader sense we may define it as the outbreak of open violence between people or groups of people. If Smith and a group of his henchmen aggress against Jones and Jones and his bodyguards pursue the Smith gang to their lair, we may cheer Jones on in his endeavor; and we, and others in society interested in repelling aggression, may contribute financially or personally to Jones's cause. But Jones has *no* right, any more than does Smith, to aggress against anyone else in the course of his "just war": to steal others' property in order to finance his pursuit, to conscript others into his posse by use of violence, or to kill others in the course of his struggle to capture the Smith forces. If Jones should do any of these things, he becomes a criminal as *fully* as Smith, and he too becomes subject to whatever sanctions are meted out against criminality. In fact, if Smith's crime was theft, and Jones should use conscription to catch him, or should kill others in the pursuit, Jones becomes more of a criminal than Smith, for such crimes against another person as enslavement and murder are surely far worse than theft. . . .

Suppose that Jones, in the course of his "just war" against the ravages of Smith, should kill a few innocent people, and suppose that he should declaim, in defense of this murder, that he was simply acting on the slogan, "Give me liberty or give me death." The absurdity of this "defense" should be evident at once, for the issue is not whether Jones was willing to risk death personally in his defensive struggle against Smith; the issue is whether he was willing to kill other people in pursuit of his legitimate end. For Jones was in truth acting on the completely indefensible slogan "Give me liberty or give *them* death," surely a far less noble battle cry.

The libertarian's basic attitude toward war must then be: it is legitimate to use violence against criminals in defense of one's rights of person and property; it is completely impermissible to violate the rights of *other* innocent people. War, then, is only proper when the exercise of violence is rigorously limited to the individual criminals. We may judge for ourselves how many wars or conflicts in history have met this criterion.

It has often been maintained, and especially by conservatives, that the development of the horrendous modern weapons of mass murder (nuclear weapons, rockets, germ warfare, etc.) is only a difference of *degree* rather than *kind* from the simpler weapons of an earlier era. Of course, one answer to this is that when the degree is the number of human lives, the difference is a very big one. But another answer that the libertarian is particularly equipped to give is that while the bow and arrow and even the rifle can be pinpointed, if the will be there, against actual criminals, modern nuclear weapons cannot. . . . These weapons are ipso facto engines of indiscriminate mass destruction. . . . We must, therefore, conclude that the use of nuclear or similar weapons, or the threat thereof, is a sin and a crime against humanity for which there can be no justification. . . .

It is time now to bring the State into our discussion. The State is a group of people who have managed to acquire a virtual monopoly of the use of violence throughout a given territorial area. In particular, it has acquired a monopoly of aggressive violence, for States generally recognize the right of individuals to use violence (though not against States, of course) in self-defense. The State then uses this monopoly to wield power over the inhabitants of the area and to enjoy the material fruits of that power. The State, then, is the only organization in society that regularly and openly obtains its monetary revenues by the use of *aggressive* violence; all other individuals and organizations (except if delegated that right by the State) can obtain wealth only by peaceful production and by voluntary exchange of their respective products. This use of violence to obtain its revenue (called "taxation") is the keystone of State power. Upon this base the State erects a further structure of power over the individuals in its territory, regulating them, penalizing critics, subsidizing favorites, etc. The State also takes care to arrogate to itself the compulsory monopoly of various critical services needed by society, thus keeping the people in dependence upon the State for key services, keeping control of the vital command posts in society and also fostering among the public the myth that *only* the State can supply these goods and services. Thus the State is careful to monopolize police and judicial service, the ownership of roads and streets, the supply of money, and the postal service, and effectively to monopolize or control education, public utilities, transportation, and radio and television.

Now, since the State arrogates to itself the monopoly of violence over a territorial area, so long as its depredations and extortions go unresisted, there is said to be "peace" in the area, since the only violence is one-way, directed by the State downward against the people. Open conflict within the area only breaks out in the case of "revolutions" in which people resist the use of State power against them. Both the quiet case of the State unresisted and the case of open revolution may be termed "vertical violence": violence of the State against its public or vice versa.

In the modern world, each land area is ruled over by a State organization, but there are a number of States scattered over the earth, each with a monopoly of violence over its own territory. No super-State exists with a monopoly of violence over the entire world; and so a state of "anarchy" exists between the several States. . . . And so, except for revolutions, which occur only sporadically, the open violence and two-sided conflict in the world takes place *between* two or more States, that is, in what is called "international war" (or "horizontal violence"). . . .

If one distinct attribute of inter-State war is inter-territoriality, another unique attribute stems from the fact that each State lives by taxation over its subjects. Any war against another State, therefore, involves the increase and extension of taxation-aggression over its own people. Conflicts between private individuals can be, and usually are, voluntarily waged and financed by the parties concerned. Revolutions can be, and often are, financed and fought by voluntary contributions of the public. But State wars can only be waged through aggression against the taxpayer.

All State wars, therefore, involve increased aggression against the State's own taxpayers, and almost all State wars (*all*, in modern warfare) involve the maximum aggression (murder) against the innocent civilians ruled by the enemy State. On the other hand, revolutions are generally financed voluntarily and may pinpoint their violence to the State rulers, and private conflicts may confine their violence to the actual criminals. The libertarian must, therefore, conclude that, while some revolutions and some private conflicts *may* be legitimate, State wars are *always* to be condemned.

Many libertarians object as follows: "While we too deplore the use of taxation for warfare, and the State's monopoly of defense service, we have to recognize that these conditions exist, and while they do, we must support the State in just wars of defense." The reply to this would go as follows: "Yes, as you say, unfortunately States exist, each having a monopoly of violence over its territorial area." What then should be the attitude of the libertarian toward conflicts between these States? The libertarian should say, in effect, to the State: "All right, you exist, but as long as you exist at least confine your activities to the area which you monopolize." In short, the libertarian is interested in reducing as much as possible the area of State aggression against all private individuals. The only way to do this, in international affairs, is for the people of each country to pressure their own State to confine its activities to the area which it monopolizes and not to aggress against other State-monopolists. In short, the objective of the libertarian is to confine any existing State to as small a degree of invasion of person and property as possible. And this means the total avoidance of war. The people under each State should pressure "their" respective States not to attack one another, and, if a conflict should break out, to negotiate a peace or declare a cease-fire as quickly as physically possible.

Suppose further that we have that rarity—an unusually clear-cut case in which the State is actually trying to defend the property of one of its citizens. A citizen of country A travels or invests in country B, and then State B aggresses against his person or confiscates his property. Surely, our libertarian critic would argue, here is a clear-cut case where State A should threaten or commit war against State B in order to defend the property of "its" citizen. Since, the argument runs, the State has taken upon itself the monopoly of defense of its citizens, it then has the obligation to go to war on behalf of any citizen, and libertarians have an obligation to support this war as a just one.

But the point again is that each State has a monopoly of violence and, therefore, of defense only over its territorial area. It has no such monopoly; in fact, it has no power at all, over any other geographical area. Therefore, if an inhabitant of country A should move to or invest in country B, the libertarian must argue that he thereby takes his chances with the State-monopolist of country B, and it would be immoral and criminal for State A to tax people in country A *and* kill numerous innocents in country B in order to defend the property of the traveler or investor.

It should also be pointed out that there is no defense against nuclear weapons (the only current "defense" is the threat of mutual annihilation)

In 1973 a lone man on New York
City's Fifth Avenue protests U.S.
support for Portugal in that
country's lengthy war against its
Angolan colonial population.

and, therefore, that the State *cannot* fulfill any sort of defense function
so long as these weapons exist. . . .

Suppose, however, that despite libertarian opposition, war has begun
and the warring States are not negotiating a peace. What, then, should
be the libertarian position? Clearly, to reduce the scope of assault of innocent civilians as much as possible. Old-fashioned international law
had two excellent devices for this: the "laws of war," and the "laws of
neutrality" or "neutrals' rights." The laws of neutrality are designed to
keep any war that breaks out confined to the warring States themselves,
without aggression against the States or particularly the peoples of the
other nations. . . .

Does opposition to all war mean that the libertarian can never countenance change—that he is consigning the world to a permanent freez-
ing of unjust regimes? Certainly not. Suppose, for example, that the
hypothetical state of "Waldavia" has attacked "Ruritania" and annexed
the western part of the country. The Western Ruritanians now long to

be reunited with their Ruritanian brethren. How is this to be achieved? There is, of course, the route of peaceful negotiation between the two powers, but suppose that the Waldavian imperialists prove adamant. Or, libertarian Waldavians can put pressure on their government to abandon its conquest in the name of justice. But suppose that this, too, does not work. What then? We must still maintain the illegitimacy of Ruritania's mounting a war against Waldavia. The legitimate routes are (1) revolutionary uprisings by the oppressed Western Ruritanian people, and (2) aid by private Ruritanian groups (or, for that matter, by friends of the Ruritanian cause in other countries) to the Western rebels—either in the form of equipment or of volunteer personnel. . . .

We cannot leave our topic without saying at least a word about the domestic tyranny that is the inevitable accompaniment of war. The great Randolph Bourne realized that "war is the health of the State." It is in war that the State really comes into its own: swelling in power, in number, in pride, in absolute dominion over the economy and the society. Society becomes a herd, seeking to kill its alleged enemies, rooting out and suppressing all dissent from the official war effort, happily betraying truth for the supposed public interest. Society becomes an armed camp, with the values and the morale—as Albert Jay Nock once phrased it—of an "army on the march."

The root myth that enables the State to wax fat off war is the canard that war is a defense *by* the State *of* its subjects. The facts, of course, are precisely the reverse. For if war is the health of the State, it is also its greatest danger. A State can only "die" by defeat in war or by revolution. In war, therefore, the State frantically mobilizes the people to fight for *it* against another State, under the pretext that *it* is fighting for them. But all this should occasion no surprise; we see it in other walks of life. For which categories of crime does the State pursue and punish most intensely—those against private citizens or those against *itself*? The gravest crimes in the State's lexicon are almost invariably not invasions of person and property, but dangers to its *own* contentment: for example, treason, desertion of a soldier to the enemy, failure to register for the draft, conspiracy to overthrow the government. Murder is pursued haphazardly unless the victim be a *policeman,* or *Gott soll hüten,* an assassinated Chief of State; failure to pay a private debt is, if anything, almost encouraged, but income tax evasion is punished with utmost severity; counterfeiting the State's money is pursued far more relentlessly than forging private checks, etc. All this evidence demonstrates that the State is far more interested in preserving its own power than in defending the rights of private citizens.

A final word about conscription: of all the ways in which war aggrandizes the State, this is perhaps the most flagrant and most despotic. But the most striking fact about conscription is the absurdity of the arguments put forward on its behalf. A man must be conscripted to defend his (or someone else's?) liberty against an evil State beyond the borders. Defend his liberty? How? By being coerced into an army whose very raison d'être is the expunging of liberty, the trampling on all the liberties of the person, the calculated and brutal dehumanization of the soldier and his transformation into an efficient engine of murder at the whim of his "commanding officer"? Can any conceivable foreign State do anything worse to him than what "his" army is now doing for his alleged benefit? Who is there, O Lord, to defend him against his "defenders"?

Conservative Thoughts on Foreign Policy

RUSSELL KIRK

Russell Kirk was arguably the founder of postwar American conservatism, and was an icon of that movement for half a century. This excerpt is taken from Kirk's 1954 book, A Program for Conservatives.

In the present instance we contend, with an ingenuous provinciality, that all the world wants to be American. . . . Displaying an impatient perplexity which is wholly sincere, we decry as reactionary or conspiratorial or Russian-influenced anyone in foreign parts who dissents from The American Way. We manifest a yawning ignorance of the venerable principle that cultural form and substance cannot be transported intact from one people to another. We claim that everyone except feudal barons or Reds longs for tractors, Bob Hope, self-service laundries, direct primaries, clover-leaf intersections, high-school extracurricular activities, two evening newspapers, Coca-Cola, and a stylish burial at Memory Grove Cemetery.

A handful of individuals, some of them quite unused to moral responsibilities on such a scale, made it their business to extirpate the populations of Nagasaki and Hiroshima; we must make it our business to curtail the possibility of such snap decisions, taken simply on the assumptions of worldly wisdom. And the conservative can urge upon his nation a policy of patience and prudence. A "preventive" war, whether or not it might be successful in the field—and that is a question much in doubt—would be morally ruinous to us. There are circumstances under which it is not only more honorable to lose than to win, but quite truly less harmful, in the ultimate providence of God.

8

The Vietnam War

Every senator in this chamber is partly responsible for send-ing 50,000 young Americans to an early grave. This cham-ber reeks of blood.

—SENATOR GEORGE MCGOVERN,
September 1, 1970

In April 2000, twenty-thousand Vietnamese gathered in Ho Chi Minh City—formerly known as Saigon—to celebrate the twenty-fifth an-niversary of the end of what Vietnamese widely referred to as the American war. The city's mayor spoke of the millions of wartime deaths. Today, Vietnam is a relatively stable society and American and Vietnamese heads of state have since exchanged visits and promoted mutual trade and tourism.

More than half a million U.S. troops were sent to serve in what was really a civil war. B-52s dropped at least as many or more bombs on rural North Vietnam as they did on Nazi Germany. Some 58,209 American servicemen and women were killed, a disproportionate number of them conscripts, and another 153,303 wounded, many damaged in both body and mind. Millions of Southeast Asians died or suffered grievous wounds.

The U.S. was defeated by a largely guerrilla force. But was it worth it?

The U.S. government supported a post–WWII France as it sought to retain its Southeast Asian colony. That is, until 1954, when the French occupiers, having been badly defeated by the Germans and everyone else since the Napoleonic wars, were just as badly beaten by the North Vietnamese at Dien Bien Phu. They quickly abandoned their colony, leaving in their wake the U.S. as its successor, and a conference at Geneva that divided North and South Vietnam at the 17th parallel with a pledge by the conferees to hold elections. The southern ruling circles, many of whose leaders had served in the French army, and Eisenhower's combative Secretary of State, John Foster Dulles, balked at elections because they feared a North Vietnamese victory, which left their allies in the south to shape a viable government, which they never could do.

Still, in May 1961, Vice President Lyndon B. Johnson did what most American politicians who traveled to Saigon would do: chatted with generals in air-conditioned comfort, and then pontificated to the press and the nation about the victory that was just around the corner. LBJ also came away praising Ngo Dinh Diem as the "Winston Churchill of Asia," though this ersatz version of the British prime minister was to be assassinated in 1963 in a U.S.-supported coup. By the time President John F. Kennedy was killed in November 1963, he had dispatched sixteen thousand U.S. military "advisors" to Vietnam and a few more to Laos. The Americans would come to share the fate of the French.

After 1965 more and more American troops poured in, including an unending stream of reluctant American draftees. With very few exceptions virtually all congressmen and Washington hawks saw to it that their draft-eligible family members avoided active military duty. When Dick Cheney was asked why he had requested five draft deferments, which kept him safely at home, he famously answered, "I had other priorities in the '60s than military service. . . . I don't regret the decisions I made."*

At the start of U.S. military intervention, political courage was rare. The post–World War II rise of anti-colonialism was drowned out by the obsessive anti-Communism of every U.S. president and nearly every politician. "The Russians Are Coming," went the popular film of that name, which, while managing a different and happier ending, nevertheless summed up American political opinion and fears at the time.

Unlike the Senate, the House of Representatives voted unanimously to approve the Gulf of Tonkin Resolution, which responded to two alleged torpedo boat attacks by the North Vietnamese against two U.S. destroyers near the North Vietnamese coast. Before too long these dubious, exaggerated incidents—much like the post–9/11 fabrications about Saddam Hussein's Iraq having weapons of mass destruction and being involved in the terrorist attacks of that day—were used by Johnson's hard-line advisors to urge a land war on the Asian mainland, a move against which many military experts had long warned. It was also used to persuade—and frighten—the American people that distant, insignificant, and rural North Vietnam posed a major threat to their country and the Western world.

Two senatorial dissenters emerged: Wayne Morse of Oregon and Alaska's Ernest Gruening, who always voted against spending for a war he detested. In White House circles senior advisor and Undersecretary of State George Ball and outsider John Kenneth Galbraith cautioned

---

*Joan Didion, "Cheney: The Fatal Touch," *The New York Review of Books*, October 5, 2006, 55. "There was a reason, beyond the thrill of their sheer arrogance, why the words 'other priorities' stuck in the national memory," wrote Didion. "They were first uttered not in but outside the room in which Cheney's 1989 confirmation hearings [for secretary of defense] were held, to a *Washington Post* reporter who asked why the candidate for secretary of defense had sought the five (four student and one 'hardship') deferments that had prevented him from serving in Vietnam." See also Katherine Q. Seelye, "Cheney's Five Draft Deferments During the Vietnam Era Emerge as a Campaign Issue," *New York Times*, May 1, 2004, A12.

against going to war, accurately warning that a disaster lay ahead, only to be overwhelmed by Johnson's inner circle and the capital's foreign policy elite eager to "stop Communism" in Asia.

Still, cheered on by most Americans and the media, which had been schooled to believe that communists were out to conquer all and only the U.S. stood in their way, the Domino Theory, dreamed up by American theorists (that all of Southeast Asia and more would fall if Hanoi wasn't stopped; of course, no dominoes ever fell) became the unquestioned mantra until 1967–68, when at last a growing and articulate antiwar movement began taking shape, especially after the accession of Johnson's pro-war successor, Richard Nixon, and his principal adviser, Henry Kissinger.

By 1968, popular opposition to the war at home had become widespread. The nation seemed to be undergoing a nervous breakdown, especially after the murders of Martin Luther King, Jr. and Robert Kennedy—and later, in 1970, the American invasion of Cambodia and the tragic killing of Kent State and Jackson State students. Millions of antiwar college students were driven to protest, students whom Nixon dismissed as "bums."

When the Vietnam Memorial in Washington, D.C., was dedicated, and thus became a sacred shrine to the war dead, no one in political authority who had dreamed up this mad bloodletting had ever been held legally or morally accountable, thereby insuring that few if any lessons would be learned in the decades ahead.

Against the Gulf of Tonkin Resolution

SENATOR WAYNE MORSE

Wayne Morse served as a U.S. senator from Oregon from 1945 until 1969. He began his career as a Republican, but had become a Democrat by the mid-1950s. He was, as noted in our introduction, one of two senators to vote against the Gulf of Tonkin Resolution. He delivered these remarks on August 5, 1964.

Mr. President, I rise to speak in opposition to the joint resolution. I do so with a very sad heart. But I consider the resolution . . . to be naught but a resolution which embodies a predated declaration of war.

Article I, Section 8 of our Constitution does not permit the President to make war at his own discretion. Therefore I stand on this issue as I have stood before in the Senate, perfectly willing to take the judgment of history as to the merits of my cause. . . .

I yield to no other Senator, or to anyone else in this country in my opposition to communism and all that communism stands for.

In our time a great struggle, which may very well be a deathlock struggle, is going on in the world between freedom on the one hand and the totalitarianism of communism on the other.

However, I am satisfied that that struggle can never be settled by war. I am satisfied that if the hope of anyone is that the struggle between freedom and communism can be settled by war, and that course is followed, both freedom and communism will lose, for there will be no victory in that war. . . .

I say that the incident that has inspired the joint resolution we have just read is as much the doing of the United States as it is the doing of North Vietnam. For 10 years, the role of the United States in South Vietnam has been that of a provocateur, every bit as much as North Vietnam has been a provocateur. For 10 years, the United States, in South Vietnam, has violated the Geneva agreement of 1954. For 10 years, our military policies in South Vietnam have sought to impose a military solution upon a political and economic problem. For 10 years the Communist nations of that part of the world have also violated the Geneva accord of 1954.

Not only do two wrongs not make one right, but also I care not how many wrongs we add together, we still do not come out with a summation except a summation of wrong—never a right.

The American effort to impose by force of arms a government of our own choosing upon a segment of the old colony of Indochina has caught up with us. . . .

The U.S. Government knew that the matter of national and international waters was a controversial issue in Tonkin Bay. The United States also knew that the South Vietnamese vessels planned to bomb, and did bomb, two North Vietnamese islands within three to six miles of the coast of North Vietnam. Yet, these war vessels of the United States were in the vicinity of that bombing, some miles removed.

Can anyone question that even their presence was a matter of great moral value to South Vietnam? Or the propaganda value to the military totalitarian tyrant and despot who rules South Vietnam as an American puppet—General Khanh, who is really, when all is said and done, the leader whom we have put in charge of an American protectorate called South Vietnam?

It should be unnecessary to point out either to the Senate or to the American people what the position of the United States and its people would be if the tables were reversed and Soviet warships or submarines were to patrol five to eleven miles at sea while Cuban naval vessels bombarded Key West. . . .

Our charges of aggression against North Vietnam will be greeted by considerable snickering abroad.

So, too, will the pious phrases of the resolution about defending freedom in South Vietnam. There is no freedom in South Vietnam. I think even the American people know that to say we are defending freedom in South Vietnam is a travesty upon the word. We are defending General Khanh from being overthrown; that is all. We are defending a clique of military generals and their merchant friends who live well in Saigon, and who need a constantly increasing American military force to protect their privileged position. . . .

There are many congressional politicians who would evade their responsibilities as to American foreign policy in Asia by use of the specious argument that "foreign policy is a matter for the executive branch of the Government. That branch has information no Congressman has access to." Of course, such an alibi for evading congressional responsibility in the field of foreign policy may be based on lack of understanding, or a convenient forgetting of our system of checks and balances that exists and should be exercised in the relationships between and among our three coordinate and coequal branches of government.

Granted that there are many in Congress who would prefer to pass the buck to the White House, the State Department, and the Pentagon Building in respect to our unilateral American military action in Asia. And this resolution gives them the vehicle. Nevertheless, I am satisfied that once the American people come to understand the facts involved in the ill-fated military operations in Asia, they will hold to an accounting those Members of Congress who abdicate their responsibilities in the field of foreign policy. . . .

Does anyone mean to tell me that with a population of 15 million, and military forces consisting of 400,000 to 450,000 South Vietnamese troops, of various types and various services, they are incapacitated, and that we must send American boys over there to die in what amounts basically to a civil war?

Mr. President, criticism has not prevented, and will not prevent me from saying that, in my judgment, we cannot justify the shedding of American blood in that kind of war in southeast Asia. France learned that lesson. France tried to fight it for eight years, and with 240,000 casualties. The French people finally pulled down the French Government and said they had had enough.

I do not believe that any number of American conventional forces in South Vietnam, or in Asia generally, can win a war, if the test of winning a war is establishing peace. We can win military victories. We can kill millions of people, but not without losses of our own. Then, at the end of that blood march, we shall end with the same job to perform; namely, establishing peace, but in a war-wracked world, if we survive. . . .

We had to send in 15,000 American boys—at first—and we do not know with certainty how many were in the last allotment, but probably another 4,000 or 5,000 or more. And the way things are going over there today, the American people had better get ready for thousands more to be sent.

I view with great concern the danger that thousands of them will be bogged down in Asia for a long time to come. If that happens, there will be one place in the world where there will be no regrets, and that will be Moscow.

Mr. President, when the Diem government diverted itself from fighting rebels to fighting Buddhists, a coup by military protégés of the United States overthrew it. Within a few weeks, another coup replaced the Minh junta with what the American military advisers considered a more efficient military junta under General Khanh.

At no time has South Vietnam had a government of its own choosing. In fact, the Khanh junta justified its coup with the excuse that some Minh officers were pro-French, and might seek some way of neutralizing the country. What the people of South Vietnam, even those the government still controls, might want has never been given a passing thought.

Just how the present Khanh government differs from the old Bao Dai government which served as the French puppet, I have never been able to see. . . .

Many people are saying these days that getting into South Vietnam was a terrible mistake, but now that we are there, there is no point in looking back and rehashing the wisdom of it all how wrong they are. Surely when a nation goes as far down the road toward war as we have, it must know why it is there, what objective it is seeking, and whether the objective sought could possibly be achieved by any other means. . . .

Dr. Martin Luther King Jr. is pictured here speaking against the Vietnam War on February 6, 1968, at New York Avenue Presbyterian Church in Washington, D.C. He spoke under the auspices of CALCAV, an influential interfaith antiwar group.

This Chamber Reeks of Blood

GEORGE MCGOVERN

Senator George McGovern (D–SD) delivered these remarks on the Senate floor on September 1, 1970, in support of the Hatfield–McGovern amendment that would have brought the American military effort in Vietnam to an end and commenced the return of American troops to the United States.

Mr. President, the vote we are about to cast could be one of the most significant votes Senators have ever cast.

I have lived with this vote night and day since last April 30—the day before the Cambodian invasion—the day this amendment was first submitted.

I thank God this amendment was submitted when it was, because, as every Senator knows, in the turbulent days following the invasion of Cambodia and the tragedy at Kent State University, this amendment gave a constructive rallying point to millions of anguished citizens across this war-weary land.

I believe that, along with the Cooper-Church amendment, the pending amendment helped to keep the nation from exploding this summer. It was the lodestar that inspired more mail, more telegrams, more eager young visitors to our offices, more political action, and more contributions from doctors, lawyers, workers, and housewives than any other initiative of Congress in this summer of discontent.

Now this question is about to be resolved. What is the choice it presents us? It presents us with an opportunity to end a war we never should have entered. It presents us with an opportunity to revitalize constitutional government in America by restoring the war powers the Founding Fathers obliged the Congress to carry.

It gives us an opportunity to correct the drift toward one-man rule in the crucial areas of war and peace.

All my life, I have heard Republicans and conservative Democrats complaining about the growth of centralized power in the Federal executive.

Vietnam and Cambodia have convinced me that the conservatives were right. Do they really believe their own rhetoric? We have permitted the war power which the authors of the Constitution wisely gave to us as the people's representatives to slip out of our hands until it now resides behind closed doors at the State Department, the CIA, the Pentagon, and the basement of the White House. We have foolishly assumed that war was too complicated to be trusted to the people's forum—the Congress of the United States. The result has been the cruelest, the most barbaric, and the most stupid war in our national history.

Every senator in this chamber is partly responsible for sending 50,000 young Americans to an early grave. This chamber reeks of blood.

Every Senator here is partly responsible for that human wreckage at Walter Reed and Bethesda Naval and all across our land—young men without legs, or arms, or genitals, or faces, or hopes.

There are not very many of these blasted and broken boys who think this war is a glorious adventure.

Do not talk to them about bugging out, or national honor, or courage.

It does not take any courage at all for a Congressman, or a Senator, or a President to wrap himself in the flag and say we are staying in Vietnam, because it is not our blood that is being shed.

But we are responsible for those young men and their lives and their hopes.

And if we do not end this damnable war, those young men will some day curse us for our pitiful willingness to let the Executive carry the burden that the Constitution places on us.

So before we vote, let us ponder the admonition of Edmund Burke, the great parliamentarian of an earlier day: "A conscientious man would be cautious how he dealt in blood."

Let's Mind Our Own Business

GENERAL DAVID M. SHOUP

General David M. Shoup, former Commandant of the U.S. Marine Corps, delivered these remarks at the tenth Annual Junior College World Affairs Day at Pierce College in Los Angeles on May 14, 1966.

You read, you're televised to, you're radioed to, you're preached to, that it is necessary that we have our armed forces fight, get killed and maimed, and kill and maim other human beings including women and children because now is the time we must stop some kind of unwanted ideology from creeping up on this nation. The place we chose to do this is 8,000 miles away with water in between. . . .

The reasons fed to us are too shallow and narrow for students, as well as other citizens. Especially so, when you realize that what is happening, no matter how carefully and slowly the military escalation has progressed, may be projecting us toward world catastrophe. Surely, it is confusing. . . .

I want to tell you, I don't think the whole of Southeast Asia, as related to the present and future safety and freedom of the people of this country, is worth the life or limb of a single American. . . .

I believe that if we had and would keep our dirty, bloody, dollar-crooked fingers out of the business of these nations so full of depressed, exploited people, they will arrive at a solution of their own. That they design and want. That they fight and work for. And if unfortunately their revolution must be of a violent type because the "haves" refuse to share with the "have-nots" by any peaceful method, at least what they get will be their own, and not the American style, which they don't want and above all don't want crammed down their throats by Americans.

Divinity Students' Letter to Secretary of Defense Robert S. McNamara, 1967

The letter, written by students at New York's Union Theological Seminary, was signed by religious leaders and over a thousand seminarians.

Dear Mr. Secretary:

We are addressing this to you because you are Secretary of Defense, and also because we know you are a man of deep religious feeling and integrity.

We are divinity students—future ministers, priests, and rabbis—and, as you know, we have a classification in Selective Service that virtually exempts us from the draft. We are thus enabled to evade the moral dilemma that is so troubling to many other young men who face the prospect of military service—the dilemma of whether to participate in the war in Vietnam in spite of conscience or whether to refuse to serve and risk the consequences. But we are precisely the people who should be least exempted from facing basic moral issues, and our privileged status therefore adds to our dilemma. For this reason we are more and more uncomfortable about accepting deferments not available to others, as if avoiding moral dilemmas were an acceptable way of dealing with them.

Large numbers of divinity students cannot support the war in Vietnam because they believe this war is neither in the religious tradition of just wars nor in the national interest. On the other hand, most of us believe law and order as fundamental to a free society, and for that reason many who oppose the war on moral grounds are loath to counsel others to break the law by refusing to fight in Vietnam. But if those people specially charged by society with moral responsibilities do not act on their deepest convictions, surely the whole of society is in deep trouble.

We are impressed by a proposal advanced by a minority of the Marshall Commission, the General Board of the National Council of Churches, the General Assembly of the United Presbyterian Church, the Council for Christian Social Action of the United Church of Christ, Americans for Democratic Action, and other significant groups—the proposal that the Selective Service law be amended to recognize conscientious objection to a particular war. If this proposal does not seem acceptable, can you suggest any other way to avoid a confrontation between the demands of the law and those law-abiding young Americans whose conscience will not permit them to fight in Vietnam? Without some procedure that could ease such a confrontation, we fear the grave prospect of growing numbers of young men refusing to fight in Vietnam whatever the legal consequences to themselves and the political consequences to the country. Faced by such a situation, many of us would feel obliged to decline special exemptions to face the same consequences as our peers.

We look forward to hearing from you about this deeply troubling matter.

From *Fighting the Lamb's War:*
Skirmishes with the American Empire
The Autobiography of Philip Berrigan

During the 1960s, Daniel and Philip Berrigan, Roman Catholic priests, argued that the American religious establishment was complicit in the war. Relying on nonviolent civil disobedience, they and their supporters destroyed draft board records, acts for which they were sentenced to prison. Dan, who is also a poet, went on to write the play The Trial of the Catonsville Nine, *while Phil (who left the priesthood in the 1970s), despite years of imprisonment for his refusal to accept U.S. foreign policy, until his death continued protesting his government's support of nuclear weaponry.*

On May 17, 1968, my brother [Dan Berrigan] and I, along with seven others, walked into the draft board at Catonsville, Maryland. We carried file drawers into the parking lot and poured our own blood over them. We burned the files, prayed, and waited to be arrested. Dan might have stayed at Cornell, holding worship services, counseling students, and teaching a course now and then. He might have built a comfortable niche there, writing poetry, going for tenure, living out his life in genteel, wine-and-cheese obscurity. Instead, he stepped out on an existential limb, knowing that it would break, sending him, and all of us, to prison. My brother was the most valuable, the most insightful, the wisest, and perhaps the strongest member of our group.

Our efforts to communicate with the high-ranking masterminds of mass murder had been futile. We had attended nonviolent demonstrations, written letters to government leaders, and met with government officials, pleading with the government to end its genocidal campaign

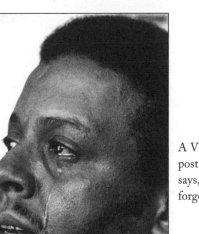

© Gordon Baer. Courtesy of Gordon Baer Collection.

A Vietnam veteran suffering from post-traumatic stress disorder says, "I prayed for survival, but forgot peace of mind."

against the Vietnamese people. Nothing worked. No one listened. "Power comes from the barrel of a gun," said Mao Tse-tung. The architects of the Vietnam War—Lyndon Baines Johnson, Robert McNamara, McGeorge Bundy, Dean Rusk—obviously agreed. We were trying to dialogue with the Mad Hatter; we were attempting to reform Big Brother. Words had lost all meaning. Euphemisms and bureaucratese abounded:

> We must destroy the village in order to save it. We must prolong the war, in order to bring about peace. We must support dictators if we wish to promote democracy.

In the context of search-and-destroy missions, saturation bombings, and free-fire zones, what did this convoluted language really mean? When officials insist on using Newspeak, how should people respond? Where is the basis for honest communication? Words didn't fail us. We tried to speak truthfully, without guile. Our attempts at dialogue with the warmakers sank into Machiavellian waters. We were speaking to the powerful, who considered us powerless and, therefore, not worth listening to.

Vietnam, we discovered, was not only a war on people. It was a war on the very meaning of human communication. Manipulating language was just one more means to achieve some Orwellian end. Words were merely rhetorical devices. Expendable as 18-year-old American boys, destructible as the Vietnamese people. The Catonsville Nine knew that we were moving even deeper into some new existential, religious, ethical territory. Escalating our opposition to the war; trying to startle the doves from the hawk's nest of the Catholic church; acting out the Christian mandate to resist evil. We were burning draft records at Catonsville to protest our government's burning children in Vietnam, and we knew that our actions would shock, anger, and alienate not only our critics, but some of our closest supporters, and certainly many Catholics as well. . . .

The Verdict

DANIEL BERRIGAN

The reference to "Judge Thomsen" in this poem about the Catonsville trial is to Roszel Thomsen, the federal judge who presided over the trial.

Everything before was a great lie.
Illusion, distemper, the judge's eye
Negro and Jew for rigorists.
The children die
Singing in the furnace. In Hell they say
Heaven is a great lie.

Years, years ago
My mother moves in youth. In her
I move, too, to birth, to youth, to this.
The judge's tic-toc is time's steel hand
Summoning
Come priest to the temple. Everything else
Is a great lie. Four walls, home, youth
Truth untried, all all is a great lie.
The truth
The judge shuts in his two eyes
Come Jesuit, the university cannot
No nor the universe, nor murdered Jesus
Imagine. Imagine! Everything before
Was a great lie.
Philip; your freedom, stature
Simplicity, the ghetto where the children
Malinger, die.
Judge Thomsen, strike with a hot hammer
The hour, the truth. The truth has birth
All former truth must die. Everything
Before—faith, hope, love itself
Was a great lie.

Learning the Hard Way

W. D. EHRHART

*W. D. Ehrhart is a writer, poet, and teacher who served in the U.S.
Marines for three years, including thirteen months in Vietnam. He
delivered these remarks to the students at George School, Newtown,
Pennsylvania, January 18, 1982.*

"He's not the same." Ann tells a women's support group about her Vietnam veteran husband whom "the war changed so drastically."

© Gordon Baer. Courtesy of Gordon Baer Collection.

Why should military conscription be of any concern to you? The United States is not at war. There is no active draft taking place at this time, and our national leaders have repeatedly insisted that they are not contemplating a military draft. The current required registration, according to the government, is only a contingency plan to cover the possibility of some unforeseeable national emergency which everyone hopes will never occur. Moreover, half of you—as women—wouldn't even be subject to such an emergency draft under present law. The other half need only register at your local post office when you turn 18, and go about your lives as always until you are too old to be drafted.

But what are the odds that you will reach that magic age which puts you beyond conscription? Fifty percent? Three to two? Five to one? I would not hazard a guess. Consider our government's open hostility toward the Sandinista government of Nicaragua. Consider our massive dependence on Middle Eastern oil, and how our government might respond if that supply is threatened or cut off. Consider that our government is sending millions of dollars of military hardware to support a right-wing government in El Salvador, and that U.S. military personnel are at this moment deployed in that country. Consider that U.S. government policymakers now openly discuss what was utterly unthinkable only a decade ago: the notion that a nuclear war can be winnable.

Consider that in 1980, then-Republican candidate for president Ronald Reagan criticized President Jimmy Carter's reinstitution of draft registration as needless and inflammatory to world peace, promising that if elected, he would end registration. Soon after his election, however, Mr. Reagan publicly endorsed retention of draft registration.

Finally, consider this: in 1954, then-Senator Lyndon Johnson publicly stated, "I am against sending American GIs into the mud and muck of Indochina on a blood-letting spree to perpetuate colonialism and white man's exploitation of Asia." In 1964, then-President Johnson campaigned successfully for re-election against Barry Goldwater on a promise to keep American GIs out of Vietnam. Four years later, while Lyndon Johnson was still president, nearly half a million American GIs were fighting in the mud and muck of Indochina, and the blood-letting spree would eventually claim the lives of 1.7 million Vietnamese, wounding 3.2 million more, and leaving 12 million homeless.

One of those half million American GIs was me. I was not even drafted; I volunteered. I based my decision on every responsible source of information I had available to me at that time. According to the information I had—information disseminated by my government and all the major news media—Communists from North Vietnam, supported by the Russians and the Chinese, were waging a terrible war of aggression against the free Republic of South Vietnam. Moreover, not only was the freedom of the South Vietnamese at stake, but because Vietnam was part and parcel of the Communist conspiracy ultimately to take over the world, my country's freedom and my own freedom were at stake. It was something called the Domino Theory.

This was all taking place about the time I was your age, and I believed sincerely that if we did not stop the communists in Vietnam, we would one day have to fight them in San Diego. I had no reason up to that point in my life to doubt either my government or my high school teachers or the *New York Times*. I believed in my country and its God-given role as leader of the Free World—that it was the finest nation on earth, that its political system and its leaders were essentially good, and that any nation or people who opposed us must be inherently bad. Furthermore, I valued my freedom, and took seriously the notion that I owed something to my country. The draft was already cranking into high gear in the spring of 1966 when I decided to turn down four college acceptances and enlist in the United States Marine Corps. I was 17 years old, nine days out of high school.

Seven months later, I found myself in Vietnam. What I found in Vietnam, however, was not at all what I had been taught to expect. The American people had been told that we were defending a free democracy. What I found was a military dictatorship rife with corruption and venality and repression. The premier of South Vietnam openly admired Adolf Hitler. Buddhist priests who petitioned for peace were jailed or shot down in the streets. Officials at every level engaged in blatant black-marketeering at astronomical profit and at the expense of their own people. And the government was clearly devoid of the support of the vast majority of the Vietnamese people.

The American people had been told that some Vietnamese civilians had been mercifully relocated into safe hamlets to protect them from the marauding Viet Cong. What I found was the wholesale forced removal of thousands of people from their ancestral homelands to poverty-stricken, misery-laden shantytowns where men had no work and women rooted through American garbage trying to find food for their children.

The American people had been told that the Viet Cong managed to perpetuate their guerrilla war only through violence and coercion inflicted upon the Vietnamese people: kidnapping, murder, impressment and theft were the tactics of the communists; unspeakable atrocities were visited upon those who refused to cooperate. But in my thirteen months in a Marine infantry battalion, I regularly witnessed and participated in

A young woman offers a flower to MPs as a symbol of peace
during an anti–Vietnam War protest at the Pentagon.

the destruction of civilian homes and sometimes whole villages, the most
brutal interrogations of civilians, and the routine killing of unarmed
men, women and children along with their crops and livestock.

The American people had been told that we were in Vietnam to defend the Vietnamese against outside aggression, but I found that we
were the aggressors, we were the foreigners, and the people we were
supposedly defending hated us because they destroyed their forests with
chemical defoliants, and burned their fields with napalm, and called the
people of Vietnam gooks, chinks, slopes and zipperheads, turning their
sons into shoeshine boys and their daughters into whores.

Make no mistake about it: there were indeed Viet Cong in Vietnam.
And they regularly tried to kill me. But they had good reason to do so,
and most of the people of Vietnam, as nearly as I could tell then and
still believe to this day, were on the side of the Viet Cong, wanting little else than for us to stop killing them and go away. In short, I discovered

that the information upon which I had based my decision to enlist had been bad information.

For my little part in the war, the government promoted me to sergeant, awarded me the Purple Heart Medal, two Presidential Unit citations, the Navy Combat Action ribbon and the Good Conduct Medal, and gave me an honorable discharge. But I could not avoid the increasingly uncomfortable feeling that my government had been playing the game with less than a full deck of cards, and that I had been had, plain and simple.

Consider this: five years after I went to Vietnam to help contain the Chinese communists—who were, remember, according to our government, supporting and directing the Viet Cong—President Richard Nixon stood on the Great Wall of China with Communist Premier Chou En Lai, smiling and shaking hands while American GIs continued to fight and die in the mud and muck of Indochina.

Consider this: eight years after I went to Vietnam to prevent the Domino Theory from tumbling into San Diego, the fall of South Vietnam to the communists was reported on the six o'clock news with hardly more impact than the story of a bad fire in Cleveland. The lives of Americans were not altered in any way. Kids continued to play ball in the park, mothers and fathers went to work, and all America geared up feverishly for the coming bicentennial celebration.

Consider this: when the Pentagon Papers—the government's own history of the war in Vietnam—became public, they revealed a stark, willful pattern of deception, misrepresentation and outright lies on the part of U.S. policymakers regarding the situation in Vietnam and the U.S. government's intentions over the entire course of the war.

But that was Vietnam; that's ancient history. What does it have to do with you? Consider how the United States has dealt with the people responsible for the Vietnam war. McGeorge Bundy, whom the Pentagon Papers identifies as the major architect of U.S. policy in Vietnam, became president of the Ford Foundation. Robert S. McNamara, Secretary of Defense under Presidents Kennedy and Johnson, became president of the World Bank. General William Westmoreland, who built up U.S. troop levels from 30,000 to 500,000, insisting all the while that he could see the light at the end of the tunnel, was promoted to Army Chief of Staff. Harold Brown, who as secretary of the Air Force called for extensive bombing of North Vietnam, was appointed Secretary of Defense by President Carter. Paul H. Nitze, a senior official in the Defense Department during the war, was appointed chief U.S. negotiator for strategic arms limitations talks by President Reagan.

In short, the people who got us into Vietnam and kept us there for a quarter of a century have continued to be and still are an integral part of the policy-making apparatus of the U.S. government. President Reagan himself has repeatedly called the U.S. war in Indochina "a noble cause."

Now consider the fates of those of us who actually fought in that noble cause. There are approximately 2.5 million of us. Forty-eight thousand of us were killed in combat. Another 10,000 of us died in Vietnam of non-combat incidents. More than 300,000 of us were wounded in action, including 21,000 permanently physically disabled. Thirteen thousand of us were diagnosed as permanently disabled due to psychological or neurological disorders.

All through the decade of the 1970s, responsible medical authorities indicated repeatedly that one-third to one-half of all Vietnam veterans suffered chronic psychological problems resulting from the war. By 1976, 500,000 of us had attempted suicide since coming home. Fifty-five thousand of us succeeded in that tragic attempt, or died of drug overdose or in single-car accidents. Yet it was not until 1979—seventeen years after the first of us were sent to Vietnam, six years after the last of us came home—that the United States government even acknowledged psychological trauma as a Vietnam-related injury and the Veterans Administration began to treat those of us with stress problems. And every year since Reagan's election in 1980, funding for those Vietnam Veterans Outreach Clinics has gotten smaller and smaller.

Consider that the jobless rate among Vietnam veterans has continued to be among the highest in the country, while the GI Bill that was supposed to enable us to go to college turned out to be hardly enough to pay for our books. Consider that Vietnam veterans have the highest divorce rate in the nation, and that as early as 1973, 32 percent of all inmates in federal prisons were Vietnam veterans. Consider that in 1980 Vietnam veterans were honored on a U.S. postage stamp, but the U.S. government still refuses to treat most Vietnam veterans afflicted with symptoms of Agent Orange poisoning, contracted by exposure in the chemical defoliants used by U.S. Forces in Vietnam. And consider that those of us who tried to tell our fellow citizens what was really happening in Vietnam were characterized by Vice President of the United States Spiro T. Agnew as "malcontents, radicals, incendiaries, civil and uncivil disobedients, yippies, hippies, yahoos, Black Panthers, lions and tigers."

And all of this has a great deal to do with you because you are the next potential crop of American war veterans. You, or your boyfriends and brothers and husbands and cousins and friends. Consider the recruiting ads current on television these days that proclaim in slick technicolor: "The Few, the Proud, the Marines"; "Air Force—a great way of life"; "The Navy: it's not just a job; it's an adventure"; "Be all you can be in today's Action Army."

Consider that the U.S. government maintains that the guerrilla movement in El Salvador is the brainchild of the Russians and the baby of the Cubans—an argument almost identical to the claims made about Vietnam twenty years ago—and this in spite of the fact that a former U.S. ambassador to El Salvador has characterized the president of the Salvadoran National Assembly as "a pathological killer." Consider that the present administration has created the largest increase in the military budget since the Second World War, and intends to double that increase by 1985. Consider that the United States is the world's largest exporter of arms and armaments. Now consider again President Reagan's changing position on draft registration.

I can't possibly tell you here all that I would like to tell you—all that I have learned in the 16 years since I sat where you are now sitting. But I can tell you a few things. I still believe that all of us owe something to our country, but I am no longer convinced that what I owe my country is military service whenever and wherever my government demands it. Furthermore, if I owe something to my country, my country also owes something to me—and to each one of you: it owes us the obligation not to ask for our lives unless it is absolutely necessary. And I believe absolutely that in the course of my lifetime and yours, the U.S. government—regardless of the particular administration or political party in power—has failed that obligation time and time again.

I will not tell you to become conscientious objectors, or to urge your friends and brothers and boyfriends to become conscientious objectors. But I sincerely hope that all of you will begin to learn the things that I failed to learn until it was too late, to question beliefs and assumptions I failed to question until the damage had been done.

I hope that none of you will ever have to face the kind of decision that I faced when I was your age. But if you do, I hope even more that you will be able to look back on your decision and honestly conclude that you made the right choice. Because you will have to live with that decision for the rest of your lives—if you live at all—and I can tell you from hard experience that the wrong choice is an awesome burden indeed.

Time on Target

W. D. EHRHART

We used to get intelligence reports
from the Vietnamese district offices.
Every night, I'd make a list

of targets for artillery to hit.
It used to give me quite a kick
to know that I, a corporal,
could command an entire battery
to fire anywhere I said.
One day, while on patrol,
we passed the ruins of a house;
beside it sat a woman
with her left hand torn away;
beside her lay a child, dead.
When I got back to base,
I told the fellows in the COC;
it gave us all a lift to know
all those shells we fired every night
were hitting something.

Hunting

W. D. EHRHART

Sighting down the long black barrel,
I wait till front and rear sights
form a perfect line on his body,
then slowly squeeze the trigger.
The thought occurs
that I have never hunted anything in my whole life
except other men.
But I have learned by now
where such thoughts lead,
and soon pass on
to chow, and sleep,
and how much longer till I change my socks.

Psychologists for Peace parade against the Vietnam War in New York City in the late 1960s.

The Fish Cheer &
I-Feel-Like-I'm-Fixin'-To-Die Rag

COUNTRY JOE & THE FISH

Country Joe & the Fish, headed by "Country" Joe McDonald and Barry "The Fish" Melton, made a name for themselves in the latter half of the 1960s with their protest music against the Vietnam War. This song, from 1965, was their biggest hit.

> *Gimme an F!*
> *F!*
> *Gimme an I!*
> *I!*
> *Gimme an S!*
> *S!*

Gimme an H!

H!

What's that spell?

FISH!

What's that spell?

FISH!

What's that spell?

FISH!

Yeah, come on all of you, big strong men,

Uncle Sam needs your help again.

He's got himself in a terrible jam

Way down yonder in Vietnam

So put down your books and pick up a gun,

We're gonna have a whole lotta fun.

And it's one, two, three,

What are we fighting for?

Don't ask me, I don't give a damn,

Next stop is Vietnam;

And it's five, six, seven,

Open up the pearly gates,

Well there ain't no time to wonder why,

Whoopee! we're all gonna die.

Well, come on generals, let's move fast;

Your big chance has come at last.

Gotta go out and get those reds—

The only good commie is the one who's dead

And you know that peace can only be won

When we've blown 'em all to kingdom come.

And it's one, two, three,

What are we fighting for?

Don't ask me, I don't give a damn,

Next stop is Vietnam;

And it's five, six, seven,

Open up the pearly gates,
Well there ain't no time to wonder why
Whoopee! We're all gonna die.
Huh!
Well, come on Wall Street, don't move slow,
Why man, this is war au-go-go.
There's plenty good money to be made
By supplying the Army with the tools of the trade,
Just hope and pray that if they drop the bomb,
They drop it on the Viet Cong.
And it's one, two, three,
What are we fighting for?
Don't ask me, I don't give a damn,
Next stop is Vietnam.
And it's five, six, seven,
Open up the pearly gates,
Well there ain't no time to wonder why
Whoopee! We're all gonna die.
Well, come on mothers throughout the land,
Pack your boys off to Vietnam.
Come on fathers, don't hesitate,
Send 'em off before it's too late.
Be the first one on your block
To have your boy come home in a box.
And it's one, two, three
What are we fighting for?
Don't ask me, I don't give a damn,
Next stop is Vietnam.
And it's five, six, seven,
Open up the pearly gates,
Well there ain't no time to wonder why,
Whoopee! We're all gonna die.

9

Iraq and the War on Terror

The troops here and across the world are fighting a global war on terror. The war reached our shores on September the 11th. . . . Our mission in Iraq is clear. We're hunting down terrorists. We're helping build a free nation that is an ally in the war on terror. We're advancing freedom in the broader Middle East. We are removing a source of violence and instability, and laying the foundation of peace for our children and grandchildren.

—PRESIDENT GEORGE W. BUSH,
address to the nation, June 28, 2005

Consider some of the consequences of the Iraq War: more than four thousand American troops killed and tens of thousands wounded, many grievously so; enormous numbers of Iraqi civilians slain; widespread war profiteering and corruption in Iraq; mercenaries and private militias; an Iraqi civil war; ethnic cleansing among Iraqis; officially sponsored torture; "rendition" (sending suspected terrorists to countries that torture prisoners); an avalanche of U.S. government lies and deliberate misinformation; a vast expansion of presidential power and castration of congressional authority; a very pro-Bush Supreme Court majority; egregious violations of habeas corpus; disregard for civil liberties; too many Democratic Party hawks; another round of "stab-in-the-back" assaults against war critics; a conformist mainstream media (both print and television); a deadening absence of concern for the huge number of Iraqi civilian casualties; the trillions of dollars spent on the war; and the continued authority and influence of the pro-war Dick Cheney and extremists demanding yet another war, this time against Iran.

By the time George W. Bush and Dick Cheney rose to power in 2001, younger second-string and well-paid neoconservatives were well established in Washington, courtesy of the capital's proliferation of think tanks and their wealthy patrons. Writing and publishing regularly, holding seminars with true believers, and knowledgeable about Washington's Byzantine political scene, theirs was a callow and myopic vision extolling "regime change" and "benevolent global hegemony"—achievable, if necessary, at the point of a gun. Their catastrophic misjudgments were grounded on nothing more than theoretical and martial posturing. Virtually none of them have any experience in active military service. Together with the belligerent Cheney and their Christian fundamentalist and liberal hawk allies, they exalt the American imperium.

Was the Iraq War about oil, economic gain, Israel, the desire to control the Middle East, 9/11, or a combination of motives that moved them to demand the invasion of Iraq and then predict a glorious victory and welcoming population? It is hard to forget the photo-op in 2004 when Bush, wearing an Air Force suit to make him appear as a combat veteran, stood on the USS Abraham Lincoln under a triumphant streamer heralding "Mission Accomplished." That scene, manufactured by the administration, once again sent the message that an America motivated by pure humanitarian instincts had prevailed against evil.

Having learned little from its early support of the Vietnam War, the media again rolled over and became the government's handmaiden.

With the exception of Knight-Ridder (now called McClatchy) and the people we include here, our major media agencies uncritically accepted the fabrications aired by the government. Lying by presidential administrations is, of course, hardly novel. The Spanish-American War, the invasion of the Philippines, entry into World War I, the repeated occupations of Caribbean and Central American mini-states, the Vietnam War, Ronald Reagan's proxy war in Central America, and the unexplained but widely approved invasions of Grenada and Panama are a few examples of presidential falsehoods that a sycophantic press made little effort to expose. On television, only a handful of critics were allowed on the air. Why, then, should government policies and politicians change? Since the end of the Cold War, one presidential administration after another failed to consider alternative foreign policies. American pugnacity and the absence of serious diplomacy will surely lead to new wars in the years ahead, unless challenged by future presidents, Congresses, and the American people.

Against War with Afghanistan

U.S. REPRESENTATIVE BARBARA LEE

Representative Barbara Lee (D-CA) was the only member of Congress to vote against authorizing President George W. Bush to use military force against Afghanistan. She delivered these remarks on the House floor on September 15, 2001.

Mr. Speaker, I rise today with a heavy heart, one that is filled with sorrow for the families and loved ones who were killed and injured in New York, Virginia, and Pennsylvania. Only the most foolish or the most callous would not understand the grief that has gripped the American people and millions across the world.

This unspeakable attack on the United States has forced me to rely on my moral compass, my conscience, and my God for direction.

September 11 changed the world. Our deepest fears now haunt us. Yet I am convinced that military action will not prevent further acts of international terrorism against the United States.

I know that this use-of-force resolution will pass although we all know that the President can wage a war even without this resolution. However difficult this vote may be, some of us must urge the use of restraint. There must be some of us who say, let's step back for a moment and think through the implications of our actions today—let us more fully understand its consequences.

We are not dealing with a conventional war. We cannot respond in a conventional manner. I do not want to see this spiral out of control. This crisis involves issues of national security, foreign policy, public safety, intelligence gathering, economics, and murder. Our response must be equally multifaceted.

We must not rush to judgment. Far too many innocent people have already died. Our country is in mourning. If we rush to launch a counterattack, we run too great a risk that women, children, and other noncombatants will be caught in the crossfire.

Nor can we let our justified anger over these outrageous acts by vicious murderers inflame prejudice against all Arab Americans, Muslims, Southeast Asians, or any other people because of their race, religion, or ethnicity.

Finally, we must be careful not to embark on an open-ended war with neither an exit strategy nor a focused target. We cannot repeat past mistakes.

In 1964, Congress gave President Lyndon Johnson the power to "take all necessary measures" to repel attacks and prevent further aggression. In so doing, this House abandoned its own constitutional responsibilities and launched our country into years of undeclared war in Vietnam.

At that time, Sen. Wayne Morse, one of two lonely votes against the Tonkin Gulf Resolution, declared, "I believe that history will record that we have made a grave mistake in subverting and circumventing the Constitution of the United States. . . . I believe that within the next century, future generations will look with dismay and great disappointment upon a Congress which is now about to make such a historic mistake."

Senator Morse was correct, and I fear we make the same mistake today. And I fear the consequences.

I have agonized over this vote. But I came to grips with it in the very painful yet beautiful memorial service today at the National Cathedral. As a member of the clergy so eloquently said, "As we act, let us not become the evil that we deplore."

We Stand Passively Mute

SENATOR ROBERT BYRD

Senator Robert Byrd (D–WV) delivered this speech on the Senate floor on February 12, 2003.

To contemplate war is to think about the most horrible of human experiences. On this February day, as this nation stands at the brink of battle, every American on some level must be contemplating the horrors of war.

Yet, this Chamber is, for the most part, silent—ominously, dreadfully silent. There is no debate, no discussion, no attempt to lay out for the nation the pros and cons of this particular war. There is nothing.

We stand passively mute in the United States Senate, paralyzed by our own uncertainty, seemingly stunned by the sheer turmoil of events. Only on the editorial pages of our newspapers is there much substantive discussion of the prudence or imprudence of engaging in this particular war.

Reverend William Sloan Coffin, an army and CIA veteran, Presbyterian minister, and leader of SANE/FREEZE (now called Peace Action), is pictured here in the 1980s. His religious faith inspired his work for peace and civil rights. During the Vietnam War, Coffin, Dr. Benjamin Spock, and others were convicted of helping draft resisters, a verdict rejected on appeal. Before his death in 2006, he said, "The war against Iraq is as disastrous as it is unnecessary . . . the worst war in American history."

And this is no small conflagration we contemplate. This is no simple attempt to defang a villain. No. This coming battle, if it materializes, represents a turning point in U.S. foreign policy and possibly a turning point in the recent history of the world.

This nation is about to embark upon the first test of a revolutionary doctrine applied in an extraordinary way at an unfortunate time. The doctrine of preemption—the idea that the United States or any other nation can legitimately attack a nation that is not imminently threatening but may be threatening in the future—is a radical new twist on the traditional idea of self-defense. It appears to be in contravention of international law and the U.N. Charter. And it is being tested at a time of worldwide terrorism, making many countries around the globe wonder if they will soon be on our—or some other nation's—hit list. High level Administration figures recently refused to take nuclear weapons off the table when discussing a possible attack against Iraq. What could be more destabilizing and unwise than this type of uncertainty, particularly in a world where globalism has tied the vital economic and security interests of many nations so closely together? There are huge cracks emerging in our time-honored alliances, and U.S. intentions are suddenly subject to damaging worldwide speculation. Anti-Americanism based on mistrust, misinformation, suspicion, and alarming rhetoric from U.S. leaders is fracturing the once solid alliance against global terrorism which existed after September 11.

Here at home, people are warned of imminent terrorist attacks with little guidance as to when or where such attacks might occur. Family members are being called to active military duty, with no idea of the duration of their stay or what horrors they may face. Communities are being left with less than adequate police and fire protection. Other essential services are also short-staffed. The mood of the nation is grim. The economy is stumbling. Fuel prices are rising and may soon spike higher.

This Administration, now in power for a little over two years, must be judged on its record. I believe that that record is dismal.

In that scant two years, this Administration has squandered a large projected surplus of some $5.6 trillion over the next decade and taken us to projected deficits as far as the eye can see. This Administration's domestic policy has put many of our states in dire financial condition, under-funding scores of essential programs for our people. This Administration has fostered policies which have slowed economic growth. This Administration has ignored urgent matters such as the crisis in health care for our elderly. This Administration has been slow to provide adequate funding for homeland security. This Administration has been reluctant to better protect our long and porous borders.

In foreign policy, this Administration has failed to find Osama bin Laden. In fact, just yesterday we heard from him again marshaling his forces and urging them to kill. This Administration has split traditional alliances, possibly crippling, for all time, international order-keeping entities like the United Nations and NATO. This Administration has called into question the traditional worldwide perception of the United States as well-intentioned peacekeeper. This Administration has turned the patient art of diplomacy into threats, labeling, and name-calling of the sort that reflects quite poorly on the intelligence and sensitivity of our leaders, and which will have consequences for years to come.

Calling heads of state pygmies, labeling whole countries as evil, denigrating powerful European allies as irrelevant—these types of crude insensitivities can do our great nation no good. We may have massive military might, but we cannot fight a global war on terrorism alone. We need the cooperation and friendship of our time-honored allies as well as the newer-found friends whom we can attract with our wealth. Our awesome military machine will do us little good if we suffer another devastating attack on our homeland which severely damages our economy. Our military manpower is already stretched thin and we will need the augmenting support of those nations who can supply troop strength, not just sign letters cheering us on.

The war in Afghanistan has cost us $37 billion so far, yet there is evidence that terrorism may already be starting to regain its hold in that region. We have not found bin Laden, and unless we secure the peace in Afghanistan, the dark dens of terrorism may yet again flourish in that remote and devastated land.

Pakistan as well is at risk of destabilizing forces. This Administration has not finished the first war against terrorism and yet it is eager to embark on another conflict with perils much greater than those in Afghanistan. Is our attention span that short? Have we not learned that after winning the war one must always secure the peace?

And yet we hear little about the aftermath of war in Iraq. In the absence of plans, speculation abroad is rife. Will we seize Iraq's oil fields, becoming an occupying power which controls the price and supply of that nation's oil for the foreseeable future? To whom do we propose to hand the reigns of power after Saddam Hussein?

Will our war inflame the Muslim world, resulting in devastating attacks on Israel? Will Israel retaliate with its own nuclear arsenal?

Will the Jordanian and Saudi Arabian governments be toppled by radicals, bolstered by Iran which has much closer ties to terrorism than Iraq?

Could a disruption of the world's oil supply lead to a worldwide recession? Has our senselessly bellicose language and our callous disregard of the interests and opinions of other nations increased the global race to join the nuclear club and made proliferation an even more lucrative practice for nations which need the income?

In only the space of two short years this reckless and arrogant Administration has initiated policies which may reap disastrous consequences for years.

One can understand the anger and shock of any president after the savage attacks of September 11. One can appreciate the frustration of having only a shadow to chase and an amorphous, fleeting enemy on which it is nearly impossible to exact retribution.

But to turn one's frustration and anger into the kind of extremely destabilizing and dangerous foreign policy debacle that the world is currently witnessing is inexcusable from any Administration charged with the awesome power and responsibility of guiding the destiny of the greatest superpower on the planet. Frankly, many of the pronouncements made by this Administration are outrageous. There is no other word.

Yet this chamber is hauntingly silent. On what is possibly the eve of horrific infliction of death and destruction on the population of the nation of Iraq—a population, I might add, of which over 50 percent is under age 15—this chamber is silent. On what is possibly only days before we send thousands of our own citizens to face unimagined horrors of chemical and biological warfare—this chamber is silent. On the eve of what could possibly be a vicious terrorist attack in retaliation for our attack on Iraq, it is business as usual in the United States Senate.

We are truly "sleepwalking through history." In my heart of hearts I pray that this great nation and its good and trusting citizens are not in for a rudest of awakenings.

To engage in war is always to pick a wild card. And war must always be a last resort, not a first choice. I truly must question the judgment of any president who can say that a massive unprovoked military attack on a nation which is over 50 percent children is "in the highest moral traditions of our country." This war is not necessary at this time. Pressure appears to be having a good result in Iraq. Our mistake was to put ourselves in a corner so quickly. Our challenge is to now find a graceful way out of a box of our own making. Perhaps there is still a way if we allow more time.

An Open Letter to My Fellow Veterans

CAMILLO "MAC" BICA

As a veteran recovering from his experiences as a United States Marine Corps officer during the Vietnam War, Camillo "Mac" Bica, a professor of philosophy at the School of Visual Arts in New York City, founded, and coordinated for five years, the Veterans Self-Help Initiative. He published this open letter on March 22, 2007.

As we enter our fifth year of occupation, and as Iraq continues to degenerate into sectarian violence and civil war, I think it important that we talk, vet to vet. Real talk, talk from the heart, as we did back in Iraq, in the Nam, in Korea, on the battlefields of Europe and the Pacific. Let us put aside, for a moment, all the bunk we have been fed over the years by those who were not there. You know who I mean. The politicians and war strategists who cavalierly make war, decide tactics, and send us off to fight, bleed, and die for a cause that is uncertain or non-existent. Self-proclaimed "patriots" who, while remaining safe at home, try to convince us that the threat to our way of life—to America and to freedom—is real and grave and that the disruption of our lives and the sacrifices we make, and that our brothers and sisters make, are necessary and glorious.

It is not easy, I know, to ignore their bull, the mythology they create, and to separate fantasy from reality. Time and pain have seen to that. Maybe, in our rational minds, it is comforting to accept their lies, their brainwashing, and their changing of history. Perhaps it is even therapeutic, as a means of "readjusting," of coping with the memories and living with the experiences of war. After all, it is easier and preferable to think oneself a hero than a dupe. Easier to believe our efforts and sacrifices are necessary and noble, rather than a mistake, a waste of lives and treasure.

But in our gut, down deep in places we no longer wish to go, dark places, frightening places, we know the truth. We lived it. We were there. We saw the insanity, the horror, the chaos, the suffering, and the death. Think back. Clear your mind. We killed and were killed. We held our brothers and sisters in our arms, embraced them as they breathed their last breath. Their screams will forever echo in our minds. Final glances we will remember for the rest of our lives. Can you hear their cries? Can you smell the smells? Is the adrenalin flowing? Are you there?

Now think. Where is the glory, or the necessity? What is the purpose, or the strategy? Can you feel it? The fear? The frustration? The futility? The waste? The profound sadness? The horror? This is the reality of war, a reality that we know and those who make war try to hide. Memories and knowledge we try to forget, or suppress, or change. This vulnerability they exploit. And from need and from the fear that our efforts and sacrifices and those of our lost comrades will be defiled or diminished should war be seen as it truly is, we embrace their mythology and their lies. While the truth may certainly be tragic and anxiety-provoking, we must realize that the cost of a false sense of comfort is unacceptably high and that we forget or ignore the realities and lessons of war at our peril, and at the peril of our children.

For those of us who have experienced the trauma and horror of the battlefield, or suffered the loss or injury of a loved one, accepting the truth about war, though difficult and disconcerting, will ultimately prove uplifting and curative. When we realize the deception and the mythologizing of war, and begin to see clearly, it becomes apparent that our legacy, dignity, self-respect, and integrity rest not upon fantasy, lies, and fabrications. We have proved our patriotism, selflessness, valor, and nobility, not with shallow rhetoric but by our actions and our sacrifices on the field of battle.

We who know war for what it truly is have a profound responsibility to again come forward, shoulder to shoulder, and bear witness to the truth about war. If our sacrifices and those of our brothers and sisters whose lives were cut short by war, are to have any meaning at all, we must raise our voices in unison. We must warn those who make war lightly—or are ignorant of its consequences and send other children to kill and to die in battle—that we reject their mythology and their rhetoric of false patriotism and will not unquestioningly and blindly support unjust, unnecessary, and immoral wars.

Perhaps war is a reality that will not soon go away, and sacrifices on the field of battle will again be required. But by demanding truth and recognizing war as it truly is, by questioning purpose and necessity, by ensuring a clarity of vision rather than the blind compliance some wish to portray as patriotism, we will ensure that war remains a means of last resort, that no other person will again have to kill, die, or grieve the loss of their son or daughter for a cause that is misguided. We will ensure that those who dare to initiate such wars and connive to use deception and myth to encourage participation and support are held responsible for their crimes against humanity.

Let us make this our legacy. Welcome home.

I Lost My Son to a War I Oppose; We Were Both Doing Our Duty

ANDREW J. BACEVICH

Andrew J. Bacevich is a professor of international relations at Boston University and author of The New American Militarism: How

Americans Are Seduced by War (2005), among other books. This article appeared in the Washington Post *on May 27, 2007.*

Parents who lose children, whether through accident or illness, inevitably wonder what they could have done to prevent their loss. When my son was killed in Iraq earlier this month at age 27, I found myself pondering my responsibility for his death.

Among the hundreds of messages that my wife and I have received, two bore directly on this question. Both held me personally culpable, insisting that my public opposition to the war had provided aid and comfort to the enemy. Each said that my son's death came as a direct result of my antiwar writings.

This may seem a vile accusation to lay against a grieving father. But in fact, it has become a staple of American political discourse, repeated endlessly by those keen to allow President Bush a free hand in waging his war. By encouraging "the terrorists," opponents of the Iraq conflict increase the risk to U.S. troops. Although the First Amendment protects antiwar critics from being tried for treason, it provides no protection for the hardly less serious charge of failing to support the troops—today's civic equivalent of dereliction of duty.

What exactly is a father's duty when his son is sent into harm's way?

Among the many ways to answer that question, mine was this one: As my son was doing his utmost to be a good soldier, I strove to be a good citizen.

As a citizen, I have tried since September 11, 2001, to promote a critical understanding of U.S. foreign policy. I know that even now, people of good will find much to admire in Bush's response to that awful day. They applaud his doctrine of preventive war. They endorse his crusade to spread democracy across the Muslim world and to eliminate tyranny from the face of the Earth. They insist not only that his decision to invade Iraq in 2003 was correct but that the war there can still be won. Some—the members of the "the-surge-is-already-working" school of thought—even profess to see victory just over the horizon.

I believe that such notions are dead wrong and doomed to fail. In books, articles and op-ed pieces, in talks to audiences large and small, I have said as much. "The long war is an unwinnable one," I wrote in this section of the *Washington Post* in August 2005. "The United States needs to liquidate its presence in Iraq, placing the onus on Iraqis to decide their fate and creating the space for other regional powers to assist in brokering a political settlement. We've done all that we can do."

Not for a second did I expect my own efforts to make a difference. But I did nurse the hope that my voice might combine with those of others—teachers, writers, activists and ordinary folks—to educate the public about the folly of the course on which the nation has embarked. I hoped that those efforts might produce a political climate conducive to change. I genuinely believed that if the people spoke, our leaders in Washington would listen and respond.

This, I can now see, was an illusion.

The people have spoken, and nothing of substance has changed. The November 2006 midterm elections signified an unambiguous repudiation of the policies that landed us in our present predicament. But half a year later, the war continues, with no end in sight. Indeed, by sending more troops to Iraq (and by extending the tours of those, like my son, who were already there), Bush has signaled his complete disregard for what was once quaintly referred to as "the will of the people."

To be fair, responsibility for the war's continuation now rests no less with the Democrats who control Congress than with the president and his party. After my son's death, my state's senators, Edward M. Kennedy and John F. Kerry, telephoned to express their condolences. Stephen F. Lynch, our congressman, attended my son's wake. Kerry was present for the funeral mass. My family and I greatly appreciated such gestures. But when I suggested to each of them the necessity of ending the war, I got the brush-off. More accurately, after ever so briefly pretending to listen, each treated me to a convoluted explanation that said in essence: Don't blame me.

To whom do Kennedy, Kerry and Lynch listen? We know the answer: to the same people who have the ear of George W. Bush and Karl Rove—namely, wealthy individuals and institutions.

Money buys access and influence. Money greases the process that will yield us a new president in 2008. When it comes to Iraq, money ensures that the concerns of big business, big oil, bellicose evangelicals and Middle East allies gain a hearing. By comparison, the lives of U.S. soldiers figure as an afterthought.

Memorial Day orators will say that a GI's life is priceless. Don't believe it. I know what value the U.S. government assigns to a soldier's life: I've been handed the check. It's roughly what the Yankees will pay Roger Clemens per inning once he starts pitching next month.

Money maintains the Republican/Democratic duopoly of trivialized politics. It confines the debate over U.S. policy to well-hewn channels. It preserves intact the clichés of 1933–45 about isolationism, appeasement and the nation's call to "global leadership." It inhibits any serious accounting of exactly how much our misadventure in Iraq is costing. It ignores completely the question of who actually pays. It negates democracy, rendering free speech little more than a means of recording dissent.

This is not some great conspiracy. It's the way our system works.

In joining the Army, my son was following in his father's footsteps: Before he was born, I had served in Vietnam. As military officers, we shared an ironic kinship of sorts, each of us demonstrating a peculiar knack for picking the wrong war at the wrong time. Yet he was the better soldier—brave and steadfast and irrepressible.

I know that my son did his best to serve our country. Through my own opposition to a profoundly misguided war, I thought I was doing the same. In fact, while he was giving his all, I was doing nothing. In this way, I failed him.

Why Did Bush Destroy Iraq?

PAUL CRAIG ROBERTS

Paul Craig Roberts wrote the 1981 Kemp-Roth bill that cut income-tax rates and was assistant secretary of the treasury in the Reagan administration. He served as associate editor of the Wall Street Journal *editorial page and contributing editor of* National Review. *He is author or coauthor of eight books, including* The Supply-Side Revolution *(Harvard University Press). This was his Creators Syndicate column for March 13, 2006.*

March 20 is the third anniversary of the Bush regime's invasion of Iraq. U.S. military casualties to date are approximately 20,000 killed, wounded, maimed, and disabled. Iraqi civilian casualties number in the tens of thousands. Iraq's infrastructure is in ruins. Tens of thousands of homes have been destroyed. Fallujah, a city of 300,000 people, had 36,000 of its 50,000 homes destroyed by the U.S. military. Half of the city's former population are displaced persons living in tents.

Thousands of Iraqis have been detained in prisons, and hundreds have been brutally tortured. America's reputation in the Muslim world is ruined.

The Bush regime expected a short "cakewalk" war to be followed by the imposition of a puppet government and permanent U.S. military bases. Instead, U.S. military forces are confronted with an insurgency that has denied control over Iraq to the U.S. military. Chaos rules, and civil war may be coming on top of the insurgency.

On March 9, U.S. Defense Secretary Donald Rumsfeld, the man who has been totally wrong about Iraq, told Congress that if the unprecedented violence in Iraq breaks out in civil war, the U.S. will rely primarily on Iraq's security forces to put down civil war.

What Iraqi security forces? Iraq does not have a security force. The Shia have a security force, the Sunnis have a security force, and the

Kurds have a security force. The sectarian militias control the streets, towns, and cities. If civil war breaks out, the "Iraqi security force" will dissolve into the sectarian militias, leaving the U.S. military in the middle of the melee.

Is this what "support the troops" means?

President Bush's determination to remain in Iraq despite the obvious failure of the attempted occupation puts Bush at odds with the American public and with our troops. Polls show that a majority of Americans believe that the invasion of Iraq was a mistake and that our troops should be withdrawn. An even larger majority of the troops themselves believe they should be withdrawn.

Yet Bush, who is incapable of admitting a mistake, persists in a strategic blunder that is turning into a catastrophe.

Bush's support has fallen to 34 percent.

The war's out-of-pocket cost to date is approximately $300 billion—every dollar borrowed from foreigners. Economic and budgetary experts have calculated that the ultimate cost of Bush's Iraq war in terms of long-term care for veterans, interest on borrowed money, and resources diverted from productive uses will be between $1 trillion and $2 trillion.

What is being achieved for this enormous sacrifice?

No one knows.

Every reason we have been given for the Iraqi invasion has proved to be false. Saddam Hussein had no weapons of mass destruction. Reports from UN weapons inspectors, top level U.S. intelligence officials, Secretary of the Treasury Paul O'Neill, and leaked top-secret documents from the British cabinet all make it unequivocally clear that the Bush regime first decided to invade Iraq and then looked around for a reason.

Saddam Hussein had no terrorist connection to Osama bin Laden and no role in the 9/11 attack. Hussein was a secular ruler totally at odds with bin Laden's Islamist aims. Every informed person in the world knew this.

When the original justifications for the U.S. invasion collapsed, Bush said that the reason for the invasion was to rid Iraq of a dictator

An October 2005 anti–Iraq War vigil outside the Armed Forces Recruiting Station in Times Square, New York City, marks two thousand dead U.S. troops.

and to put a democracy in its place. Despite all the hoopla about democracy and elections, no Iraqi government has been able to form, and the country is on the brink of civil war. Some Middle East experts believe that violence will spread throughout the region.

The brutal truth is that America's responsibility is extreme. We have destroyed a country and created political chaos for no reason whatsoever.

Seldom in history has a government miscalculated as badly as Bush has in Iraq. More disturbingly, Bush shows no ability to recover from his mistake. All we get from our leader is pigheaded promises of victory that none of our military commanders believe.

Our entire government is lost in confusion. One day Vice President Cheney and Defense Secretary Rumsfeld tell us that we are having great success in training an Iraqi military and will be able to begin withdrawing our troops in a year. The next day they tell us that we will be fighting the war for decades.

Bush's invasion of Iraq was a mistake. Bush's attempt to cover up his mistake with patriotism will ultimately discredit patriotism.

By permission of Paul Craig Roberts and Creators Syndicate, Inc.

It's Mother's Day Again and We're *Still* at War

MURRAY POLNER

Murray Polner, coeditor of this volume, published this article on Mother's Day 2007.

After the carnage of the Second World War, the members of the now defunct Victory Chapter of the American Gold Star Mothers in St. Petersburg, Florida, knew better than most what it was to lose their sons, daughters, husbands and other near relatives in war. "We'd rather not talk about it," one mother, whose son was killed in WWII, told the *St. Petersburg Times* fifteen years after the war ended. "It's a terrible scar that never heals. We hope there will never be another war so no other mothers will have to go through this ordeal." But thanks to our wars in Vietnam, Grenada, Panama, and the Gulf War—not to mention our proxy wars around the globe—and now Iraq, too many Moms now have to mourn family members lost to wars dreamed up by demagogic politicians.

But Mother's Day is now upon us. Few Americans know that Mother's Day was initially suggested by two peace-minded mothers, Julia Ward Howe, a long-forgotten nineteenth-century antislavery activist and suffragette who wrote the "Battle Hymn of the Republic," and Anna Reeves Jarvis, mother of eleven, who influenced Howe and once asked her fellow Appalachian townspeople, badly polarized by the Civil War, to remain neutral and help nurse the wounded on both sides.

Howe had lived through the barbarism of the Civil War, which led her to ask a question that's as relevant today as it was in her time: "Why do not the mothers of mankind interfere in these matters, to prevent the waste of that human life of which they alone bear and know the costs?" Mother's Day, she insisted, "should be devoted to the advocacy of peace doctrines."

Though not a mother, my favorite female opponent of war and imperialism was the forgotten poet and feminist Katherine Lee Bates who wrote "America the Beautiful" as a poem in 1895, which is now virtually our second national anthem. The poem I love best is her "Glory," in which an officer heading for the front says goodbye to his tearful mother.

> Again he raged in that lurid hell
> Where the country he loved had thrown him.
> "You are promoted!" shrieked a shell.
> His mother would not have known him.

More recently there was Lenore Breslauer, a mother of two, who helped found Another Mother for Peace during the Vietnam War and coined their marvelous slogan: "War is not healthy for children and other living beings." Years later I came to know three mothers named Carol who started Mothers and Others Against War in 1979 to protest Jimmy Carter's resurrection of draft registration. They stayed on to battle Ronald Reagan's proxy wars in Central America.

On this Mother's Day, while yet another American war drags on and on, we could use more of the anger and dissenting voices of countless women who have joined together to protest sacrificing their sons and daughters as cannon fodder, as Russian mothers have done protesting Moscow's invasions of Afghanistan and Chechnya. In Argentina and Chile, mothers and grandmothers marched against the murders of the American-supported butchers who ran their nations during the late '70s and '80s. And in this country, the anti-Iraq movement has been led by women demonstrating in essence against people who believe "War is a glorious golden thing . . . invoking Honor and Praise and Valor and Love of Country"—as a disillusioned and bitter Roland Leighton, an obscure British combat soldier of WWI wrote cynically to his fiancée, the British antiwar writer Vera Brittain.

Sadly, on this Mother's Day, peace seems further away than ever. How many more war widows and grieving parents do we need? Do we need yet another war memorial to the dead in Washington? Do we really need to continue disseminating the myth that an idealistic America always fights for freedom and democracy?

On Mother's Day 2007 thousands of American soldiers have already been killed, and many more have been wounded in body and mind, not to mention tens of thousands of Iraqis. They all had mothers.

Inaugurating Endless War

PATRICK J. BUCHANAN

Patrick J. Buchanan, political commentator and best-selling author, served in three White Houses. He ran for the Republican presidential nomination in 1992 and 1996, winning the New Hampshire primary in the latter year, and as the nominee of the Reform Party in 2000. This was his Creators Syndicate column for January 26, 2005.

Where Woodrow Wilson was going to make the world safe for democracy, George W. Bush is going him one better. President Bush is going to make the whole world democratic. As he declared in his inaugural address, our "great objective" is "ending tyranny" on earth.

And how does the president propose to achieve it?

> So, it is the policy of the United States to seek and support the growth of democratic movements and institutions in every nation and culture, with the ultimate goal of ending tyranny in our world.

The president is here asserting a unilateral American right to interfere in the internal affairs of every nation on earth, without regard to whether these nations have threatened us or attacked us. Their domestic politics are now our concern, because if they are not democratic, we are not secure.

Let it be said: This is a formula for endless collisions between this nation and every autocratic regime on earth and must inevitably lead to endless wars. And wars are the death of republics.

President Bush also plans to badger and hector foreign leaders on the progress they are making, or failing to make, in attaining U.S. standards of liberty and freedom:

> We will persistently clarify the choice before every ruler and nation: The moral choice between oppression, which is always wrong, and freedom, which is eternally right. . . . We will encourage reform in other governments by making clear that success in our relations will require the decent treatment of their own peoples. . . .

One awaits with anticipation the next visit of the Saudi crown prince. And as there are at least 50 autocracies or tyrannies in Africa, the Middle East, and Asia, questions arise.

If President Musharraf refuses to yield dictatorial powers, will Bush sanction Pakistan, and risk his overthrow and the transfer of his nuclear weapons to pro-Taliban generals sympathetic to al-Qaeda?

If Beijing declares its treatment of dissidents to be none of Bush's business, will Bush impose sanctions and enrage a regime ruling 1.3 billion people with whom we have $200 billion in annual trade?

When a Chinese fighter crashed a U.S. reconnaissance plane and Beijing held its crew hostage, Bush meekly apologized. Now, he's going to take these xenophobic Chinese communists to the woodshed?

If President Putin tells Bush the oligarch Mikhail Khodorkovsky will stay in prison and he will decide how elections are run in Russia, what is Bush going to do? Isolate him and drive Russia into the arms of China, as we have already done with our sanctions on Burma?

If the Saudis reject democracy, are we going to stop buying their oil? Somewhere, Osama is praying that Bush will undermine the Saudi monarchy, as another democracy-worshiper, Jimmy Carter, helped to undermine the Shah—after whom we got the Ayatollah.

President Bush is championing a policy of interventionism in the internal affairs of every nation on earth. But did we not learn from

9/11 that intervention is not a cure for terrorism, it is the cause of terrorism?

Clearly, the president does not understand this, or believe it. For in his inaugural, he describes 9/11 as the day "when freedom came under attack." But Osama bin Laden did not dispatch his fanatics to ram planes into the World Trade Center because he hated our Bill of Rights. He did it because he hates our presence and our policies in the Middle East.

President Bush says we have no other choice than to end tyranny on earth because the "survival of liberty in our land increasingly depends on the success of liberty in other lands." But this is ahistorical.

The world has almost always been a cesspool of despotisms, but America has always been free. We have retained our liberty by following the counsel of Washington and staying out of foreign wars that were not America's wars. It has been when we intervened in wars where our vital interests were not imperiled—crushing the Philippine insurrection, World War I, invading Iraq—that America has come to grief.

Occupying the Philippines led us to intervention in Asia, war with Japan and, soon after, wars to defend the South Korean and Indochinese remnants of the Japanese empire. Wilson's war gave us the Versailles peace treaty that tore a defeated Germany apart and imposed unpayable debts on her people, leading directly to Hitler.

The invasion of Iraq has reaped a harvest of hatred in the Arab world, cost us 10,000 dead and wounded and $200 billion, and created a new training ground and haven for terrorists to replace the one we cleaned out in Afghanistan.

In declaring it to be America's mission in the world to end tyranny on earth, President Bush is launching a crusade even more ambitious and utopian than was Wilson's. His crusade, too, will end, as Wilson's did, in disillusionment for him and tragedy for his country.

Career Diplomat John Brady Kiesling Resigns

John Brady Kiesling, a career diplomat who has served in American embassies around the world, submitted this letter of resignation in February 2003. It appeared in the New York Times.

Dear Mr. Secretary:

I am writing you to submit my resignation from the Foreign Service of the United States and from my position as Political Counselor in U.S. Embassy Athens, effective March 7. I do so with a heavy heart. The baggage of my upbringing included a felt obligation to give something back to my country. Service as a U.S. diplomat was a dream job. I was paid to understand foreign languages and cultures, to seek out diplomats, politicians, scholars and journalists, and to persuade them that U.S. interests and theirs fundamentally coincided. My faith in my country and its values was the most powerful weapon in my diplomatic arsenal.

It is inevitable that during twenty years with the State Department I would become more sophisticated and cynical about the narrow and selfish bureaucratic motives that sometimes shaped our policies. Human nature is what it is, and I was rewarded and promoted for understanding human nature. But until this Administration it had been possible to believe that by upholding the policies of my president I was also upholding the interests of the American people and the world. I believe it no longer.

The policies we are now asked to advance are incompatible not only with American values but also with American interests. Our fervent pursuit of war with Iraq is driving us to squander the international legitimacy that has been America's most potent weapon of both offense and defense since the days of Woodrow Wilson. We have begun to dismantle the largest and most effective web of international relationships the world has ever known. Our current course will bring instability and danger, not security.

The sacrifice of global interests to domestic politics and to bureaucratic self-interest is nothing new, and it is certainly not a uniquely American problem. Still, we have not seen such systematic distortion of intelligence, such systematic manipulation of American opinion, since the war in Vietnam. The September 11 tragedy left us stronger than before, rallying around us a vast international coalition to cooperate for the first time in a systematic way against the threat of terrorism. But rather than take credit for those successes and build on them, this Administration has chosen to make terrorism a domestic political tool, enlisting a scattered and largely defeated Al Qaeda as its bureaucratic ally. We spread disproportionate terror and confusion in the public mind, arbitrarily linking the unrelated problems of terrorism and Iraq. The result, and perhaps the motive, is to justify a vast misallocation of shrinking public wealth to the military and to weaken the safeguards that protect American citizens from the heavy hand of government. September 11 did not do as much damage to the fabric of American society as we seem determined to do to ourselves. Is the Russia of the late Romanovs really our model, a selfish, superstitious empire thrashing toward self-destruction in the name of a doomed status quo?

We should ask ourselves why we have failed to persuade more of the world that a war with Iraq is necessary. We have over the past two years done too much to assert to our world partners that narrow and mercenary U.S. interests override the cherished values of our partners. Even where our aims were not in question, our consistency is at issue. The model of Afghanistan is little comfort to allies wondering on what basis we plan to rebuild the Middle East, and in whose image and interests. Have we indeed become blind, as Russia is blind in Chechnya, as Israel is blind in the Occupied Territories, to our own advice, that overwhelming military power is not the answer to terrorism? After the shambles of post-war Iraq joins the shambles in Grozny and Ramallah, it will be a brave foreigner who forms ranks with Micronesia to follow where we lead.

We have a coalition still, a good one. The loyalty of many of our friends is impressive, a tribute to American moral capital built up over a century. But our closest allies are persuaded less that war is justified than that it would be perilous to allow the U.S. to drift into complete solipsism. Loyalty should be reciprocal. Why does our President condone the swaggering and contemptuous approach to our friends and allies this Administration is fostering, including among its most senior officials. Has *oderint dum metuant* really become our motto?

I urge you to listen to America's friends around the world. Even here in Greece, purported hotbed of European anti-Americanism, we have more and closer friends than the American newspaper reader can possibly imagine. Even when they complain about American arrogance, Greeks know that the world is a difficult and dangerous place, and they want a strong international system, with the U.S. and EU in close partnership. When our friends are afraid of us rather than for us, it is time to worry. And now they are afraid. Who will tell them convincingly that the United States is as it was, a beacon of liberty, security, and justice for the planet?

Mr. Secretary, I have enormous respect for your character and ability. You have preserved more international credibility for us than our policy deserves, and salvaged something positive from the excesses of an ideological and self-serving Administration. But your loyalty to the President goes too far. We are straining beyond its limits an international system we built with such toil and treasure, a web of laws, treaties, organizations, and shared values that sets limits on our foes far more effectively than it ever constrained America's ability to defend its interests.

I am resigning because I have tried and failed to reconcile my conscience with my ability to represent the current U.S. Administration. I have confidence that our democratic process is ultimately self-correcting, and hope that in a small way I can contribute from outside to shaping policies that better serve the security and prosperity of the American people and the world we share.

America has to be big enough to admit a mistake and bring it to an end.

Iraq Comes Home: Soldiers Share the Devastating Tales of War

EMILY DEPRANG

Emily DePrang, a freelance writer, wrote this essay for the June 29, 2007, issue of the Texas Observer.

Statistics are one way to tell the story of the approximately 1.4 million servicemen and women who've been to Iraq and Afghanistan. According to a study published in the *New England Journal of Medicine* in 2004, 86 percent of soldiers in Iraq reported knowing someone who was seriously injured or killed there. Some 77 percent reported shooting at the enemy; 75 percent reported seeing women or children in imminent peril and being unable to help. Fifty-one percent reported handling or uncovering human remains; 28 percent were responsible for the death of a noncombatant. One in five Iraq veterans return home seriously impaired by post-traumatic stress disorder (PTSD).

Words are another way. Below are the stories of three veterans of this war, told in their voices, edited for flow and efficiency but otherwise unchanged. They bear out the statistics and suggest that even those who are not diagnosably impaired return burdened by experiences they can neither forget nor integrate into their postwar lives. They speak of the inadequacy of what the military calls reintegration counseling, of the immediacy of their worst memories, of their helplessness in battle, of the struggle to rejoin a society that seems unwilling or unable to comprehend the price of their service. Strangers to one another and to me, they nevertheless tried, sometimes through tears, to communicate what the intensity of an ambiguous war has done to them.

One veteran, Sue Randolph, put it this way: "People walk up to me and say, 'Thank you for your service.' And I know they mean well, but I want to ask, 'Do you know what you're thanking me for?'" She, Rocky, and Michael Goss offer their stories here in the hope that citizens will begin to know.

*   *   *

Michael Goss, 29, served two tours in Iraq. He grew up in Corpus Christi and returned there after his other-than-honorable discharge. He lives with his brother. He is divorced and sees his children every other weekend while working the graveyard shift as a bail bondsman. He is quietly intelligent, thoughtful and attentive, always saying "ma'am" and opening the door for people. He struggles with severe PTSD and is obsessed with learning about the insurgency by studying reports and videos online. He is awaiting treatment from the Veterans Administration. He has been waiting for over a year.

Michael Goss:

I gave the Army seven years. It was supposed to be my career. I did two tours in Iraq, in 2003 and 2005. But during the last one, I started to get depressed. I lost faith in my chain of command. I became known as a rogue NCO. That's how I got my other-than-honorable discharge.

One night they said to me, "Sgt. Goss, gather your best guys." I say, "Where we going?" They say, "Don't worry about it, just come on." So we get in the car and go. We drive three blocks away, and there's six dead soldiers on the ground. They say, "You're casualty collecting tonight." I'm not prepared for that. I wasn't taught how to do that. But you're there. So you pick them up, and you put them in a body bag, pieces by pieces, and you go back to your unit, and you stand inside your room. And they're like, "You're going on a patrol, come on." You're like, "Hang on a minute. Let me think about what

I just did here." I just put six American guys in damn body bags. No-body's prepared for that. Nobody's prepared for that thing to blow up on the side of the road. You're talking, and you're driving, and then something blows up, and the next thing you know, two of your guys are missing their faces. They just want you to get up the next day and go, go, let's do it again, you're a soldier. Yeah, I got the sol-dier part, okay?

It gets to the point where they numb you. They numb you to death. They numb you to anything. You come back, and it starts com-ing back to you slowly. Now you gotta figure out a way to deal with it. In Iraq you had a way to deal with it, because they kept pushing you back out there. Keep pushing you back out into the streets. Go, go, go. Hey, I just shot four people today. Yeah, and in about four hours you're going to go back out, and you'll probably shoot six more. So let's go. Just deal with it. We'll fix it when we get back. That's basically what they're telling you. We'll fix it all when we get back. We'll get your head right and everything when we get back to the States. I'm sorry, it's not like that. It's not supposed to be like that. All the soldiers have post-traumatic stress disorder, and they're like, "Hey, you're good. You went to counseling four times, you can go back to Iraq. It's okay." No. It doesn't work that way.

I have PTSD. I know when I got it—the night I killed an eight-year-old girl. Her family was trying to cross a checkpoint. We'd just shot three guys who'd tried to run a checkpoint. And during that mess, they were just trying to get through to get away from it all. And we ended up shooting all them, too. It was a family of six. The only one that survived was a 13-month-old and her mother. And the worst part about it all was that where I shot my bullets, when I went to see what I'd shot at, there was an eight-year-old girl there. I tried my best to bring her back to life, but there was no use. But that's what trig-gered my depression.

When I got out of the Army, I had 10 days to get off base. There was no reintegration counseling. As soon as I got back, nobody gave a f— about anything except that piece of paper that said I got everything out of my room. I got out of the Army, and everything went to s— from there.

My wife ended up finding another guy. I'm getting divorced, and I'm fighting for custody. She wants child support, the house, the car, the boys.

I get three nights off a week. And I drink and take pills to help me sleep at night. I do what I can to help myself. I talk to friends. Soldiers who were there. Once in a while one of my old soldiers will call me, drunk off his ass, crying about the stuff he saw in Iraq. And all I can do is tell him, "You and me both are going to have to find a way to work this out." That's the only thing I can tell him.

I do martial arts, that's what I do. I go in a cage and I fight. It helps take my mind off things. I get hurt, but I can't feel it. I don't feel it until after it's all over with.

So let's put this in perspective now. I got two Iraq tours, multiple kills, I picked up plenty of dead bodies, American bodies, enemy bodies. I killed an eight-year-old girl, which still haunts me to this day. I come back home. My wife finds somebody else. I'm sleeping on my brother's couch while she has the apartment, the kids, the car, everything that we worked on together. I work as a bail bondsman making $432 a week, which all goes to my brother. I have to fight just to see my boys because she's at the point where she thinks I don't deserve to see my kids because I haven't had help for my PTSD. She's scared I might do something stupid. And the VA won't help me out because of my other-than-honorable discharge. What else do you want to know?

Every month the VA sends me a letter saying I'm still under review. I'm like, I couldn't care less about the money. I don't care about disability percentage. I want you to tell me to go to this f—— doctor here and go get help. That's what I want them to tell me. If they think I don't deserve money because I got kicked out with an other-than-honorable discharge, fine. But don't tell me I'm cured all of a sudden, because I'm not. I still have my nightmares, anxiety attacks, panic attacks, I still see the glitter from the IED blowing up when I'm going down the street. I still see the barrette in her hair when I carried her out of the car to the ambulance when she was bleeding all over me. I still see all that. And there's nothing that I can do about that now.

* * *

Rocky, 26, prefers to remain anonymous. He joined the Army shortly before the attacks of Sept. 11, 2001, and went to Iraq in 2004 for one year and a day. A Houston native, he lives alone now in a Dallas apartment, goes to community college and works in construction. He's funny, playful and handsome, and carries a pool cue in his trunk to be ready for a game at any time. He doesn't tell people he's a veteran. He doesn't like to talk about it. This story is an exception.

Rocky:

I was one of those kids that could have been handed anything on a silver platter. But I really worked hard for everything anyway, because I wanted to prove myself. And my parents, who would have given me anything, ruled with an iron fist. And I was patriotic. So it seemed like everything in my life pointed to the Army as the way to go.

I was 20. I'm sure I was different then. I don't know how. I know how I am now. I assume that the character traits that I show now are the core set of values that I left with. My sense of pride, hard work. Everything I have, I made out of nothing.

You get to see what people are made of over there. You get to see how shallow people are, how weak they are. How strong they can be in horrible moments. And then how the people you should be looking up to are hiding, and you have to look out for them. You get to really see what a person is made of.

And over there, I learned to read people. I know what they're going to do before they do it. After seeing the same movements before you get shot at or bombed, the same symptoms of the city and the people around you—it's a fluid movement. Doors close, people disappear, and all of a sudden you're like, okay guys, hunker down, it's about to hit us. And all of a sudden, you're under fire.

People would pop shots at us and pop back. They'd have a setup where they have a bomb in the road, and everybody sits by the windows when they set off an IED. When we're looking at what's going on, everybody's laughing and pointing and smiling after your buddy's sitting there bleeding. So I held them all responsible. Everybody that was in the guilty range.

If there was gunfire coming from a window, I shot into that window and made sure nothing was coming back out at me. One time, there was an RPG shooter shooting at me. He hit a Bradley in front of us, and we were in a Humvee. He hit the Bradley in front of us, and the round didn't go off. It got stuck in the mud. So the Bradley rolled back, and we rolled back. And I had to shoot the position-caller before I could shoot the actual shooter. He didn't have a gun, but I knew what he was doing. He was the one calling out what's going on. He was on the phone. So I sent a shot up 20 feet above him and below him and to the side of him. And he just stood there. On his phone, talking the whole time. Innocent people run. The bad guys stay and fight. If they're not running, they're going to be calling. That's the way I see it. So I shot him. If you freaked out and stood still, I'm sorry. I cannot take this chance again. You have to start making these moral decisions. Better to be judged by 12 than carried by six. You're caught in the f—— middle of it.

After that, now I think, well, now I'm damned. Now I've done the worst thing. There's not much more worse you can do than shoot an unarmed person. It's not just, man, now I got to f—— deal with this. It's like, man, I hope nobody saw that, because I'll go to jail, too. You feel so horrible. You kind of die inside. There's really nothing beneath me now. I'm at the bottom of the barrel. You're worried about salvation and people finding out these dirty little secrets. It's not something that you wanted to do. It might be something that you had to do, that you accidentally did. Things happen. And then there's the whole fear of going to jail for trying to do what's right for your country—it's bad. Sometimes you think people are shooting at you, and you'd rather just chance it because you're hoping they don't have an armor-piercing round.

But I'm not going to bow down. I know what I'm made of—do you? Most people have no idea what matters. When I'm standing at the gates and I see St. Peter, I'll say, lemme in. I try to do right now. I don't want to hurt anybody's feelings. I go to school, maybe I'll earn a midlevel job. Just fly under the radar. I don't want any attention. I just want to be away from people. Not many people call me still. I keep it real dim in my apartment. I like it calm and quiet. This is what life's made of. Being able to relax and be safe. Watch a movie, play some video games. Just to sit back and have fun with your friends. That's beautiful.

*   *   *

Sue Randolph, 39, grew up in Saudi Arabia and earned her master's degree in Arabic at the University of Michigan. After her service in 2003, she moved to Houston with her husband, a geologist. She now works in satellite communications and raises her 3-year-old daughter, a self-identified "princess," and a 2-month-old kitten named Sparkles. Randolph's family goes kayaking and hiking on weekends. She is clever, quick-witted, passionate and kind. She still struggles with anxiety while driving and when she's near crowds. She finds news about the war upsetting and frustratingly inaccurate.

Sue Randolph:

I joined the Army because I had $65,000 in student loans and didn't know how I was going to make payments. Since I had a master's in political science—Middle East studies and Arabic—I ended up doing translation as part of the search for weapons of mass destruction. For a year, my team drove around behind the 3rd Infantry getting shot at, getting mortared, looking at warehouses of documents, chemicals, and parts of things that could be WMDs. I mean, you name it, we did it. We talked to people. We went into people's houses.

The technological level of the things I saw wasn't anywhere near anything [former Secretary of State] Colin Powell talked about. The buildings we went into, wiring was on the outside of the walls. I didn't see anything like the equipment you'd see in a fifth-grade science lab. The most technically advanced thing we saw was a 12-volt car battery hooked up to bedsprings for torture. But not anything on the chemical or biological level.

Iraq looks like it's straight out of the Bible. It's mud brick, it's falling down. It's kids with sticks herding goats. There's like three high-rises in all of Baghdad, and those are the only ones you'll ever see on any newscast. The rest of it is mud brick falling down.

At the time, I would see little girls on the side of the road, and I felt like I was part of a big machine that was going to help them have a better life. At the time. Now, looking at all of the lack of evidence for us being there except GW throwing a temper tantrum, frankly I feel—not used, because I signed up for it—but I feel like we were there for no good reason. Eventually Saddam would have been overthrown, either by his own people or through Iran or someone else, and change would have come. It wouldn't have been on our timetable, but it would have happened. I don't think it was worthwhile at all.

When I went back to my base in Germany, it was like a bad dream. It was like nothing happened. Then I got out of the Army and came back to the States. Once you leave the Army, there's no reintegration help of any kind. Unless you went looking for it, there was nothing. And even if you went looking for it, you had to dig.

The military says that they're giving exit counseling and reintegration. What they're calling reentry counseling, in my experience, was, "Don't drink and drive. Pay your bills on time. Don't beat your spouse. Don't kick your dog." All of these things that once you've reached a certain age, you're supposed to know. None of it is, "If you have discomfort with dealing with crowds, if you don't feel comfortable with your spouse, if you can't sleep in a bed, if you don't want to drive down the road because you think everything is a bomb, here's what to do." No psychological or de-stress counseling is involved in this reintegration to garrison. And that's just if you're staying in the Army. If you're leaving the Army, you get, "Here's how to write a resume."

They don't prepare you to leave. Hell, they didn't prepare me to be there. I was going into people's houses trying to tell the wife and kids as we're segregating them out from the men that we're the good guys. But they're crying because one of their kids got killed because he was up there sleeping on the roof when we decided to bust into their house. I mean, that's crazy. But we're the good guys. Now I have to deal with that for the next 20 or 30 years. I have a 3-year-old. I deal with that every day.

I think we are going to end up like after Vietnam if we're not careful. The Vietnam guys were treated really horribly, and whether they came back and quietly went back to their lives or not, they were all stereotyped in a criminal negative. And I'm afraid if we as a society don't learn what we didn't do for those guys, we're going to have that in spades. We don't have low-end kind of industry jobs for them like working in the auto plant, so they're not going to be supporting their families. And they're going to be angry. They're going to feel like they're owed. Do we get everybody counseling as soon as they get out, mandatory 90-day counseling? I don't know how. But there isn't enough money in this country right now to make some of these guys feel like what they went through was worthwhile.

We have no comprehension of the psychological cost of this war. I know kids in Iraq who killed themselves. I know kids that got killed.

Okay, that's apparently the price of doing business. But multiply me by two million. If I'm fairly high-functioning, what about the ones that aren't? They're going back to small-town America, and their families aren't going to know what to do with them. It's like, what do we do with Johnny now?

10

Americans Confront War

"It is forbidden to kill; therefore all murderers are punished un-less they kill in large numbers and to the sound of trumpets."

—VOLTAIRE

In this final chapter Americans from the past two centuries address various aspects of the subject of war.

John Quincy Adams on U.S. Foreign Policy

John Quincy Adams, who would be elected president in 1824, delivered the speech from which these remarks are excerpted before the House of Representatives on July 4, 1821.

And now, friends and countrymen, if the wise and learned philosophers of the elder world, the first observers of nutation and aberration, the discoverers of maddening ether and invisible planets, the inventors of Congreve rockets and Shrapnel shells, should find their hearts disposed to enquire what has America done for the benefit of mankind?

Let our answer be this: America, with the same voice which spoke herself into existence as a nation, proclaimed to mankind the inextinguishable rights of human nature, and the only lawful foundations of government. America, in the assembly of nations, since her admission among them, has invariably, though often fruitlessly, held forth to them the hand of honest friendship, of equal freedom, of generous reciprocity.

She has uniformly spoken among them, though often to heedless and often to disdainful ears, the language of equal liberty, of equal justice, and of equal rights.

She has, in the lapse of nearly half a century, without a single exception, respected the independence of other nations while asserting and maintaining her own.

She has abstained from interference in the concerns of others, even when conflict has been for principles to which she clings, as to the last vital drop that visits the heart.

She has seen that probably for centuries to come, all the contests of that Aceldama, the European world, will be contests of inveterate power, and emerging right.

Wherever the standard of freedom and Independence has been or shall be unfurled, there will her heart, her benedictions and her prayers be.

But she goes not abroad in search of monsters to destroy.

She is the well-wisher to the freedom and independence of all.

She is the champion and vindicator only of her own.

She will commend the general cause by the countenance of her voice, and the benignant sympathy of her example.

She well knows that by once enlisting under other banners than her own, were they even the banners of foreign independence, she would involve herself beyond the power of extrication, in all the wars of interest and intrigue, of individual avarice, envy, and ambition, which assume the colors and usurp the standard of freedom.

The fundamental maxims of her policy would insensibly change from liberty to force. The frontlet upon her brows would no longer beam with the ineffable splendor of freedom and independence; but in its stead would soon be substituted an imperial diadem, flashing in false and tarnished lustre the murky radiance of dominion and power.

She might become the dictatress of the world. She would be no longer the ruler of her own spirit. . . .

[America's] glory is not dominion, but liberty. Her march is the march of the mind. She has a spear and a shield: but the motto upon her shield is, Freedom, Independence, Peace. This has been her Declaration: this has been, as far as her necessary intercourse with the rest of mankind would permit, her practice.

Mother's Day Proclamation

JULIA WARD HOWE

Julia Ward Howe (1819–1910), abolitionist and feminist, composed her Mother's Day Proclamation in 1870, in the wake of the American Civil War and the Franco-Prussian War.

Arise then . . . women of this day!
Arise, all women who have hearts!
Whether your baptism be of water or of tears!
Say firmly:
"We will not have questions answered by irrelevant agencies,
Our husbands will not come to us, reeking with carnage,
For caresses and applause.
Our sons shall not be taken from us to unlearn
All that we have been able to teach them of charity, mercy and
patience.
We, the women of one country,
Will be too tender of those of another country
To allow our sons to be trained to injure theirs."

From the voice of a devastated Earth a voice goes up with
Our own. It says: "Disarm! Disarm!
The sword of murder is not the balance of justice."
Blood does not wipe our dishonor,
Nor violence indicate possession.
As men have often forsaken the plough and the anvil
At the summons of war,
Let women now leave all that may be left of home
For a great and earnest day of counsel.
Let them meet first, as women, to bewail and commemorate the dead.
Let them solemnly take counsel with each other as to the means
Whereby the great human family can live in peace . . .
Each bearing after his own time the sacred impress, not of Caesar,
But of God—
In the name of womanhood and humanity, I earnestly ask
That a general congress of women without limit of nationality,
May be appointed and held at someplace deemed most convenient
And the earliest period consistent with its objects,
To promote the alliance of the different nationalities,
The amicable settlement of international questions,
The great and general interests of peace.

The Valuation of Human Life in War

ELIHU BURRITT

*Elihu Burritt, a prominent nineteenth-century peace activist, believed in
the use of peaceful means to bring about the end of slavery, and condemned
the American Peace Society for supporting the Civil War. He rejected the
society's claim that while it opposed international wars, it supported the
mere suppression of an insurrection, which it claimed the war was. Burritt
contemptuously dismissed its argument "that this terrible conflict, in which*

each party is arraying 500,000 armed men against the other, is not war but
quelling a mob on the part of the Federal Government. . . . I feel that this
sophistry and position have shorn the locks of the Society of all the strength
of principle; and I have been saddened to silence."

In this essay, Burritt speaks of the effects of war on the natural sympathy
people otherwise have for their suffering fellow men.

If there is one sentiment that more than another marks the civilization of
the present day, it is the interest felt in human life. Sympathy with human
suffering is the most distinctive characteristic of our age. Never before in
the world's history were there such associated efforts to diminish or prevent suffering. The societies organized for this purpose are almost innu-
merable. Great calamities by fire, pestilence, or famine are almost
drowned by the flood of benevolence thus brought to bear upon them.
The great heart of the community has thus become very sensitive to every
kind of suffering, want, or wrong. How the whole nation is distressed at
the news of the explosion of fire-damp in a coal mine, by which a score—
perhaps a hundred—working-men lose their lives! The Queen on her
throne telegraphs to the scene of the disaster to make inquiry or express
her sympathy. In thousands of family circles the fate of the poor colliers is
deplored with deep commiseration. Money pours in from all directions to
support and comfort the mourning widows and orphans.

A shipwreck, a railway accident, or any other catastrophe which destroys human life, produces the same feeling in the community. Sometimes a single life put in peril will fill a nation's heart with anxiety and
grief. For instance, take the case of Dr. Livingstone, the African ex-
plorer. What intense and painful interest was felt, not only in England,
but in other countries, in his fate! What costly expeditions were fitted
out to seek for him in the hot wilds of that distant continent! Then
think of Sir John Franklin, and of the feeling which his fate inspired
throughout the civilized world.

Now compare the feeling with which the community hears of the loss
or peril of a few human lives by these accidents with which the news of the

death or mutilation of thousands of men, equally precious, on the field of battle is received. How different is the valuation! How different in universal sympathy! War seems to reverse our best and boasted civilization, to carry back human society to the dark ages of barbarism, to cheapen the public appreciation of human life almost to the standard of brute beasts. This has always seemed to me one of war's worst works, because it destroys also the sense of the ruin and misery which the sword makes in the world.

And this demoralization of sentiment is not confined to the two or three nations engaged in war; it extends to the most distant and neutral nations, and they read of thousands slain or mangled in a single battle with but a little more human sensibility than they would read the loss of so many pawns by a move on a chess-board. With what deep sympathy the American nation, even to the very slaves, heard of the suffering in Ireland by the potato famine! What ship-loads of corn and provisions they sent over to relieve that suffering! But how little of that benevolent sympathy and of that generous aid would they have given to the same amount of suffering inflicted by war upon the people of a foreign country! This, I repeat, is one of the very worst works of war. It is not only the demoralization, but almost the transformation, of human nature. We can generally ascertain how many lives have been lost in war. The tax-gatherer lets us know how much money it costs. But no registry kept on earth can tell us how much is lost to the world by this insensibility to human suffering which a war produces in the whole family circle of nations.

Four Bloody Lies of War, from Havana 1898 to Baghdad 2003

HARVEY WASSERMAN

Harvey Wasserman is author of numerous books, including Harvey Wasserman's History of the United States; Solartopia!; Our Green-Powered Earth, A.D. 2030; *and* A Glimpse of the Big Light: Losing

Parents, Finding Spirit, *all available at HarveyWasserman.com. This essay appeared in the* Columbus (Ohio) Free Press *on May 8, 2005.*

The Bush Administration's lies about its rationales for attacking Iraq fit a pattern of deceit that has dragged America into at least three other unjust and catastrophic wars.

The "smoking gun" documents that emerged in the recent British election confirm the administration had decided to go to war and then sought "intelligence" to sell it.

But conscious, manipulative lies were also at the root of American attacks on Cuba in 1898, U.S. intervention into World War I in 1917 and in Vietnam. These lies are as proven and irrefutable as the unconscionable deception that dragged the U.S. into Iraq in 2003.

In each case, these lies of war have caused horrific human slaughter, the destruction of human rights and liberties, and financial disaster.

In Cuba, the 1898 sinking of the battleship *Maine* brought the U.S. into war with Spain. The people of Cuba, Puerto Rico and the Philippines were in revolt against the crumbling Spanish empire. Media baron William Randolph Hearst, the era's Rupert Murdoch, wanted a war to sell papers and promote "jingo" power. He portrayed the Spaniards as barbaric rapists and worse. In the name of democracy and freedom, Hearst and pro-war fanatics like Theodore Roosevelt demanded U.S. intervention.

Republican President William McKinley, personal hero of today's White House dirty trickster Karl Rove, dutifully sent the battleship *Maine* into Havana harbor. Suddenly, it blew up, killing some 250 American sailors.

Spain was blamed, and Hearst got his war. Having just conquered and annexed what had been the sovereign monarchy of Hawaii, the Americans now annexed Puerto Rico and installed colonial regimes in Cuba and the Philippines.

But Filipino guerrillas waged a jungle resistance that dragged into the new century. Thousands died in the quagmire. An angry anti-imperial movement sprung up here amongst farmers, labor unions and intellectuals like Samuel Clemens, whose writings under the pen name Mark Twain remain among the fiercest critiques of the perils of empire.

And guess what! New underwater technology has shown that the *Maine* actually blew up from the inside. Definitive scientific analysis says the Spaniards could not have sunk it. The explosion that brought it down most likely came from a faulty boiler or a munitions misfire, but definitely not from a Spanish mine or torpedo.

The Spanish-American War, with all its bloody imperial slaughter, had been sold on a lie.

As was U.S. intervention in World War I. In 1915, as part of a blockade against Great Britain, the Germans downed the passenger ship *Lusitania,* on its way from New York to London. More than a thousand people died, many of them Americans.

President Woodrow Wilson screamed that Germany had violated international law. As Hearst had done to the Spaniards, Wilson portrayed "the Huns" as merciless, bloodthirsty barbarians.

The Germans argued that the *Lusitania* had been carrying weapons, and that they were within their rights to sink her. A substantial majority of Americans angrily opposed U.S. intervention, saying only bankers would profit and that war would divert us from the real issues of unionization, poverty and Robber Baron domination of American industry.

In the face of an anti-imperial majority, Wilson withdrew troops he had sent into Mexico, then ran as a "peace candidate" in 1916 on the slogan "He Kept Us Out of War."

But in April 1917, reviving bloody images of the *Lusitania,* Wilson dragged the U.S. into the slaughter. More than 100,000 Americans died. Under cover of war, federal marshals burned and blew up offices of the Socialist Party and radical unions like the Industrial Workers of the World. Wilson shredded the Bill of Rights and jailed, deported or killed thousands of organizers. Eugene V. Debs, the beloved leader of the American labor movement, was thrown in federal prison. The ideological left was crushed.

Yet another depiction of Americans opposed to their government's continual wars.

Wilson did tip the military balance for Britain and France. But his high-minded rhetoric about a League of Nations and a balanced peace fell into chaos. The Allies demanded reparations which helped feed the Nazi movement and an even greater slaughter in World War II. Wilson suffered a stroke and left the country in shambles.

And guess what! Deep sea divers recently found the *Lusitania*, its sunken hull laden with illegal armaments. As the Germans had claimed, the ship was violating international law. Like McKinley, Wilson had duped America into a catastrophic intervention based on "faulty intelligence."

Likewise, Vietnam, which hysterical cold warriors portrayed as the key domino in a global struggle against communism. The U.S. had canceled 1956 elections which would have given to Ho Chi Minh control of a unified Vietnam. But nationalist guerillas were clearly on the brink of wresting South Vietnam from Western control.

In 1964 North Vietnamese allegedly fired on two U.S. ships in the Gulf of Tonkin. While campaigning as a peace candidate, Lyndon Johnson used the incident to win Congressional approval for unlimited intervention. By 1967 he'd sent some 550,000 U.S. troops into Southeast Asia.

A mirror image of the earlier war in the Philippines, Vietnam may rank as the greatest of all modern American catastrophes. It split and alienated a generation, poisoned American politics, spawned a toxic cadre of dirty tricksters and marked the downturn of the American economy. The war destroyed Johnson's Great Society, and has rendered every American tangibly poorer in more ways than can be counted.

And guess what! The Gulf of Tonkin incident probably never happened. According to then–Secretary of Defense Robert McNamara, the Vietnamese may never actually have fired shots that may or may not have put a few bullet holes in one or two U.S. ships. Even if they did, any such attack had zero military significance.

Like the *Maine* and *Lusitania*, the guns of Tonkin were nothing more than lies of war.

Bitter debate still also rages over the origins of World War II and Korea. Many argue that Franklin Roosevelt knew the Japanese were going to attack Pearl Harbor, and that he let it happen. Some also say that South Korea attacked North Korea, not vice-versa.

At least in terms of public consensus, these two stories still lack definitive smoking guns. But the *Maine*, the *Lusitania* and the Tonkin Gulf are known, irrefutable quantities.

To which we now must add George W. Bush's lies of Iraq. The war was primarily sold as a way to destroy Saddam Hussein's Weapons of Mass Destruction. The world was also told Saddam was involved in the 9/11 attacks on the U.S., and was trying to get nuclear bombs.

These were all lies. The British memos proving the Bush and Blair Administrations knew Saddam did not have WMDs, was not involved in 9/11 and had no way to make atomic weapons are now public monuments. Like the *Maine*, *Lusitania* and Tonkin, the proofs are tangible and irrefutable.

What happened to the perpetrators of those previous lies?

In 1901, William McKinley became the third sitting president (after Lincoln and Garfield) to be assassinated. Theodore Roosevelt then dragged the Philippine slaughter to its tragic conclusion. Only when his young son Quentin was killed in World War I did T. R. question the glories of imperial conquest.

Woodrow Wilson's debilitating stroke came as he imposed the most intense attack on civil liberties in U.S. history destroying the Socialist Party and the ideological left. He was succeeded by the affable Warren G. Harding, who freed Eugene V. Debs from federal prison, then himself died in office (of apparent food poisoning) amidst a sea of scandal.

After Tonkin, Lyndon Johnson's presidency descended into Wilsonian chaos. A ferocious anti-war movement forced him to duck out of running for re-election. Richard Nixon then took the lies of war to a whole new level, expanding the slaughter in Southeast Asia and becoming the first U.S. president to resign in disgrace.

Nixon's "dirty trickster" disciples Karl Rove and Dick Cheney have now poisoned this nation with yet another ghastly lie of war. Their hopeless Iraqi slaughter has become the modern definition of cynical deceit, human butchery and economic ruin.

Exactly what will happen to us and to the liars that have dragged us into this latest bloody quagmire remains to be seen.

But history does not indicate a pretty outcome.

The Glory of War

LLEWELLYN H. ROCKWELL, JR.

Llewellyn Rockwell is president of the libertarian Ludwig von Mises Institute and editor in chief of LewRockwell.com, the world's most heavily trafficked libertarian Web site. This essay appeared in 2005.

In 1977, American Christians Against Torture organized a campaign to protest the use of torture in times of peace and war. This demonstration—possibly in response to American support for General Pinochet's Chile—was staged on the steps of the U.S. Capitol in April of the same year.

© Kathleen Cameron. Courtesy of Kathleen Cameron Collection.

The bloom on the rose of war eventually fades, leaving only the thorns. By the time this takes place, most everyone has already begun the national task of averting the eyes from the thorns, meaning the awful reality, the dashed hopes, the expense, the lame, the limbless, the widows, the orphans, the death on all sides, and the resulting instability. The people who still take an interest are those who first took an interest in war: the power elite, who began the war for purposes very different from that which they sold to the public at the outset.

Thus does the American public not care much about Iraq. It is not quite as invisible as other nations that were the subject of national obsessions in the recent past. Hardly anyone knows who or what is running El Salvador, Nicaragua, Haiti, Libya, Serbia, or Somalia, or any of the other formerly strategic countries that once engaged national attention.

In fact, the president of Nicaragua, Enrique Bolanos (never heard of him, huh?) is visiting the White House next week in hopes of soliciting support for the upcoming election, which could prove to be dicey since the old U.S. nemesis Daniel Ortega is running and gaining some support on a consistently anti-U.S. platform. Should he win, one can imagine the White House swinging into high gear about how Nicaragua is harboring communists, er . . . terrorists. Or maybe not. Maybe he will rule the country and never make a headline. It is all up to the state.

Why the state goes to war is not a mystery—at least the general reasons are not mysterious. War is an excuse for spending money on its friends. It can punish enemies that are not going with the program. It intimidates other states tempted to go their own way. It can pave the way for commercial interests linked to the state. The regime that makes and wins a war gets written up in the history books. So the reasons are the same now as in the ancient world: power, money, glory.

Why the bourgeoisie back war is another matter. It is self-evidently not in their interest. The government gains power at their expense. It spends their money and runs up debt that is paid out of taxes and inflation. It fosters the creation of permanent enemies abroad who then work to diminish our security at home. It leads to the violation of privacy and civil liberty. War is incompatible with a government that leaves people alone to develop their lives in an atmosphere of freedom.

Nonetheless, war with moral themes—we are the good guys working for God and they are the bad guys doing the devil's work—tends to attract a massive amount of middle-class support. People believe the lies, and, once exposed, they defend the right of the state to lie. People who are otherwise outraged by murder find themselves celebrating the same on a mass industrial scale. People who harbor no hatred toward foreigners find themselves attaching ghastly monikers to whole classes of foreign peoples. Regular middle-class people, who otherwise struggle to eke out a flourishing life in this vale of tears, feel hatred well up within them and confuse it for honor, bravery, courage, and valor.

Why? Nationalism is one answer. To be at war is to feel at one with something much larger than oneself, to be a part of a grand historical project. They have absorbed the civic religion from childhood—Boston tea, cherry trees, log cabins, Chevrolet—but it mostly has no living presence in their minds until the state pushes the war button, and then all the nationalist emotions well up within them.

Nationalism is usually associated with attachment to a particular set of state managers that you think can somehow lead the country in a particular direction of which you approve. So the nationalism of the Iraq war was mostly a Republican Party phenomenon. All Democrats are suspected as being insufficiently loyal, of feeling sympathy for The Enemy, or defending such ideas as civil liberty at a time when the nation needs unity more than ever.

You could tell a Republican nationalist during this last war because the words peace and liberty were always said with a sneer, as if they didn't matter at all. Even the Constitution came in for a pounding from these people. Bush did all he could to consolidate decision-making power unto himself, and even strongly suggested that he was acting on God's orders as Commander in Chief, and his religious constitutionalist supporters went right along with it. They were willing to break as many eggs as necessary to make the war omelet. I've got an archive of a thousand hate mails to prove it.

But nationalism is not the only basis for bourgeois support for war. Long-time war correspondent Chris Hedges, in his great book *War Is a Force that Gives Us Meaning* (Anchor, 2003) argues that war operates as a kind of canvas on which every member of the middle and working class can paint his or her own picture. Whatever personal frustrations exist in your life, however powerless you feel, war works as a kind of narcotic. It provides a means for people to feel temporarily powerful and important, as if they are part of some big episode in history. War then becomes for people a kind of lurching attempt to taste immortality. War gives their lives meaning.

Hedges doesn't go this far but if you know something about the sociology of religion, you can recognize what he is speaking of: the sacraments. In Christian theology they are derived from periodic ceremonies in the Jewish tradition that cultivate the favor of God, who grants our lives transcendent importance. We receive sacraments as a means of gaining propitiation for our sins, an eternal blessing on worldly choices, or the very means of eternal life.

War is the devil's sacrament. It promises to bind us not with God but with the nation state. It grants not life but death. It provides not liberty but slavery. It lives not on truth but on lies, and these lies are themselves said to be worthy of defense. It exalts evil and puts down the good. It is promiscuous in encouraging an orgy of sin, not self-restraint and thought. It is irrational and bloody and vicious and appalling. And it claims to be the highest achievement of man.

It is worse than mass insanity. It is mass wallowing in evil.

And then it is over. People oddly forget what took place. The rose wilts and the thorns grow but people go on with their lives. War no longer inspires. War news becomes uninteresting. All those arguments with friends and family—what were they about anyway? All that killing and expense and death—let's just avert our eyes from it all. Maybe in a few years, once the war is out of the news forever and the country we smashed recovers some modicum of civilization, we can revisit the event and proclaim it glorious. But for now, let's just say it never happened.

That seems to be just about where people stand these days with the Iraq War. Iraq is a mess, hundreds of thousands are killed and maimed, billions of dollars are missing, the debt is astronomical, and the world seethes in hatred toward the conquering empire. And what does the warmongering middle class have to say for itself? Pretty much what you might expect: nothing.

People have long accused the great liberal tradition of a dogmatic attachment to peace. It would appear that this is precisely what is necessary in order to preserve the freedom necessary for all of us to find true meaning in our lives.

Do we reject war and all its works? We do reject them.

Put Away the Flags

HOWARD ZINN

Howard Zinn, a World War II bombardier, is the author of the best-selling
A People's History of the United States. *This essay appeared in the July
3, 2006, issue of the* Progressive.

On this July 4, we would do well to renounce nationalism and all its
symbols: its flags, its pledges of allegiance, its anthems, its insistence in
song that God must single out America to be blessed.

Is not nationalism—that devotion to a flag, an anthem, a boundary
so fierce it engenders mass murder—one of the great evils of our time,
along with racism, along with religious hatred?

These ways of thinking—cultivated, nurtured, indoctrinated from
childhood on—have been useful to those in power, and deadly for those
out of power.

National spirit can be benign in a country that is small and lacking
both in military power and a hunger for expansion (Switzerland, Nor-
way, Costa Rica and many more). But in a nation like ours—huge, pos-
sessing thousands of weapons of mass destruction—what might have
been harmless pride becomes an arrogant nationalism dangerous to others and to ourselves.

Our citizenry has been brought up to see our nation as different
from others, an exception in the world, uniquely moral, expanding into
other lands in order to bring civilization, liberty, democracy.

That self-deception started early.

When the first English settlers moved into Indian land in Massachusetts Bay and were resisted, the violence escalated into war with the
Pequot Indians. The killing of Indians was seen as approved by God,
the taking of land as commanded by the Bible. The Puritans cited one
of the Psalms, which says: "Ask of me, and I shall give thee, the hea-

Burning a facsimile of a draft card, Daniel Ellsberg, a former marine, protests President Jimmy Carter's proposal to reinstate draft registration in 1979. Ellsberg once worked for the RAND Corporation, the Defense Department, and the State Department at the U.S. embassy in Saigon. In 1969, he copied highly classified documents, later called the Pentagon Papers, revealing, as he said, "patterns of official deception" and gave them to the *New York Times* and the *Washington Post*. He was arrested, but his case was dismissed after it was discovered that Watergate burglars working for the Nixon administration had illegally searched his psychiatrist's office.

then for thine inheritance, and the uttermost parts of the Earth for thy possession."

When the English set fire to a Pequot village and massacred men, women and children, the Puritan theologian Cotton Mather said: "It was supposed that no less than 600 Pequot souls were brought down to hell that day."

On the eve of the Mexican War, an American journalist declared it our "Manifest Destiny to overspread the continent allotted by Providence." After the invasion of Mexico began, the *New York Herald* announced: "We believe it is a part of our destiny to civilize that beautiful country."

It was always supposedly for benign purposes that our country went to war.

We invaded Cuba in 1898 to liberate the Cubans, and went to war in the Philippines shortly after, as President McKinley put it, "to civilize and Christianize" the Filipino people.

As our armies were committing massacres in the Philippines (at least 600,000 Filipinos died in a few years of conflict), Elihu Root, our secretary of war, was saying: "The American soldier is different from all other soldiers of all other countries since the war began. He is the advance guard of liberty and justice, of law and order, and of peace and happiness."

We see in Iraq that our soldiers are not different. They have, perhaps against their better nature, killed thousands of Iraqi civilians. And some soldiers have shown themselves capable of brutality, of torture.

Yet they are victims, too, of our government's lies.

How many times have we heard President Bush and Secretary of Defense Donald Rumsfeld tell the troops that if they die, if they return without arms or legs, or blinded, it is for "liberty," for "democracy"?

One of the effects of nationalist thinking is a loss of a sense of proportion. The killing of 2,300 people at Pearl Harbor becomes the justification for killing 240,000 in Hiroshima and Nagasaki. The killing of 3,000 people on Sept. 11 becomes the justification for killing tens of thousands of people in Afghanistan and Iraq.

And nationalism is given a special virulence when it is said to be blessed by Providence. Today we have a president, invading two countries in four years, who announced on the campaign trail last year that God speaks through him.

We need to refute the idea that our nation is different from, morally superior to, the other imperial powers of world history.

We need to assert our allegiance to the human race, and not to any one nation.

War Is a Government Program

SHELDON RICHMAN

Sheldon Richman, an antiwar libertarian and editor of the Foundation for Economic Education's periodical the Freeman, *wrote this essay for* Freedom Daily, *the publication of the Future of Freedom Foundation, in 2007.*

June 1 is the 227th anniversary of the birth of Carl von Clausewitz, the influential Prussian military theorist and historian. Clausewitz is best known for writing in his book, *On War*, "War is not merely a political act, but also a real political instrument, a continuation of political commerce, a carrying out of the same by other means."

These words come to mind whenever I hear conservative enthusiasts for the Iraq occupation complain about political interference with military operations. They don't understand the most basic fact of war: it is a government program. So why aren't people who claim to be suspicious of other government programs suspicious of war? I can see only two reasons, neither of them flattering: power lust or nationalistic zeal.

Many of us grow up believing that government reflects the will of the people. But skeptics know better. Government has assumed more and more control over private life not because the people demanded it, but because power-seekers and privilege-seekers sought outlets for their ambitions. They then propagandized the public until a sufficient number of people came to believe government control was good for them. ("Public" education has been remarkably effective in this regard.)

The story is similar with war. Politicians start wars for political reasons. They may seek to control resources or a foreign population. Or they may want to secure existing interests that could be at risk without war. The military is a means to political ends.

Writer, poet, and antiwar activist Grace Paley is here protesting Wall Street's investments in nuclear weapons and nuclear power. (Paley described her activism as "combative pacifism.") About fifteen hundred people were arrested on October 29, 1979, for blocking access to the New York Stock Exchange.

War always has a domestic side. Ruling classes hold power so that they may live off the toil of the domestic population. And because the ruled far outnumber the rulers, ideology and propaganda are necessary to maintain the allegiance of the subject population. War is useful in keeping the population in a state of fear and therefore trustful of their rulers. H. L. Mencken said it well: "The whole aim of practical politics is to keep the populace alarmed (and hence clamorous to be led to safety) by menacing it with an endless series of hobgoblins, all of them imaginary."

War is more dangerous than other government programs and not just for the obvious reason—mass murder. Foreign affairs and war planning seem to justify secrecy, shutting the supposedly sovereign people out of the government's scheming. Politicians would have a hard time justifying secrecy in domestic affairs. But it is routine in war-related matters. So much for government's adventures mirroring the people's wishes.

Americans Confront War

Most unappreciated of all is that war is the midwife of intrusive bureaucracy. James Madison understood this. "Of all the enemies of true liberty, war is, perhaps, the most to be dreaded, because it comprises and develops the germ of every other. War is the parent of armies; from these proceed debts and taxes; and armies, and debts, and taxes are the known instruments for bringing the many under the domination of the few. . . . No nation can preserve its freedom in the midst of continual warfare."

On their own, people do not go to war, and without compulsion they would never pay for it—they have better things to do with their money. Herman Goering, Hitler's second in command, understood this: "Of course the people don't want war. . . . But after all, it's the leaders of the country who determine the policy, and it's always a simple matter to drag the people along, whether it's a democracy or a fascist dictatorship or a Parliament or a Communist dictatorship."

Mencken knew this too: "Wars are seldom caused by spontaneous hatreds between people, for peoples in general are too ignorant of one another to have grievances and too indifferent to what goes on beyond their borders to plan conquests. They must be urged to the slaughter by politicians who know how to alarm them."

War is politics. And that's no compliment.

Reflections on War and Its Consequences

LAWRENCE S. WITTNER

Lawrence S. Wittner is professor of history at the State University of New York, Albany. His latest book is Toward Nuclear Abolition: A History of the World Nuclear Disarmament Movement, 1971 to the Present. *He wrote this essay in 2006.*

The shift of the Iraq War from what its early proponents claimed would be a cakewalk to what most current observers—including the small group of neocons who originally championed it—consider a disaster suggests that war's consequences are not always predictable.

Some wars, admittedly, work out fairly well—at least for the victors. In the third of the Punic Wars (149–146 B.C.), Rome's victory against Carthage was complete, and it obliterated that rival empire from the face of the earth. For the Carthaginians, of course, the outcome was less satisfying. Rome's victorious legions razed the city of Carthage and sowed salt in its fields, thereby ensuring that what had been a thriving metropolis would become a wasteland.

But even the victors are not immune to some unexpected and very unpleasant consequences. World War I led to 30 million people killed or wounded and disastrous epidemics of disease, plus a multibillion-dollar debt that was never repaid to U.S. creditors and, ultimately, fed into the collapse of the international financial system in 1929. The war also facilitated the rise of Communism and Fascism, two fanatical movements that added immensely to the brutality and destructiveness of the twentieth century. Certainly, World War I didn't live up to Woodrow Wilson's promises of a "war to end war" and a "war to make the world safe for democracy."

Even World War II—the "good war"—was not all it is frequently cracked up to be. Yes, it led to some very satisfying developments, most notably the destruction of the fascist governments of Germany, Italy, and Japan. But people too often forget that it had some very negative consequences. These include the killing of 50 million people, as well as the crippling, blinding, and maiming of millions more. Then, of course, there was also the genocide carried out under cover of the war, the systematic destruction of cities and civilian populations, the ruin of once-vibrant economies, the massive violations of civil liberties (e.g., the internment of Japanese-Americans in concentration camps), the establishment of totalitarian control in Eastern Europe, the development and use of nuclear weapons, and the onset of the nuclear arms race. This grim toll leaves out the substantial number of rapes, mental breakdowns, and postwar murders unleashed by the war.

During the Reagan administration's proxy war in Nicaragua, Abbie Hoffman protests outside the U.S. embassy in Managua in 1984.

The point here is not that World War II was "bad," but that wars are not as clean or morally pure as they are portrayed.

Curiously, pacifists have long been stereotyped as sentimental and naïve. But haven't the real romantics of the past century been the misty-eyed flag-wavers, convinced that the next war will build a brave new world? Particularly in a world harboring some 30,000 nuclear weapons, those who speak about war as if it consisted of two noble knights, jousting before cheering crowds, have lost all sense of reality.

This lack of realism about the consequences of modern war is all too pervasive. During the Cuban missile crisis, it led Defense Secretary Robert McNamara to warn top U.S. national security officials against their glib proposal to bomb the Soviet missile sites. That's not the end, he insisted. That's just the beginning! After the crisis, President Kennedy was delighted that war with the Soviet Union had been averted—a war that he estimated would have killed 300 million people.

How do we account for the romantic view of war that seems to overcome portions of society on a periodic basis? Certainly hawkish government officials, economic elites, and their backers in the mass media have contributed to popular feeble-mindedness when it comes to war's consequences. And rulers of empires tend to become foolish when presented with supreme power. But it is also true that some people revel in what they assume is the romance of war as a welcome escape from their humdrum daily existence. Nor should this surprise us, for they find similar escape in romantic songs and novels, movies, spectator sports, and, sometimes, in identification with a "strong" leader.

Of course, war might just be a bad habit—one that is difficult to break after persisting for thousands of years. Even so, people will give it up only when they confront its disastrous consequences. And this clear thinking about war might prove difficult for many of them, at least as long as they prefer romance to reality.

Left-Right Alliance Against War?

JON BASIL UTLEY

Jon Basil Utley is the Robert A. Taft Fellow at the Ludwig von Mises Institute, and a former correspondent for Knight/Ridder in South America. He wrote this essay in 2007 for Foreign Policy in Focus.

Americans opposed to war are a distinct minority. If the Iraq War were going well, most Americans would support it. Yet the Iraq venture has been such a disaster for America that peace groups have a chance to expose the pro-war interests in the nation and advance an alternative foreign policy based on law and international cooperation. Incredible war costs, a growing police state at home, loss of allies, and tremendous anti-Americanism abroad have given most Americans pause about our foreign policies.

Even so, Washington is on the verge of extending the war with an attack on Iran. To change American policy, we need to understand the differences between the antiwar movements on the Left and the Right before identifying how they might cooperate.

The leadership of both political parties supports war and empire. The Republican establishment's war promoters include the big conservative foundations, congressional leadership, old-line media such as *National Review* and the *Wall Street Journal* op-ed page, and the Religious Right's Armageddonites. The recent Conservative Political Action Committee (CPAC) meeting suppressed any antiwar debate, while speaker after speaker denounced foreigners, immigrants, and Arabs. Cheers resonated for PATRIOT Act architect John Yoo, and John Bolton was a banquet speaker. The current Republican presidential front-runners all favor continuing the wars in the Middle East.

Against the above some lonely libertarians and a very few constitutional conservatives opposed attacking Iraq, both in 2003 and before the first Gulf War in 1990. Although many Republicans opposed the Kosovo war, they did so mainly because a Democrat, Bill Clinton, started it. The rationale for that U.S. intervention, like with Iraq, was also based on falsifications.

Most Democratic congressional leaders also voted for the Iraq war. Outsider Howard Dean, a vocal opponent of the war, was blown away by the Democratic establishment in 2004. In a recent *Washington Post* analysis, political scientist Tony Smith explains why the Democrats can't put together a successful vote against the Iraq war. Many of the Democrats, according to Smith, are influenced by an ideology of using American military power for Wilsonian ends. They take their cues from "special interests . . . that want an aggressive policy—globalizing corporations, the military-industrial complex, the pro-Israel lobbies, those who covet Middle Eastern oil." The policies of these powerful "neoliberals," Smith writes, coincide with those of the "neo-conservatives."

War is Washington's big business. The military-industrial complex has never been more profitable. Last year, 15,300 earmarks for defense spending went to projects carefully designed to gain adherents in every state. The F–22 fighter plane, for instance, has 1,000 subcontractors in 43 states. Electronic chips and secret superweapons are so complicated that profits can be hidden all along the production line well beyond the scrutiny of outsiders. Even newly planned missiles for Poland to "defend Europe" from Iran may be less about a grand strategic design than simply about selling more arms. Russia's resultant concerns and European dismay are considered inconsequential.

Over and over, Washington's War Party trumps the views of most business interests as well as the foreign policy and academic establishment. The consequences of Washington having made enemies of nearly a quarter of the human race, the Muslims, are only now unfolding. Yet the War Party continues to look for new conflicts, next with China, to justify the vast budget for weaponry mostly irrelevant to the War on Terror. The recent CPAC meeting and much of the conservative media are, for instance, full of dire warnings of a great Chinese military threat to America.

To change Washington from its cowboy, shoot-first approach to a more cooperative stance with other nations is not just a matter of defeating George Bush. Opposing new wars, whether in Iran or elsewhere, requires cooperation of the Left together with libertarians and constitutional conservatives. There is now a convergence of interests. The Left today is a minority and can't expect to win power alone. The Republicans, because of the war, are splitting apart. Concern for deficits and constitutional freedoms have driven out libertarians, while immigration issues split business interests from the cultural conservatives.

To work together, the Left and Right must first confront their differences. There are past animosities and fundamental divergences in worldviews. Arguments that move one side have little effect on the other. In general the Left is more focused on America's shortcomings and emotional issues, while the Right fears the outside world and looks to simplistic military solutions for most problems.

More specifically, the Left tends to make moral arguments about foreign policy. For instance, the Left's concern over the death of innocent civilians in war—collateral damage—has little resonance with the Right. But the Right, at least some of it, has a pragmatic concern that such killing makes America even more hated and perhaps less safe. Most on the Right, however, argue that America is hated anyway, so more killing makes little difference. After all, our president has told us that we are hated because we are so good.

Many on the Left also think that it is immoral to make foreign policies based solely on U.S. national interest, a term that for them means business interests. Most conservatives know little and care little about the outside world. Leftists are generally more knowledgeable, but they know and care little about business or economic growth if such conditions cause economic injustice. Then there are the disagreements over how to use resources. Arguing that warfare is intrinsic to capitalism, much of the Left wants to use the war disaster to profoundly change America. The anti-war Right attributes the war to a takeover of foreign policy by former leftists, the neoconservatives, and to an unleashed military-industrial complex.

But the categories also are losing their meaning. The Left no longer means confiscatory taxes and welfare-state socialism. The Right no longer means balanced budgets, small government, and constitutional freedoms. Today other political divisions are more meaningful, such as between empire and republic, free traders and protectionists, pro- and anti-immigration interests, constitutionalists vs. Big Government. These all transcend Left and Right.

Also, there are common issues that can unite the moderate antiwar movements on both sides of the political spectrum. The common threat of trillions of dollars for unending wars already threatens both tax cuts and social welfare.

The growing police state at home and consequent erosion of civil liberties can also unify the two camps. Police State Republicans now run the party. There is little complaint at the dominant conservative think-tanks and foundations, for example, over PATRIOT Act excesses and expanding police powers. But many old-line conservatives have objected, including the American Conservative Union (which sponsors CPAC), the new *American Conservative* magazine, tax fighter Grover Norquist, Paul Weyrich, former congressman Bob Barr, and a few others. The libertarian institutes have sponsored many speakers and publications, and the Cato Institute has already cooperated with the American Civil Liberties Union on these issues. But the conservative war establishment has overwhelmed these voices. Equally, most of the Religious Right shows little concern for police-state measures. After all, millions of them believe the world will end soon, so what does the Constitution matter? Notably also, almost all their top leaders (except Chuck Colson and Pat Nolan of Prison Fellowship and author Rick Warren) supported the torture of prisoners of war. Only now, with new leadership, has the National Association of Evangelicals dared to condemn torture.

The Left, being on the outs, now has much more concern for the constitutional rule of law and international law. However the Left also has a long history, when it was in power, of caring little for constitutional niceties, especially on economic matters. Even today, the Left would go to war for Darfur regardless of consequences, as it once decimated Haiti's economy with an economic blockade under Clinton. In attacking Serbia, the Left did not demand any U.N. resolutions but used NATO for legitimacy, which severely undermined the pro-Western democratic forces in Russia.

In many ways America has become like Rome, moving inexorably toward empire and a police state. A majority of Americans will always trade away their freedoms for supposed security. A few more terrorist attacks will weaken our constitutional protections even further. Democracies cannot run empires. So, empire will mean losing our democracy. Empire will also mean the constant risk of "mistakes" that can trigger nuclear or biological warfare.

Those of us with similar concerns on both Right and Left need more communication with each other. We need to study how we can work together. Brink Lindsay of the Cato Institute gives us one example with his manifesto on how to bring together libertarians with liberals.

We must also be mindful of the challenges. Christian reconstructionist Gary North argues that Left-Right alliances have rarely worked: witness how the Left, except for figures like Randolph Bourne and Eugene Debs, abandoned its internationalism and went nationalistic in support of U.S. entry into World War I. He argues that "each side should do its best to convince its own followers. We know our own side's accents and hot buttons."

Here, however, are some ways of transcending Left-Right concerns and forging an anti-imperial coalition.

Explain to Americans how other nations also seek security, that negotiation is not "un-American," that Reagan too negotiated.

Work against a U.S. attack on Iran and the spread of war, which could end up wrecking world trade. Work to bring in Japan and South Korea, which depend upon Arabian Gulf oil, to publicly pressure Bush not to attack.

Bring in the business community. Much of it fears blowback from growing anti-Americanism abroad. The hi-tech industries in particular want peace to protect their intellectual property rights. Remember: Andrew Carnegie was a founding member of the Anti-Imperialist League.

The improvements to our civil defense are woefully inadequate and incompetently behind schedule. We all know the prime targets: our big coastal cities, tunnels, reservoirs, and industrial ports such as the Houston Ship Canal. We need biological defense, hospital resources, and fallout shelters much more than we need new submarines. More consciousness about these risks might make more Americans aware of the connection between our bombing of foreigners and their acts of terrorism against us.

Conservatives should join Leftist antiwar demonstrations, but with their own placards and banners. I have seen such at antiwar marches in Washington, and they are effective and draw attention. I wrote about this during the Kosovo war, because only Leftists make big antiwar events.

Each side needs to publicize the other's antiwar resources. On the Right the conservative establishment has been very successful in suppressing antiwar views.

Courtesy of the Fellowship of Reconciliation/Doug Hostetter.

Protesters demonstrate in New York City on June 3, 1999, against U.S. bombing.

Attend each other's meetings (though this can be counterproductive if the meetings are dominated by the extremist yahoos on the Right or America-haters on the Left).

Promote travel, international conferences, and foreign views, especially for the young.

Secure divided government so that each branch will investigate the other and help restrain its abuses of power.

Work for term limits, still the best way to limit Leviathan, and bring in younger, less compromised congressmen and women.

Remind Republicans that when they provide the president with ever more nearly dictatorial powers, it may well be a Hillary Clinton who enforces them.

There remains much that divides Left and Right. But, particularly as these designations lose their meaning, there is much that unites us as well. Opposition to American empire can serve as the banner that welcomes us into the one big tent of people opposed to war, an Anti-Imperialist League for the twenty-first century.

Great Antiwar Films
A List by Butler Shaffer

I have grown weary of the war lovers taking over every holiday and exploiting them for their own deadly ambitions. Turning the Fourth of July into a celebration of militaristic statism (see the old Bing Crosby musical *Holiday Inn*) was bad enough. But then seeing a Santa Claus in a flag-draped Uncle Sam suit on a Christmas card a couple of years ago was simply too much.

Memorial Day is one holiday on which I often hold an antiwar film festival, inviting a few friends—who, being friends of mine, have no need to be reminded of the evils of warfare—to watch what I consider the best of the films that bring war into disrepute. Instead of going out to a cemetery to join an "honor guard" gang to play "Taps" and fire their rifles to celebrate the deaths of victims of warfare, I suggest such an antiwar film festival for your own consideration.

Some of the films I find most effective are the following (each with one to three stars reflecting my opinion as to its importance):

Aftermath: The Remnants of War One of the most powerful of all antiwar films, particularly since it doesn't show any battle scenes. It is a documentary, produced by the Canadian Film Board, of the various messes that the war system leaves to the rest of mankind to deal with decades after the wars have ended (e.g., the unexploded munitions from World Wars I and II that continue to kill French farmers each year).

All Quiet on the Western Front Lewis Milestone's film won Oscars in 1930 for best film and best director. A very good antiwar film—from the perspective of some young Germans. I particularly like it because it stars one of the few real heroes from Hollywood, Lew Ayres, who refused to be conscripted into the army during World War II, a decision that virtually ruined his Hollywood career.

While on the topic of "heroes," I would *exclude* any and all war films by John Wayne who, more than anyone else, helped Hollywood glorify wartime butchery, even as he managed to keep himself out of the war. Sound like any presidents?

*** *The Americanization of Emily*   My favorite antiwar film. This James Garner–Julie Andrews picture is quite good. The most powerful portion of it is the garden scene, in which Garner and Andrews are talking with Andrews's mother about war. Garner's impassioned soliloquy on the nature of war, with emphasis on the wives and mothers who keep the bloodbaths going by honoring them, packs more wallop than just about any other film. Garner's character ends up declaring that it will be cowards—such as himself—who will save the world.

* *Apocalypse Now*   An excellent Vietnam War–era film with dark and darkside overtones.

** *The Battle of Algiers*   A 1965 film done in a pseudo-documentary style, it dramatizes the decade-long struggle of Algerians against their French occupiers. This motion picture affords viewers insights into the current responses of Iraqis to their American occupiers.

*** *Breaker Morant*   This is the story of Australian soldiers during the Boer War against whom phony murder charges are made in order to facilitate the political machinations of bringing the war to an end. It illustrates, quite well, how soldiers—treated by the state as nothing more than fungible resources for its exploitation—can be sacrificed both on and off the battlefield.

** *Catch–22*   The film adaptation of Joseph Hiller's treatment of the "normal" insanity of the war system, based on his own wartime experiences.

*** *Children of Men*   A futuristic film set in an Orwellian England, where endless wars against endless enemies have become the norm. Throughout the world, most women have become infertile, threatening the extinction of the human species. A woman has become pregnant, and most of the film is taken up with trying to get her to a country that would harbor her and her unborn child. This is a very dark and violent film—someone is always in the process of killing others, bombing buildings, etc. What is encouraging, however, is that none of the warring factions are presented as "good" guys fighting the "bad" guys. It is the anti-life nature of the war system itself—with mankind as the endangered species—that dominates the movie.

** *Das Boot* and ** *Letters from Iwo Jima* Two films that address the horrors of warfare from the perspectives of those on the "other" side: in the first, Germans, in the second, Japanese. The latter is Clint Eastwood's highly praised picture.

** *The Deer Hunter* A powerful, not-for-the-squeamish look at the Vietnam War. In 1978, it won Oscars for best picture and best supporting actor (Christopher Walken).

** *Dr. Strangelove* Another Stanley Kubrick offering that involves an Air Force general who decides to start a war with the Soviet Union. As with *The Mouse That Roared*, Peter Sellers plays a number of roles. A film that gets better with time.

** *Duck Soup* The Marx brothers' slapstick assault on the war system, with Groucho as Freedonia's prime minister declaring war on a neighboring country for no apparent reason. My favorite line in the film is when, in the course of battle, Groucho tells the others that they are fighting for Mrs. Teasdale's (who's played by Margaret Dumont) honor, "which is probably more than she ever did."

** *Gallipoli* A film by one of my favorite directors, Peter Weir. It takes place in World War I and does a moving job of showing the disillusionment of young men caught up in the ersatz "glory" of war.

** *Grand Illusion* A 1937 film by director Jean Renoir, *Grand Illusion* focuses on the futility of the war system. That the German government tried to destroy this film when it first came out provides some evidence of its importance.

** *Hearts and Minds* Winner of an Oscar for best documentary, *Hearts and Minds* deals with the events and machinations that led to the Vietnam War. No clearer example of the hypocrisy of the United States' alleged efforts to bring "freedom" to Southeast Asia is found than in the effort of the federal government to have this film formally censored so that Americans could not learn what their "representative" [political] thugs had been up to.

** *Johnny Got His Gun*   A Dalton Trumbo film set in World War I, told from the perspective of an all-but-dead wounded soldier. The darkest of the films I'm recommending.

*** *Joyeux Noël*   A recent film depicting an actual pause in battle—on Christmas Eve—during World War I. French, German, and British soldiers met in a no-man's-land to exchange candy and cigarettes, converse, and even play an abbreviated game of soccer.

*** *King of Hearts*, or *Le Roi de Coeur*   A Philippe de Broca film set in World War I, in which a soldier played by Alan Bates, is sent into a French town to check things out, unaware that the inhabitants have left the town and the residents of the local mental asylum have taken their places. Very good comedy.

* *Lord of War*   This movie deals more with the underbelly of post–Cold War arms trafficking than with wars themselves (although there is plenty of bloodletting for any pro-war vampires). Pay attention to the credits following the film. They inform us that the five nations most heavily involved in selling arms to the rest of the world are also the five permanent members of the United Nations Security Council!

* *M*A*S*H*   Anyone not familiar with Robert Altman's dark comedic look at war—the Korean War being the one in question—has probably been out in the desert too long.

* *The Mouse That Roared*   Jack Arnold's classic starring Peter Sellers. A European duchy figures the best way out of its financial difficulties is to wage war on America and then receive postwar foreign aid.

*** *Oh! What a Lovely War*   A British musical comedy (originally a stage show) set in World War I. The ending scene, in particular, will bring tears to the eyes of those who abhor the systematic killing of people. One of my all-time favorites!

** *Paths of Glory*   A Stanley Kubrick film starring Kirk Douglas. A general sends his men on a suicide mission. When the mission fails, a few soldiers are arbitrarily selected to be tried—and executed—for cowardice.

** *Platoon* and ** *Full Metal Jacket*   These are potent films providing a soldier's perspective on the dehumanizing, life-destroying nature of war. As one who believes that the gore and broken bodies of those killed in wars should be regularly shown on television—so that the Sean Hannitys, the Rush Lim-baughs, the Bill O'Reillys, et al., can get a snootful of the system they so adore—these films provide a good secondary source. *Platoon* won an Oscar for best picture.

** *The Quiet American* (2002)   The adaptation of Graham Greene's novel deals with the behind-the-scenes manipulations that led to America's in-volvement in the Vietnam War. Don't waste your time with the 1958 version, which treats Greene's novel as a murder mystery, not a political intrigue.

*** *Shenandoah*   The best antiwar film with a consistent libertarian [and pacifist] message. Jimmy Stewart plays a Virginia farmer—with a large fam-ily—who has no use for the Civil War and its intrusions upon his property. When I first sat through this film over forty years ago, I kept waiting for Stewart to cave in and see the errors of his ways. He never does. Some won-derful lines that you'll not soon forget. One of the very few films that later became a stage play. If you haven't seen this one, where have you been?

** *Slaughterhouse-Five*   Kurt Vonnegut's novel, from which this film is adapted, offers the same basic theme of the normalcy of institutionalized insanity from the perspective of a soldier. I once saw a lengthy interview (on C-SPAN, as I recall) of Heller and Vonnegut together. Vonnegut related a conversation he had had with a friend on a troopship coming back from Eu-rope. Vonnegut asked his friend, "What did you learn from all of this?" To which the other man replied, "Never to believe your own government."

* *Three Kings*   Set in the first Gulf War, there is an abundance of the blood-bath that defines every war. What is of particular interest in this film, how-ever, is the impact war has on the noncombatant refugees. A very nice ending from their perspective.

** *A Very Long Engagement*   Perhaps, as a motion-picture production, this is artistically the best film of all I have recommended. While set in wartime (World War I), with plenty of battlefield insanity, it is essentially a love story involving a young woman intent on finding her fiancé—is he alive or dead?—after the war. There is also a very interesting character: a prostitute bent on revenge against corrupt military officers.

*** *Wag the Dog*   For those who reject, out of hand, the idea that political con-spiracies exist—unless, of course, one is talking about conspiracies perpetrated by "bad guys"—this film may prove either troublesome or enlightening. In an age when the best way to satirize something is to make a factual report of it, this film of a contrived war engineered to enliven a presidential reelection campaign has all the ring of a documentary. A must for any modern film festival.

*** *Why We Fight*   A powerful documentary—in which Karen Kwiatkowski, Chalmers Johnson, and Gore Vidal carry most of the intellectual load—on the nature and history of the post–World War II American war-making system. It won the Grand Jury Prize at the 2005 Sundance Film Festival. *Warning!* Do not confuse this with the pro-war series of the same name, produced during World War II by one of my un-favorite directors, Frank Capra.

Butler Shaffer is a professor at Southwestern University School of Law, and author of In Restraint of Trade: The Business Campaign Against Competition, 1918–1938. *He is a frequent columnist for LewRockwell.com, where this list first appeared.*

Bibliography

Abrams, Ray H. *Preachers Present Arms.* Herald Press, 1969.

Albrecht-Carrie, Rene. *The Meaning of the First World War.* Prentice-Hall, 1965.

Alter, Norma M. *Vietnam Protest Theatre: The Television War on Stage.* Indiana University Press, 1996.

Anderson, David L. and John Ernst, eds. *The War That Never Ends: New Perspectives on the Vietnam War.* University Press of Kentucky, 2007.

Barkan, Stephen E. *Protestors on Trial: Criminal Justice in the Southern Civil Rights and Vietnam Antiwar Movements.* Rutgers University Press, 1978.

Barry, Jan and W. D. Ehrhart, eds. *Demilitarized Zones: Veterans After Vietnam.* East River Anthology, 1976.

Baskir, Lawrence M. and William A. Strauss. *Chance and Circumstance: The Draft, the War and the Vietnam Generation.* Knopf, 1978.

Beidler, Philip D. *American Wars, American Peace.* University of Georgia Press, 2007.

_____. *Late Thoughts on an Old War.* University of Georgia Press, 2004.

Beisner, Robert L. *Twelve Against Empire: The Anti-Imperialists 1898–1900.* McGraw-Hill, 1971.

Bennett, W. Lance and David Paletz. *Taken By Storm: The Media, Public Opinion and U.S. Foreign Policy in the Gulf War.* University of Chicago Press, 1994.

Bennett, W. Lance, Regina Lawrence and Steven Livingston. *When the Press Fails: Political Power and the News Media from Iraq to Katrina.* University of Chicago Press, 2007.

Bernstein, Iver. *The New York City Draft Riots: Their Significance for American Society and Politics in the Age of the Civil War.* Oxford University Press, 1990.

Berrigan, Daniel. *To Dwell in Peace: An Autobiography.* Harper & Row, 1987.

_____. *The Trial of the Catonsville Nine.* Beacon Press, 1970.

Berrigan, Philip and Fred A. Wilcox. *Fighting the Lamb's War: Skirmishes with the American Empire.* Common Courage Press, 1996.

Bess, Michael. *Choices Under Fire: Moral Dimensions of World War II.* Knopf, 2006.

Bill, James A. *George Ball: Behind the Scenes in U.S. Foreign Policy.* Yale University Press, 1998.

Brock, Peter. *Pacifism in the United States: From the Colonial Era to the First World War.* Princeton University Press, 1968.

Bourne, Randolph. *War and the Intellectuals.* Harper & Row, 1964.

Burke, Joanna. *An Intimate History of Killing: Face to Face Killing in Twentieth Century Warfare.* Basic Books, 1999.

Caputo, Philip. *A Rumor of War.* Holt, Rinehart & Winston, 1977.

Carroll, James. *An American Requiem: God, My Father, and the War that Came Between Us.* Houghton Mifflin, 1996.

Cohen, Carl. *Civil Disobedience: Conscience, Tactics and the Law.* Columbia University Press, 1971.

Cooney, Robert and Helen Michalowski. *The Power of the People: Active Nonviolence in the United States.* Peace Press, 1977.

Cowan, Paul, Nick Egleson and Nat Hentoff, with Barbara Herbert and Robert Hall. *State Secrets: Police Surveillance in America.* Holt, Rinehart & Winston, 1974.

Crow, John Armstrong. *The Epic of Latin America,* 4th ed. University of California Press, 1992.

Cruttwell, C.R.M.F. *A History of the Great War, 1914–1918.* Chicago Academy Publishers, 2007.

Cumings, Bruce. *The Origins of the Korean War.* 2 vols. Princeton University Press, 1981 and 1990.

_____. *War and Television.* Verso, 1992.

Davies, Peter. *The Truth of Kent State: A Challenge to the American Conscience.* Farrar, Straus & Giroux, 1973.

Davis, James K. *Assault on the Left: The FBI and the Sixties Antiwar Movement.* Praeger, 1997.

DeBenedetti, Charles, ed. *Peace Heroes in Twentieth Century America.* Indiana University Press, 1986.

DeBenedetti, Charles with Charles Chatfield. *An American Ordeal: The Antiwar Movement of the Vietnam Era.* Syracuse University Press, 1990.

Dellinger, David. *From Yale to Jail: The Life Story of a Moral Dissenter.* Pantheon, 1993.

Denson, John V., ed. *The Costs of War: America's Pyrrhic Victories.* Transaction Publishers, 1999.

Destler, Chester. *American Radicalism, 1865–1901.* Quadrangle Books, 1966.

De Voto, Bernard. *The Year of Decision: 1846.* Little, Brown, 1943.

Draper, Theodore. *A Very Thin Line: The Iran-Contra Affairs.* Hill & Wang, 1991.

Drinnon, Richard. *Violence in the American Experience: Winning the West.* New American Library, 1979.

Egendorf, Arthur. *Healing from the War: Trauma and Transformation After Vietnam.* Houghton Mifflin, 1985.

Ehrhart, W. D. *Vietnam-Perkasie: A Combat Marine Memoir.* McFarland, 1983.

_____. *Busted: A Vietnam Veteran in Nixon's America.* University of Massachusetts Press, 1995.

Ekirch, Arthur A. Jr., *The Civilian and the Military: A History of the American Anti-militarist Tradition.* Oxford University Press, 1965.

Eller, Cynthia. *Conscientious Objectors and the Second World War: Moral and Religious Arguments in Support of Pacifism.* Praeger, 1991.

Elmer, Jerry. *Felon for Peace: The Memoir of a Vietnam-Era Draft Resister.* Vanderbilt University Press, 2005.

Fick, Nathaniel. *One Bullet Away: The Making of a Marine Officer.* Houghton Mifflin, 2005.

Finn, James. *Protest: Pacifism and Politics: Some Passionate Views on War and Nonviolence.* Random House, 1967.

Fleischman, Harry. *Norman Thomas: A Biography, 1884–1968.* Norton, 1969.

Flynn, John T. *As We Go Marching.* Doubleday, 1944.

Foley, Michael S. *Confronting the War Machine: Draft Resistance During the Vietnam War.* University of North Carolina Press, 2003.

Franklin, John Hope. *From Slavery to Freedom.* Knopf, 1974.

Fredrickson, George M. *Big Enough to Be Inconsistent: Abraham Lincoln Confronts Slavery and Race.* Harvard University Press, 2008.

Frey-Wouters and Robert S. Laufer. *Legacy of a War: The American Soldier in Vietnam.* M. E. Sharpe, 1986.

Friedman, Leon and Burt Neuborne. *Unquestioning Obedience to the President: The ACLU Case Against the Legality of the War in Vietnam.* Norton, 1972.

Fussell, Paul. *The Great War and Modern Memory.* Oxford, 1991.

_____. *The Norton Book of Modern War.* Norton, 1991.

Gatewood, William B. Jr., *"Smoked Yankees" and the Struggle for Empire: Letters from Negro Soldiers, 1898–1902.* University of Arkansas Press, 1987.

_____. *Black Americans and the White Man's Burden.* University of Illinois Press, 1975.

Gaylin, Willard. *In the Service of their Country: War Resisters in Prison.* Grosset and Dunlap, 1970.

Gentry, Curt. *J. Edgar Hoover: The Man and the Secrets.* Norton, 1991.

Ginger, Ray. *The Bending Cross: A Biography of Eugene V. Debs.* Rutgers University Press, 1949.

Gioglio, Gerald R. *Days of Decision: An Oral History of Conscientious Objectors in the Military during the Vietnam War.* Broken Rifle Press, 1989.

Glasser, Ronald J. *365 Days.* George Braziller, 1971.

Gordon, William A. *Four Dead in Ohio: Was There a Conspiracy at Kent State?* North Ridge Books, 1995.

Gray, Francine Du Plessix. *Divine Disobedience: Profiles in Catholic Radicalism.* Knopf, 1970.

Halberstam, David. *The Coldest Winter: America and the Korean War.* Hyperion, 2007.

Hall, Simon. *Peace and Freedom: The Civil Rights and Antiwar Movements in the 1960s.* University of Pennsylvania Press, 2005.

Harris, David. *Our War: What We Did in Vietnam and What It Did to Us.* Times Books, 1996.

Hedeman, Ed, ed. *Guide to War Tax Resistance.* New York: War Resisters League, 1983.

Heineman, Kenneth. *Campus War: The Peace Movement at American State Universities in the Vietnam Era.* New York University Press, 1994.

Herr, Michael. *Dispatches.* Vintage International, 1991. (Herr was a war correspondent in Vietnam.)

Hersey, John. *Hiroshima.* Knopf, 1969.

Hersh, Seymour. *The Price of Power: Kissinger in the Nixon White House.* Summit Books, 1983.

Hickey, Donald. *The War of 1812: A Forgotten Conflict.* University of Illinois Press, 1989.

Higgs, Robert. *Crisis and Leviathan: Critical Episodes in the Growth of American Government.* Oxford University Press, 1987.

Hine, Robert V. and John Mack Faragher. *Frontiers: A Short History of the American West.* Yale University Press, 2007.

Hoganson, Kristin L. *Fighting for American Manhood: How Gender Politics Provoked the Spanish-American and Philippine-American Wars.* Yale University Press, 1998.

Howell-Koehler, Nancy, ed. *Vietnam: The Battle Comes Home: A Photographic Record of Post-Traumatic Stress with Selected Essays.* Photographs by Gordon Baer. Morgan & Morgan, 1984.

Hummel, Jeffrey Rogers. *Emancipating Slaves, Enslaving Free Men: A History of the Civil War.* Open Court, 1996.

Hunt, Andrew E. *The Turning: A History of Vietnam Veterans Against the War.* New York University Press, 1999.

Jeffreys-Jones, Rhodri. *Peace Now! American Society and the Ending of the Vietnam War.* Yale University Press, 1999.

Johnson, Robert D. *Ernest Gruening and the American Dissenting Tradition.* Harvard University Press, 1998.

Karp, Walter. *The Politics of War.* Franklin Square Press, 2003.

Kelner, Joseph and James Munves. *Kent State Coverup.* Harper & Row, 1980.

Kingston, Maxine Hong, ed. *Veterans of War, Veterans of Peace.* Koa Books, 2006.

Kinzer, Stephen. *Overthrow: America's Century of Regime Change from Hawaii to Iraq.* Times Books, 2007.

Klement, Frank L. *Lincoln's Critics: The Copperheads of the North.* White Mane Books, 1999.

Kovic, Ron. *Born on the Fourth of July.* McGraw-Hill, 1976.

Kruckewitt, Joan. *The Death of Ben Linder: The Story of a North American in Sandinista Nicaragua.* Seven Stories Press, 1999.

Lafore, Laurence. *The Long Fuse: An Interpretation of the Origins of World War I.* J. B. Lippincott, 1965.

Latimer, John. *1812: War with America.* Harvard University Press, 2007.

Latty, Yvonne and Max Cleland. *In Conflict: Iraq War Veterans Speak Out on Duty, Loss and the Fight to Stay Alive.* Polipoint Press, 2006.

Levy, Howard and David Miller. *Going to Jail: The Political Prisoner.* Grove Press, 1970.

Lifton, Robert Jay. *Home from the War: Vietnam Veterans—Neither Victims nor Executioners.* Simon & Schuster, 1973.

Linfield, Michael. *Freedom Under Fire: U.S. Civil Liberties in Times of War.* South End Press, 1990.

Linn, Brian. *The Philippine War, 1899–1902.* University Press of Kansas, 2000.

Lofland, John. *Polite Protestors: The American Peace Movement of the 1980s.* Syracuse University Press, 1993.

MacPherson, Myra. *Long Time Passing: Vietnam and the Haunted Generation.* Doubleday, 1984.

Mayer, Milton. *What Can a Man Do?* University of Chicago Press, 1964.

McDonald, Archie P. *The Mexican War: Crisis for American Democracy.* D.C. Heath, 1969.

McPherson, James. *The Negro's Civil War.* Pantheon, 1965.

Meconis, Charles A. *With Clumsy Grace: The American Catholic Left, 1962–1975.* Seabury Press, 1979.

Merk, Frederick. *The Monroe Doctrine: American Expansionism 1843–1849.* Random House, 1966.

Miller, William D. *A Harsh and Dreadful Love: Dorothy Day and the Catholic Worker Movement.* Liveright, 1973.

Milne, David. *America's Rasputin: Walt Rostow and the Vietnam War.* Hill & Wang, 2008.

Moorehead, Caroline. *Troublesome People: The Warriors of Pacifism.* Adler & Adler, 1987.

Morrison, Samuel Eliot, Frederick Merk, and Frank Freidel. *Dissent in Three American Wars.* Harvard University Press, 1970.

Mueller, John. *Policy and Opinion in the Gulf War.* University of Chicago Press, 1994.

Mullen, Peg. *Unfriendly Fire.* University of Iowa Press, 1995.

Neal, William Patrick. "Senator Wayne L. Morse and the Quagmire of Vietnam, 1964–1968." PhD dissertation, University of Oregon, 1979.

O'Sullivan, John and Alan Meckler. *The Draft and Its Enemies: A Documentary History.* University of Illinois Press, 1974.

Patterson, James T. *Mr. Republican: A Biography of Robert A. Taft.* Houghton Mifflin, 1972.

Paul, Ron. *A Foreign Policy of Freedom: 'Peace, Commerce, and Honest Friendship.'* Foundation for Rational Economics and Education, 2007.

————. *The Revolution: A Manifesto.* Grand Central, 2008.

Pessen, Edward. *Losing Our Souls: The American Experience in the Cold War.* Ivan R. Dee, 1997.

Peterson, H. C. and Gilbert C. Fite. *Opponents of War, 1917–1918.* University of Washington Press, 1968.

Polner, Murray. *No Victory Parades: The Return of the Vietnam Veteran.* Holt, Rinehart & Winston, 1971.

Polner, Murray, ed. *When Can I Come Home? A Debate on Amnesty for Exiles, Anti-War Prisoners and Others.* Doubleday Anchor, 1972.

Polner, Murray and Jim O'Grady. *Disarmed and Dangerous: The Radical Lives and Times of Daniel and Philip Berrigan.* Basic Books, 1997.

Puller, Lewis. *Fortunate Son.* Grove Weidenfeld, 1991.

Radosh, Ronald. *Prophets on the Right: Profiles of Conservative Critics of American Globalism.* Simon & Schuster, 1975.

Raskin, Marcus and Robert Spero. *The Four Freedoms Under Siege: The Clear and Present Danger from Our National Security State.* Praeger, 2007.

Rogin, Michael. *Fathers and Children: Andrew Jackson and the Subjugation of the American Indian.* Knopf, 1975.

Rothbard, Murray N. *The Betrayal of the American Right.* Ludwig von Mises Institute, 2007.

Rothbard, Murray N. *The Panic of 1819: Reactions and Policies.* Columbia University Press, 1962.

Russett, Bruce. *No Clear and Present Danger.* Harper & Row, 1972.

Salvatore, Nick. *Eugene V. Debs: Citizen Socialist.* University of Illinois Press, 1982.

Schlissel, Lillian, ed. *Conscience in America.* E. P. Dutton, 1968.

Schroeder, John H. *Mr. Polk's War: American Opposition and Dissent, 1846–1848.* University of Wisconsin Press, 1973.

Schulzinger, Robert D. *A Time for War: The United States and Vietnam, 1941–1975.* Oxford University Press, 1997.

Secunda, Eugene and Terence P. Moran. *Selling War to America: From the Spanish American War to the Global War on Terror.* Praeger, 2007.

Seeley, Robert, ed. *The Handbook of Nonviolence.* Lakeville Press, 1986.

Sellers, Charles G. *James K. Polk.* Vol. 2: *The Continentalist, 1843–1846.* Princeton University Press, 1966.

Sheehan, Cindy. *Peace Mom: A Mother's Journey through Heartache to Activism.* Atria, 2006.

Sibley, Mulford Q. and Philip E. Jacoby. *Conscription of Conscience.* Cornell University Press, 1952.

Silbey, David J. *A War of Frontier and Empire: The Philippine-American War, 1899–1902.* Hill & Wang, 2007.

Simons, Donald L. *I Refuse: Memories of a Vietnam War Objector.* Broken Rifle Press, 1992.

Small, Melvin. *Antiwarriors: The Vietnam War and the Battle for America's Hearts and Minds.* Rowman and Littlefield, 2002.

Stinnett, Robert B. *Day of Deceit: The Truth about FDR and Pearl Harbor.* Free Press, 2000.

Stout, Harry S. *Upon the Altar of the Nation: A Moral History of the Civil War.* Penguin, 2006.

Suskind, Ron. *The One Percent Doctrine: Deep Inside America's Pursuit of Its Enemies Since 9/11.* Simon & Schuster, 2006.

Swanberg, W. A. *Norman Thomas: The Last Idealist.* Scribner's, 1976.

Thomas, Norman and Bertram D. Wolfe. *Keep America Out of War: A Program.* Frederick A. Stokes, 1939.

Tooley, Hunt. *The Western Front: Battleground and Home Front in the First World War.* New York: Palgrave Macmillan, 2003.

Tuterow, Norman. *The Mexican-American War: An Annotated Bibliography.* Greenwood Press, 1981.

Tyler, Alice Felt. *Freedom's Ferment: Phases of American Social History to 1860.* University of Minnestota Press, 1944.

Vanaik, Achin, ed. *Selling U.S. Wars.* Olive Branch Press, 2007.

Wells, Tom. *The War Within: America's Battle over Vietnam.* University of California Press, 1994.

Williams, David. *A People's History of the Civil War.* New Press, 2005.

Wittner, Lawrence S. *Rebels Against War: America's Peace Movement, 1941–1960,* rev. ed. Temple University Press, 1984.

Wolff, Leon. *Little Brown Brother.* Doubleday, 1961.

Wood, Trish and Bobby Muller. *What Was Asked of Us: An Oral History of the Iraq War by the Soldiers Who Fought It.* Little, Brown, 2006.

Wright, Evan. *Generation Kill: Devil Dogs, Iceman, Captain America, and the New Face of American War.* G. P. Putnam's Sons, 2004.

Zaroulis, Nancy and Gerald Sullivan. *Who Spoke Up? American Protest Against the War in Vietnam, 1963–1975.* Doubleday, 1984.

Zinn, Howard. *A People's History of the United States.* Harper, 1995.

Acknowledgments

For permission to reprint the selections and photographs in this volume, grateful acknowledgment is made to those named below. Every effort has been made to obtain appropriate permission to reproduce the copyrighted material included in this book. If notified of errors or omissions, the editors and the publisher will make the necessary corrections in future editions. Thanks to:

Andrew J. Bacevich for "I Lost My Son to a War I Oppose; We Were Both Doing Our Duty"; Gordon Baer (www.gbphoto.com) for his pho tographs, which also appeared in his *Vietnam: The Battle Comes Home: A Photographic Record of Post-Traumatic Stress with Selected Essays,* edited by Nancy Howell-Koehler (Morgan & Morgan, 1984); Linda Bailey and the Cincinnati Museum (Center–Cincinnati Historical Society Library; Bill Belmont for "I-Feel-Like-I'm-Fixin'-to-Die Rag" (Words and music by Joe McDonald; © 1965, renewed 1993 by Alcatraz Corner Music BMI); Scott Bennett of Georgian Court University; Dan Berrigan, American hero; Camillo "Mac" Bica and Foreign Policy in Focus for "An Open Letter to My Fellow Veterans"; Kathleen Cameron (www.majesticfeathers.com), photographer; Wendy Chmielewski and the Swarthmore College Peace Collection; Creators Syndicate for Paul Craig Roberts's "Why Did Bush Destroy Iraq?" and Pat Buchanan's "Inaugurating Endless War." Common Courage Press for the excerpt from Philip Berrigan's *Fighting the Lamb's War;* Katie Curey and the Montana Historical Society; Emily DePrang for "Iraq Comes Home: Soldiers Share the Devastating Tales of War," which originally appeared in the *Texas Observer;* Fellowship of Reconciliation (www.forusa.org) for "Why We Refused to Register"; Foreign Policy in Focus (www.fpif.org) for Jon Basil Utley's "Left-Right Alliance Against War?"; The Future of Freedom

Foundation (www.fff.org) and Sheldon Richman for "War Is a Government Program"; John C. Goodwin, photographer; International Publishers, New York City, for Helen Keller's "Strike Against War"; John Brady Kiesling for his resignation letter; Kent State University Press for David Dellinger, "Why I Refused to Register in the October 1940 Draft and a Little of What It Led To," from *A Few Small Candles: War Resisters of World War II Tell Their Stories*, edited by Larry Gara and Lenna Mae Gara (Kent State University Press, 1999); the Ludwig von Mises Institute (Mises.org) for Murray N. Rothbard's "War, Peace, and the State"; Joe McCary and Photo Response; Randall Pink; Alex Polner for help with photographs; Geoff Price of RationalRevolution.com; the *Progressive* for Howard Zinn's "Put Away the Flags"; Anne Brooks Ranallo and the Jane Addams Collection at the University of Illinois at Chicago; Jennie Rathbun and the Houghton Library, Harvard University; *Reason* magazine for Bill Kauffman's "Real Conservatives Don't Start Wars"; Lew Rockwell and LewRockwell.com for "The Glory of War"; Stan Rosenthall (www.stanrosenthallphotography.com), photographer; Philip Runkel and Marquette University Department of Special Collections and University Archives; the *Saturday Evening Post* for Milton Mayer's "I Think I'll Sit This One Out"; Butler Shaffer for his list of antiwar films; Paul Tick, photographer of antiwar movements and people; Tam Turse (www.tamturse.com), photographer; David E. Vancil, Head of Special Collections at Illinois State University; Ethan Vesely-Flad and the Fellowship of Reconciliation for Doug Hostetter and Brad Lyttle photographs; Harvey Wasserman for "Four Bloody Lies of War"; and Lawrence S. Wittner for "Reflections on War and Its Consequences." A few more debts to acknowledge. "Time on Target" is reprinted from *To Those Who Have Gone Home Tired,* (Thunder's Mouth Press, 1984); "Learning the Hard Way" is reprinted from *In the Shadow of Vietnam: Essays 1977–1991,* (McFarland & Co., Inc., 1991); and "Hunting" is reprinted from *Beautiful Wreckage: New & Selected Poems,* (Adastra Press, 1999); all by permission of author W. D. Ehrhart. Thanks to Jeffrey Herbener, Paul Binder, and Laurie Gibson for their suggestions for this volume. Thanks also to Mark van Wienen, editor of *Rendezvous with Death: American Poems of the Great War* (University of Illinois Press, 2002), for answering questions about World War I poetry. Finally, thanks to copy editor Eleanor Duncan; production editor Laura Stine; assistant editor Alix Sleight; William Frucht, Basic Books executive editor; and our indefatigable literary agent, Philip Spitzer.

About the Editors

Murray Polner is the author of *No Victory Parades: The Return of the Vietnam Veteran, Branch Rickey: A Biography,* and *Rabbi: The American Experience.* He coauthored (with Jim O'Grady) *Disarmed and Dangerous: The Radical Lives & Times of Daniel & Philip Berrigan,* edited *When Can I Come Home? A Debate on Amnesty for Exiles, Anti-War Prisoners and Others* and coedited (with Stefan Merken) *Peace, Justice and Jews: Reclaiming Our Tradition.* Polner's writings have appeared in the *New York Times, Columbia Journalism Review, Nation, Washington Monthly, Commonweal, Newsday, Present Tense, Jewish Week* and many others. Polner served in the U.S. Army and is a history book review editor for George Mason University's History News Network (www.historynewsnetwork.org/books).

Thomas E. Woods, Jr., is the *New York Times* best-selling author of *The Politically Incorrect Guide to American History,* and the first-place winner in the 2006 Templeton Enterprise Awards for his book *The Church and the Market.* His other books include *The Church Confronts Modernity, 33 Questions About American History You're Not Supposed to Ask* and (with Kevin R. C. Gutzman) *Who Killed the Constitution?* He is also coeditor of *Exploring American History: From Colonial Times to 1877,* an eleven-volume encyclopedia. Woods's writing has appeared in dozens of periodicals, including the *American Historical Review, Christian Science Monitor, Investor's Business Daily, New Oxford Review, University Bookman, Catholic World Report, Inside the Vatican,* and *Human Rights Review.* He is senior fellow in American history at the Ludwig von Mises Institute in Auburn, Alabama, and maintains a Web site at www.ThomasEWoods.com.

Index